THINKING CONFEDERATES

THINKING CONFEDERATES
Academia and the Idea of Progress in the New South

Dan R. Frost

The University of Tennessee Press / Knoxville

Published in cooperation with the United States Civil War Center.

The paper used in this book meets the minimum requirements
of ANSI/NISO Z39.48-1992 (R 1997) (Permanence of Paper).
The binding materials have been chosen for strength and durability.

Library of Congress Cataloging-in-Publication Data

Frost, Dan R., 1961–
Thinking Confederates : academia and the idea of progress
in the new South / Dan R. Frost. — 1st ed.
p. cm.
Includes bibliographical references.
ISBN 1-57233-104-6 (cl.: alk. paper)
1. Education, Higher—Southern States—History—19th century.
2. Educational change—Southern States—History—19th century.
3. United States—History—Civil War, 1861–1865—Veterans.
I. Title.
LA230.5.S6 F76 2000
370'.975—dc21   00-009485

Pour Annick

Contents

Acknowledgments

I would like to express my appreciation to the many people who helped me to develop and finish this book. I would first like to thank Karl Roider and Edward McLaughlin; albeit unknowingly, they set me on the road to conceiving this project. At Louisiana State University's Hill Memorial Library, I would like to thank Faye Phillips and her staff for helping me get started. Indeed, all the archivists and librarians at all of the research institutions that I visited deserve my utmost thanks. Gerry Anders deserves credit for his critique of an early draft of the manuscript. I would also like to thank Nancy Midgette for her recommendations for improving the text. Mavis Bryant's and Stan Ivester's assistance also proved invaluable.

I am thankful to Edward Muir and Victor Stater for their support during the early stages of this project. It is especially important for me to thank Paul Paskoff, not only for his knowledge of scientific education in the antebellum South, but also for the complete confidence he has expressed in this work.

I owe a special debt to Gaines Foster for the insights concerning the New South which he shared with me. Now that the work is completed, I recognize his influence even more than I did during the time I was researching, writing, and revising.

David Madden, founding director of the United States Civil War Center, was crucial to the success of this project. Without his faith and fervor, this book would not yet be finished.

Charles Royster provided enthusiastic intellectual and moral support that gave me the confidence to pursue and complete this book. Furthermore, his work as a historian has inspired me more than he can know.

I am particularly grateful to Jennifer Siler of the University of Tennessee Press, for her unflinching support. She guided me through the perils of publishing, and for that she always will have my heartfelt thanks.

Only space limitations prevent me from taking an entire page to express my gratitude to Chuck Shindo. I do not know how I ever could have proceeded without his extremely perceptive comments and observations. His friendship, from the beginning of this project through its conclusion, has been invaluable.

Finally, my family has been crucial to the completion of this book. My parents have given me their confidence and encouragement. Most important, my wife Annick, through her love, enthusiasm, tolerance, and strength, enabled me to finish. It is ultimately to her that I owe any success I might have.

Introduction

In 1889, Amory Dwight Mayo, Massachusetts native and Unitarian minister, observed while addressing a Nashville meeting of the National Educational Association: "From General Robert Lee, down, a large number of eminent military men were summoned to the office of president and professor in the collegiate schools—revived or newly established in the years after 1865." No other Southern gentlemen, Mayo continued, had "done so much in the educational revival of the past twenty years as these men; who hung up sword to wield the professor's 'pointer' and retired from the well-fought field of arms to maneuver, on the blackboard, the columns of symbolic signs that prophesy the coming civilization of a continent."[1]

Mayo's observation revealed his understanding of convictions prevalent among Confederate officers who entered academia. These officers combined the hope of postbellum reconciliation with a millennial idea of progress. Both Mayo's assessment of the role former Confederate veterans played in revitalizing Southern higher education and his insight into the mind of postbellum Southern academics, however, generally have been ignored or rejected.

In Anne Rivers Siddons's novel, *Hill Towns,* fictional Trinity College, high in the mountains of the Southern interior, hired "a great many unemployed Confederate officers." They gave students a classical education that fit them for life in the "Christian gentlemen's South." The conservative image of these academics is drawn from a historical interpretation that views former Confederate officers as loyal to attitudes prevalent in the Old South and hostile to change. Consequently, Confederate veterans who entered academia after the war are depicted as wedded to classical education and stubbornly resistant to innovations in curricula and teaching methods that occurred elsewhere in the United States in this era. The ideas of these Southern academics have gone largely unexamined because these individuals have been denied the status of intellectuals.[2]

Yet the Civil War generation of Southern academics, and especially former Confederate officers among them, embraced innovative academic policies and developed a forward-looking ideology for the South in the postbellum period. Confederate veterans served as presidents and professors at most state universities, agricultural and mechanical colleges, and military schools, and at many private schools. At such institutions, these men introduced and implemented scientific and technical curricula for training chemists; civil, mechanical, and mining engineers; geologists; and scientific agriculturalists, whose expertise promised to transform the South into a modern society. These Southern academics also created an idea of progress[3] that inspired and supported their activities and policies for creating a New South. They defined progress as the inevitable movement of civilization toward perpetual scientific and social achievements.

Former Confederates who entered academia were familiar with the South's strenuous wartime attempt to industrialize, in order to compete with the North's advantage in materiel. Emory Thomas argues that the impact of this industrialization revolutionized Confederate society. He states, however, that this "revolutionary experience did not survive the total defeat and destruction of the Confederate state."[4]

In fact, Union victory could not eliminate the intellectual and psychological effects of industrialization. Many Southern military and civilian officers who participated in the Confederacy's attempt to transform the South from an agrarian society into an industrial one brought that background with them into academia after the war. This "revolutionary experience" convinced postbellum Southern supporters of scientific education that their section needed to acquire and implement the technical skills necessary for progress and to wean itself from economic, if not political, dependence on the North.

Progressivist[5] Southern academics also believed that scientific examination of historical facts revealed the inevitability of Confederate defeat. These academics blamed their side's defeat on the North's overwhelming industrial advantage, which they often attributed to the superior technical education Northern schools provided their students. Most antebellum Southern academics, progressivist scholars believed, had feared progress and consequently had failed to equip college graduates with the practical scientific skills necessary to compete with the North economically, industrially, and militarily. The progressivist academics' postbellum belief in the inevitability of the Confederacy's defeat allowed them to deny their responsibility for losing the war.

At the same time, the scientific investigation of history offered the scholars the opportunity to prove to an exultant North the justness of the South's cause. Unbiased historical research, they argued, would prove that white Southerners had waged a war in defense not of slavery, but of Constitutional principles. This faith in history and progress contained both dialectical and millennial elements. Providence required the dialectical confrontation between an industrial North and an agrarian South, followed by a Union victory, because the latter was required in order to convince Southerners to embrace modern progress. With the problems of secession and slavery settled forever, the reunited nation could fulfill its millennial destiny through unmatched material and social progress and continue its role as the hope of nations.

Northern academics and intellectuals accepted much of their Southern counterparts' progressive paradigm because it corresponded well with their own ideas about progress. For Southern academics, however, progress did not entail abandoning their Lost Cause. Rather, future progress was closely tied to a proper understanding and respect for the past. Progressivist academics connected the idea of a scientifically progressive New South with that of a historically satisfying Lost Cause. They saw these not as antithetical ideologies or as convictions that needed reconciling, but as intimately linked creeds. It is not surprising that Southern academics joined science and history in this manner, because the idea of progress is a view of history closely tied to technological advancement. Roger Nisbet observes that "respect for and acceptance of the past are absolutely vital to the theory of progress; without a past, . . . no principle of development, no stages emerging from one another, and no linear projection to the future are possible."[6] Progressivist academics created a Lost Cause past capable of sustaining their hopes for a New South future. The means by which progress would be carried forward was higher education: scientific historical training to redeem the Old South, along with applied science training to bring about the New South. Although Southern adherents of progress generally believed in its inevitability, they also believed that society needed to work actively to attain it.

Southern progressivist academics, like most Americans, advocated a laissez-faire society: free markets, religious liberty, academic freedom, free association (save between the races), and decentralized government. They believed that competition, in all areas of life, acted as a major component in the creation of progress. These Southern academics drew on Victorian ideas about progress and education—as elaborated by Darwin, Huxley, Spencer, and others—to forge a view of progress they believed met the needs of the devastated South.

These academics believed that government should provide education, especially scientific education, to enable individuals to compete more effectively and therefore accelerate Southern progress. Their advocacy of tax-supported schools enabled them to accept that government might operate to stimulate progress in other areas, too. They often championed state government action to ban child labor, enforce prohibition of liquor, promote public health, and regulate railroads, all in the name of progress. Additionally, their embrace of progress led some progressivist academics to suggest that African Americans also might advance, especially materially (though never as far or as fast as other Americans). Southern progressivists also called for an expanded role for white women when warranted by their intellectual talents or manual skills.

The progressivist expectations of the Civil War generation of academics and their allies went largely unfulfilled. Beyond the turn of the century, the region continued to trail the North economically. Most white Southerners ignored academic appeals—delivered at agricultural and mechanical fairs, alumni association meetings, and commencement exercises; and reported in newspapers—to help effect progress in the South. They refused to provide the costly state and private aid to higher education that academics thought necessary to fuel the New South. White Southerners thus failed to meet the expectations of New South academics. Still, these academics managed to change the curricular orientation of the schools they controlled from classical to modern, even if they could not always fund their new programs adequately. Furthermore, the image of progress they forged in these years endured to the point that the subsequent generation of postbellum academics adopted their predecessors' progressivist ideals.

It is not true that postbellum Southern academics possessed little or no mind.[7] Public and private sentiments expressed by Southern scholars, and the curricular reforms they enacted in their schools, indicate the existence of a coherent progressivist philosophy at the forefront of Southern academic thought. During the tumultuous postwar years, these thinking Confederates constructed a vision of Southern progress that would allow a rebuilt and reconciled South to share fully in the nation's material wealth and spiritual brilliance. They exchanged their swords for pointers and implemented educational policies that they believed would enable graduates to realize that vision.

Chapter 1

Progress and Academia in the Antebellum South

Most antebellum Southern academics, intellectuals, and other spokesmen for higher education approached the idea of progress—the perpetual material and spiritual (or moral) improvement of the human race—cautiously, because they feared that potentially it threatened slavery. In order to mitigate their fears, they made the institution of slavery a prerequisite for progress. They therefore could not construe anything that threatened slavery as progress, including the industrialization that they associated with free labor and abolition. To protect slavery, they necessarily rejected academic innovations that might lead to industrialization. The Northern academy associated with material progress the industrialism that produced such technological advances as railroads, steamships, and telegraphs. In contrast, the Southern academy identified material progress not with industrialization, but with the physical benefits generated by slave labor and accrued by slaveholders. And, whereas most Northern academics identified abolition as spiritual progress, their Southern counterparts argued that slavery provided for spiritual progress by providing the owners of slaves, freed from menial labor, opportunities to improve language, law, manners, morals, and the social graces identified with advancing civilization. The classical studies that dominated the curricula of Southern antebellum state universities and denominational colleges reflected their professors' conservative attitudes toward progress. A minority of Southern educational advocates, however, discounted any threat that the idea of progress might pose to slavery. Inspired by the material aspect of progress, they attempted curricular reform, particularly the expansion of programs in applied science, in an effort to equip Southerners with the technical skills needed to compete with the North, despite the latter's industrial advantage.

The half-century that followed American independence witnessed sporadic attempts to establish Southern state colleges and provide them curricula beyond the classics which dominated American higher education. The 1776 constitution of the State of North Carolina charged that all "useful learning shall be duly encouraged and promoted in one or more [public] Universities." The University of North Carolina finally opened in 1795. Over the next twenty-five years, the legislatures of Georgia, South Carolina, and Virginia also established state schools, which typically received state land grants to provide for their endowments.[1]

The South's first state universities attempted to establish curricula that included some scientific and utilitarian training in the areas of architecture, astronomy, bookkeeping, botany, chemistry, geology, mineralogy, navigation, and surveying. Classical studies quickly rose to prominence, however. Such studies included elocution, Greek, Latin, logic, moral philosophy, and theoretical pure mathematics. These courses also prepared students for the professions of law, medicine, and theology. Under this traditional system of collegiate instruction, professors taught the "pure" sciences—the study of science for its own sake—and ignored their potential utilitarian value. Professors deemed practical applications of scientific discoveries inconsequential or plebeian. Although nascent sciences offered new possibilities for instructing students, including teaching natural science through illustrative experiments, faculty usually taught all collegiate courses using the recitation method. Students memorized portions from texts or lectures and verbally repeated, or "recited," these passages to the professor. The instructor awarded the student points based upon the precision of his performance.[2]

The Southern state university most commonly associated with early-nineteenth-century scientific education, the University of Virginia, opened in 1825. The university's foremost supporter, Thomas Jefferson, believed that classical instruction in ancient languages, pure mathematics, moral philosophy, and theology suited Old World aristocrats but not New World republicans. The curriculum he proposed for the University of Virginia included astronomy, botany, commerce, geography, modern languages, and zoology. Jefferson reserved his highest praise for the study of agriculture, which he called "the crown of all other sciences."[3]

The extreme importance Jefferson placed upon agricultural instruction is readily understandable. The classical idea that civilizations undergo cycles of birth, growth, decay, and death haunted Jefferson and most republicans of his generation. They believed hunting and gathering characterized society at its birth. The subsequent agricultural stage represented a youthful period of growth. The formation of an urban stage, indicative of a society's maturity and decline, followed. Republicans believed that American society stood at the agricultural phase of development, which they considered the most prosperous and beneficial. At this point, society consisted primarily of yeoman farmers, whose independence enabled them to act virtuously by placing public interest above self-interest. Republicans hoped to delay the urban stage, brought about as available land decreased in the wake of population growth. Such conditions led to overcrowded cities consisting of impoverished and selfish masses who were dependent upon manufacturers for their subsistence. Both laboring and commercial interests then would be unable to resist turning to the government for support, which subsequently would usurp everyone's liberty and right to property.

Republicans hoped that the West might offer land enough to prevent the evils of overpopulation indefinitely.[4]

Western lands, however, did not solve the republicans' ideological crisis. They discovered that American farmers were producing more than the domestic market consumed. Unless farmers located new markets, the limited demand threatened to reduce yeomen to subsistence agriculture, which offered little incentive to labor because it promised no rewards beyond mere existence. Republicans turned to foreign markets to prevent such an occurrence. Yet they feared that overseas trade would stimulate the importation of European luxuries, which would promote acquisitiveness and self-interest, and therefore threaten virtue. Many republicans comforted themselves with the belief that agrarian life would enable Americans to import luxuries without becoming corrupt.

Thus, republicans abandoned their classical opposition to commercial development and instead encouraged trade, in the hope of maintaining their agrarian republic. European blockades, American embargoes, and the War of 1812, however, closed ports to American shipping and demonstrated the unreliability of foreign markets. Their limited potential ultimately forced republicans to accept manufactures. They believed such industry was necessary to encourage farmers to produce beyond subsistence by providing them with a domestic market of nonagricultural workers. Republicans hoped the ability of laborers to move westward and obtain their independence through agriculture would force manufacturers to keep wages above subsistence level and thus guarantee the virtue of urban workers.[5]

Jefferson's educational thinking mirrored the republican ideological journey from abhorrence to acceptance of a commercial and manufacturing economy. Although Jefferson maintained his support for agricultural education, the nation's economic vulnerability led him to embrace other types of practical scientific instruction as well. Jefferson wrote in 1814 that he wanted Virginia to build a place "where every branch of science, deemed useful at this day and in our country should be taught in the highest degree." The institution he proposed included schools of agriculture, military science, and "technical philosophy." Jefferson claimed that the last school would train carpenters, distillers, machinists, opticians, and other craftsmen.[6]

Jefferson hoped to protect American independence through the discovery and dissemination of useful knowledge necessary for the development of commerce and manufacturing. He also believed that scientific instruction promised to elevate the masses beyond mere subsistence. Jefferson noted that individuals who applied science to their labors benefited both themselves and the public. Therefore, science promised to reconcile self-interest and public interest so as to maintain the republic's virtue. "Science," Jefferson wrote to Josiah Meigs, "is indispensably necessary for the support of a Republican government." Jefferson's pedagogical prescription for avoiding cyclical decay emphasized instruction in technical studies which promised to sustain the republic.[7]

Jefferson's optimistic view resulted from his observation that scientific inventions continually elevated the human physical condition, allowing people the leisure to cultivate their moral faculties. Jefferson denied "that man is fixed, by the law of his nature, at a given point; that his improvement is a chimera, and the hope delusive of rendering ourselves wiser, happier or better than our forefathers were." Humankind's rapidly increasing ability to change the environment through the application of science to physical problems convinced Jefferson of the likelihood of continued improvement. "[W]e need look back half a century," Jefferson observed, "to times which many now living remember well, and see the wonderful advances in the sciences and arts which have been made in that period." He credited much of this progress to education.[8]

Jefferson believed that improvement, or progress, was possible because knowledge accumulated and passed from generation to generation provided the basis for the discovery of new knowledge. He wrote to his somewhat skeptical friend John Adams, "You possess . . . too much science, not to see how much is still ahead of you, unexplained and unexplored. Your own consciousness must place you as far before our ancestors as in the rear of our posterity." Jefferson also noted that science itself prevented retrogression. "The art of printing alone, and the vast dissemination of books," Jefferson stated, "will maintain the mind where it is" if "hordes" of "barbarians" ever threatened the world's knowledge.[9]

Yet, for all Jefferson's faith that humankind could be improved, he never fully accepted the idea of unlimited progress, embraced by later nineteenth-century progressivists. "I see a prospect of great advancement in the happiness of the human race," Jefferson wrote in 1822, "and that this may proceed to an indefinite, although not infinite, degree." Earlier he had written that, while the generational transmission of accumulated knowledge must advance the well-being of humankind, this progression would not occur "*infinitely*, as some have said, but *indefinitely*, and to a term which no one can fix or foresee." Despite his faith in generational improvement, Jefferson, during the crisis over slavery in Missouri (1819–20), feared that the present generation had failed to match the wisdom of its fathers. The Missouri Compromise notwithstanding, Jefferson lamented that the sons had risked the Union over mere political considerations. He lamented that the sacrifices made "by the generation of 1776, to acquire self-government and happiness to their country, is to be thrown away by the unwise and unworthy passions of their sons."[10]

Jefferson's qualified vision of progress represents a transition from traditional republican fears concerning cycles to a new enthusiasm for perpetual progress that increasingly marked the intellectual temper of the nineteenth century. Confronted by the scientific progress of the recent past yet haunted by classical theories of inescapable cycles, Jefferson placed his faith in education and utilitarian science to help republican society prevent decay. He never seriously considered the possibility of infinite scientific or social progress, yet he doubted the likelihood of intellectual retrogression. Science and society would advance to some unforeseen point at which progress ceased but retrogression would not occur. What happened after this point Jefferson's teleology failed to specify. Unlike Christian millenarians who believed in humankind's ability to reform itself in preparation for the Second Coming and subsequent Christian paradise, Jefferson's doubts about the perfectibility of human nature forced him to discount the possibility of a similar scientific and secular utopia. "I do not, with some enthusiasts," Jefferson noted, "believe that the human condition will ever advance to such a state of perfection as that there shall no longer be pain or vice in the world."[11]

Nonetheless, Jefferson believed that his plans for the University of Virginia promised to advance human progress for as long as possible. With much of his modern curriculum in place shortly after the university opened, Jefferson died sanguine about his school's prospects. The university also provided an elective system that allowed students to select their own course of instruction. This avenue differed from the single classical course of study usually required by colleges. Many of the school's offerings, however, stressed the classics, and, over time, the university de-emphasized instruction in applied science. The university's engineering program, for example, collapsed in the wake of an economic depression in the 1840s.[12]

Public favor for utilitarian state universities started to dissipate by the end of the 1820s. The Yale Report of 1828 reaffirmed academic orthodoxy with its claim that mental discipline, instilled into students by the recitation of the classics, remained the proper objective of collegiate education. The report influenced curricular development in schools nationwide, especially in the numerous denominational colleges that appeared in the aftermath of the Second Great Awakening. Evangelical sects, especially Baptists and Methodists, had viewed colleges as places that taught infidelity. These Protestant denominations' ambivalence about a formally educated clergy had inhibited evangelical enthusiasm for higher learning. Gradually they modified their attitudes toward colleges and came to the conclusion that, given proper guidance, such institutions could help spread the Gospel. To fulfill this mission, the denominational colleges provided students with moral and religious training which took precedence over other academic concerns.[13]

To determine the exact number of collegiate schools before the Civil War is an extremely frustrating—indeed, virtually impossible—task. Many antebellum schools closed shortly after opening, due to inadequate financial support. Numerous institutions carrying the prestigious appellation "college" or "university" actually operated as secondary schools. One survey found that 172 colleges were organized between 1830 and 1860, with an attrition rate of nearly 23 percent. Protestant denominations formed the vast majority of these predominantly classical schools in rural communities. These institutions served from fewer than a dozen to over three hundred students. Students accepted by these schools ranged between thirteen and thirty years of age. The faculty usually varied between six and twelve members.[14]

Land speculators, Christian ministers, and unemployed educators encouraged communities to build colleges. These promotional endeavors frequently resulted in the development of redundant academic institutions and the duplication of educational efforts. Critics of these parallel ventures argued that they dispersed the capital necessary to provide for academically and financially sound colleges. J. D. B. De Bow's *Commercial Review* complained of the high failure rate and poor quality of Louisiana's schools. This publication observed in 1846 that the state historically had chartered and endowed many colleges, all of which had fallen "entirely short of anything that might have been expected from them." The *Review* contended that adequate support for a single but financially healthy institution would have been preferable to the twenty-odd weak schools previously promoted by the state.[15]

The growth of denominational colleges especially produced what historian Richard Hofstadter called the "great retrogression" in American higher education. Sectarian colleges, he argued, retarded the development of modern curricula.[16] Some academics nevertheless worked to move higher education away from its classical orientation. Francis Wayland, the president of Brown University from 1827 to 1855, implemented a program of utilitarian studies. His proposals sparked calls in the North and South to develop collegiate technical science programs after those in Germany and France. Between the end of the depression of the 1840s and the beginning of the Civil War, a small number of northeastern colleges and universities, including Harvard and Yale, organized scientific departments or schools that tilted Northern higher education in a slightly more practical direction.[17]

Southern supporters of practical instruction stressed the benefits that science potentially offered planters and farmers. The naturalist Benjamin L. C. Wailes, president of the fledgling agricultural society at Jefferson College in Mississippi, observed in 1841 that, in the "progress of improvement . . . new products were discovered, and new wants were supplied. Sciences before unknown, unfolding in successive ages the mysteries of nature, lent their aid, and the mechanic arts came to mitigate the toil and multiply the gains of the husbandmen." Mississippi, Wailes argued, needed manual labor schools with experimental farms to disseminate new discoveries and teach farmers to apply scientific principles in their work.[18]

Proponents of manual labor schools offered different and contradictory views of their missions. All agreed that the schools should offer poor students an opportunity to help pay for their tuition. Some backers, however, wanted the schools to teach students agricultural and mechanical science in the classroom and apply what they learned to their labors in the field or shop. Others argued for combining labor with classical instruction, believing that the latter dignified the former. Still others wanted the schools to reinforce the republican idea of personal independence obtained through one's own labor. Religious sponsors claimed that manual labor schools reinforced the biblical command to toil. The schools' curricula reflected these varied expectations.[19]

Augustus B. Longstreet, a Methodist minister and president of Emory College, wanted to join mental and manual labor "in indissoluble bonds, and to consecrate the union with the spotless robes of piety—to elevate manual labor to its legitimate rank, by blending it with mental endowments which shall *command* for it respect." He believed that the application of science to labor elevated the laborer, and that discoveries resulting from this union benefited everyone. Nevertheless, Longstreet assured Emory's youth that he did not intend to reconcile them "to a life of useless drudgery."[20]

Herein existed the primary ideological obstacle for champions of Southern utilitarian education to overcome. Southerners struggled to distinguish the "useless drudgery" that they associated with slavery from the honorable work which they construed as the "useful" application of intelligence to labor. Utilitarian education advocates tried to convince white Southerners that intelligence applied to agricultural and mechanical pursuits deserved as much respect as traditional professional knowledge. To accomplish this goal, they confronted the difficult task of either divorcing manual labor from agriculture and mechanical science or, as Longstreet suggested, elevating labor by associating it with science.[21]

William Gilham, professor of agriculture at the Virginia Military Institute (VMI) in Lexington, chose the former approach. Gilham claimed that, to attract Southern youth to the institute's proposed department of agriculture, it had to appeal to the planter class. "Our agricultural system is peculiar, and must be so," Gilham observed, "as it is modified in very many of its details by the institution of domestic slavery." He noted that slaves performed virtually all of the physical labor on Southern farms. Therefore, "our young farmers should be so educated, that they may with efficiency and skill direct the labors of others, rather than for the performance of manual labor themselves. We want scientific farmers—not mere laborers." Furthermore, Gilham believed that agricultural students should not spend time acquiring specific practical knowledge, because it never would be useful to them.[22]

The manual labor school movement could not withstand its inherent contradictions and collapsed by the mid-1840s. The schools were unprofitable for promoters and unpopular with students, who frequently rebelled against labor provisions and refused to work. One Davidson College professor disparaged that school's manual labor system as a "utopian scheme" equivalent to ill-fated attempts to raise silkworms in the South.[23]

Efforts to promote the usefulness of science for labor nevertheless continued. Northern educational reformers, including the nation's foremost proponent of public schooling, Horace Mann, argued that science applied to mechanics promised to furnish all of humankind's material desires and lessen the need for manual labor. Similar sentiments occasionally were voiced in the South. Thomas N. Wood gushed before the literary societies of the University of Alabama that the "scientific mechanist has almost annihilated distance, and has so increased the productiveness of human labor, as to give rise [to the belief] that manual labor will be entirely superseded by machinery."[24]

Nevertheless, the advantages of labor-saving machinery appeared of less immediate import to many Southerners. The expense and scarcity of free labor encouraged Northern farmers, more than slaveholding Southern planters, to embrace mechanization. Furthermore, as people who themselves engaged in little manual labor, planters lacked immediate personal incentive to develop labor-saving measures. Proslavery ideologues charged that African American slaves, locked permanently in their caste, permitted whites the leisure to pursue more exalted intellectual activities, especially elocution and other classical studies, required for advancement in politics or the professions. Planters and their sons often considered themselves above engaging in practical pursuits. Nonslaveholding farmers, economically and politically dependent upon planters, hoped to obtain slaves themselves and showed little interest in any type of education. Planters and small farmers alike generally viewed "book farming" with suspicion and preferred empirical methods of agriculture production. Both groups also opposed taxes to support public education. Planters educated their children in private schools, and small farmers needed their children's labor at home. Therefore, unlike the North, the South did not develop extensive public school systems. The South's small and politically unimportant white artisan class proved either unable or unwilling to provide public or private support for technical schools.[25]

Lettered Southerners' attitudes toward slave labor influenced their beliefs about progress and affected their attitudes toward higher education.

They understood that change, inherent in the modern idea of progress, threatened traditional authority. Therefore, their approach to progress was cautious, lest too rapid change undermine the South's labor system. James W. Massie, an intermittent professor of mathematics at VMI and a member of the Virginia House of Delegates, praised slavery in 1857 as "a conservative element in society" and claimed that it "is a mistake to suppose that *progress* necessarily involves cardinal change. Change is the child of error, like Death or Sin; progress is development, enlargement, growth."[26]

James H. Hammond, a former governor of South Carolina, told the literary societies of that state's college that it "is no paradox to say that permanence—that permanence which is created by a just, and wholesome and somewhat stringent restraint of action—is the starting point of genuine progress." Public school superintendent W. T. Walthall of Mobile, Alabama, claimed that a teacher "should be *progressive*" and "keenly and vividly suscep-tible" to improvement; however, "it is . . . still more important that he should be *conservative.*" He warned that the "age is wild with rage for fantastic novelties and pretended reformations in government, society, literature and education" and that "the growing contempt for all authority, human and divine," lay "in the false and perverted ideas of liberty and 'progress,' that . . . too often find entrance even into our schoolrooms, and tarnish the pages of our textbooks." The "false and perverted" idea feared most by Southern intellectuals was abolitionism.[27]

International abolition prevented Southern intellectuals from comfort-ably assuming that progress guaranteed the continuation of slavery. There-fore, they fashioned a progressivist vision in which slavery served as a prerequisite for human advancement. This view little resembled that of the rest of Western society. William Harper, a trustee of the University of South Carolina, shared the belief of his friend Thomas R. Dew, professor of political economy at the College of William and Mary, that slavery served as the basis for civilization. Harper argued that man refused to labor beyond what was needed to sustain his existence. "The coercion of Slavery alone," he believed, "is adequate to form man to habits of labour. Without it, there can be no accumulation of property, no providence for the future, no taste for comforts or elegancies, which are the characteristics and essentials of civilization." Harper apparently found no role for technical progress to play in alleviating the odious burden of labor and providing for the "essentials of civilization."[28]

Proslavery theorists essentially maintained a traditional republican approach to progress. Harper claimed that "progress is the condition of human affairs. Though retarded for a time by extraneous or accidental circumstances, the wheel must roll on." Population, he argued, naturally expanded, which increased the difficulty of obtaining sustenance. Competition developed among a constantly growing number of workers, thereby deflating wages and ultimately turning the unemployed into paupers. Harper and others pointed to England as evidence of the poverty, misery, and vice of the working class created by industrial free labor. Even in so-called free societies, Harper charged, "*servitude* is the condition of civilization."[29]

The South's quintessential proslavery theorist, George Fitzhugh, warned that, once the American West became overpopulated, "a refluent population [would] pour back upon the East. . . . Famine would become perennial, and revolution the common order of the day." Fitzhugh believed that such a situation already existed in Europe. The South, however, with its poor enslaved and protected from brutal wage competition, would avoid the social disorder that afflicted Europe and was destined to plague the industrial North.[30]

Southern proslavery theorists sought to delay or escape the manufacturing stage of societal progress responsible for the evils of free labor, industrialization, and urban development. They adhered to the traditional republican desire to prevent decay through spatial expansion. Massie claimed that the South's "vast and unpeopled forests" operated "as a safety-valve" making cities and manufacturers unnecessary. Southern whites, moreover, increasingly believed (as did abolitionists) that, for slavery to survive, it needed to expand—or progress—into the western territories acquired by the United States after the Mexican War. The South's intelligentsia warned that, if slavery failed to spread, the region soon would be confronted with exhausted farmland and a growing black population that would leave planters with an oversupply of agricultural labor but without viable markets for their slaves. The subsequent collapse in prices for human property ultimately would lead to economic collapse, the extinction of slavery, and societal regression.[31]

Southern intellectuals understood progress to mean material and spiritual development. One other interpretation of progress they adhered to, however, defined it as the removal of a person or object from one point on a course, passage, or journey to another point. Thus slavery operated as the basis for material progress, and societies that abandoned or lost that institution invariably progressed—or moved—cyclically from growth to maturity to decay. Southern intellectuals lacked the faith in progress expressed by their Northern and European counterparts, who regarded virtually all definitions of progress as beneficial. Although Southerners agreed with Northerners about the inevitability of progress, the latter envisioned inevitable improvement, while the former generally anticipated inevitable cycles. White Southerners believed that progress which threatened slavery was dangerous; therefore they refused to construe abolition as progress—except as a progressive stage in a declining civilization. Fear of abolitionism limited much of Southern progressivist thought to an archaic republican conception of cycles.[32]

Very few Southern intellectuals embraced the abolitionist position that slavery stifled progress. Two North Carolinians, Hinton Rowan Helper and Benjamin S. Hedrick, proved exceptions. Helper, who expatriated himself from the South, criticized slavery in his *The Impending Crisis of the South* (1857) for the impoverishment of Southern soil; the poverty of nonslaveholding whites, which prevented them from rising economically through capitalist competition for their labor; and the creation of a society that trailed the North by most educational, industrial, and material standards. Helper believed that slavery degraded all labor, and he charged that, from Delaware Bay to the Gulf of Mexico, "progress and prosperity are unknown."[33]

Hedrick, the University of North Carolina's first occupant of the "Chair of Chemistry Applied to Agriculture and the Arts," created a controversy when he revealed his desire to vote for John C. Frémont in the 1856 presidential election. A graduate of the state university, Hedrick supported Frémont's opposition to the western expansion of slavery because the professor believed that it threatened North Carolina's prosperity. Public anger against Hedrick attracted the attention of Helper, who started a correspondence with the beleaguered professor. The professor communicated to Helper that, while in attendance at a state teachers' convention in Salisbury, "quite a firm and able attempt was made to mob me." The university's board quickly fired Hedrick, who had refused to resign.[34]

Helper and Hedrick's belief that slavery, or its expansion, endangered Southern progress directly challenged the view that progress depended upon slavery. Proslavery theorists' refusal to consider the retrogressive aspects of slavery exposed their lack of concern about progress in general. If slavery retarded, instead of promoted, progress, then emancipation promised to transform Southern society constructively. If Helper, Hedrick, or any Northern abolitionist had demonstrated in any conclusive manner that slavery impeded progress, proslavery theorists most likely would have abandoned the idea of progress and defended the institution anyway. Human property and the status quo, more than progress, interested most Southern intellectuals. Nevertheless, they recognized the positive connotation the word *progress* carried in the nineteenth century, and it proved too indispensable to allow Helper, Hedrick, or anyone else to use it against them.

Southern academics and intellectuals attempted to discredit abolitionism by associating it with the host of other movements they believed proliferated in the North and led to societal decay. Albert T. Bledsoe, professor of mathematics at the University of Mississippi, decried "Socialism and Fourierism, and Fanny Wrightism, and the whole swarm of miserable *isms* that is continually buzzing in our ears." George Frederick Holmes, the first president of the University of Mississippi, denounced these, along with

"Mormonism," "St. Simonism," and "Agrarianism." Massie claimed that all "*isms* are but the efforts of individuals to congeal public sentiment to effect the same purpose which centralized government would subserve"—namely, "materialism," "Unitarianism," and "utilitarianism."[35]

Many Southern educators and their supporters reserved almost as much hostility for utilitarianism as for abolitionism. Southern classicists, intensely familiar with republican theories of cyclical growth and decay, opposed curricular reform because they associated applied science with the materialism and utilitarianism they feared led to progressive decline. William M. Wightman, president of the Methodist Southern University in Greensboro, Alabama, claimed that, in his school, "I see more than the groveling utilitarianism which would fain foster science because it may invent a machine, intensify a manure, or enlarge a crop; or in a word, help us to make more money." Wightman rhetorically asked, "Can the old Republican simplicity of manners long survive [the nation's] inundation of wealth?" Yes, he believed, as long as colleges realized they were not in the business of teaching occupations but were concerned only "with the highest possible improvement of the mind." The curriculum most capable of accomplishing this goal consisted of the Bible, the classics, belles lettres, and abstract mathematical science.[36]

Classicists believed that true education resided in an aristocracy of mind attainable only by a relatively few privileged members of society. They rejected the idea that the education of farmers and mechanics (whose occupations required utility) necessitated a superior, or even equal, level of education with that of gentlemen who chose to contemplate ancient languages and pure science. John Pratt, a professor of English literature at the University of Alabama, charged that the hostility of those who demeaned classical education emanated "from the prejudices of the uneducated mass, these prejudices are directed against an aristocracy of mind, as of wealth."[37]

Furthermore, Southern intellectuals' strict adherence to the Christian dogma of original sin required them to repudiate Northern progressivists' faith that the alleviation of poverty allowed for the spiritual improvement of individuals and therefore for the possibility for social reformation. Bledsoe, an Episcopal clergyman, blamed misguided educators, philanthropists, and statesmen, who kept the fall and depravity of humankind "so much in the back-ground," for the "countless multitude of wild and visionary schemes for the improvement of mankind." The failure to acknowledge humankind's inherent sinfulness led them to believe falsely that "men will do right, provided they are furnished with the requisite light and knowledge. As this doctrine supposes ignorance to be the only source of evil; so the only remedy it proposes is the universal diffusion of knowledge." James H. Thornwell, president of South Carolina College, criticized as "nothing better than speculative romances" the "ingenious theories which undertake, from principles of human nature, to explain the history of man's progress from barbarism to refinement." He claimed that "man was created in the image of God, and the rudeness and coarseness of uncivilized communities are states of degradation to which he has apostatized and sunk, and not his primitive and original condition."[38]

The idea that "uncivilized communities"—specifically, African societies—were degraded and depraved conveniently fit proslavery theorists' belief that Africans and African Americans were incapable of civilization. Southern intellectuals equated "civilization" with North American and European ideals of literary and technical progress. They claimed that slavery served as the only means to civilize blacks, and that, without slavery, they would return to a complete state of barbarism.[39]

Southern intellectuals adapted their Protestant religion to reinforce their proslavery and antiprogressivist attitudes. Northern and Southern Protestants believed that God allowed history to progress until Jesus Christ's return to earth. Bledsoe assured his listeners that he believed in "slow and resistless progress," despite his doubts about education's ability to alleviate human depravity. His progressivist faith, however, resided not in humankind but in Divine Providence, under which both the natural and political world "has each succeeding night, all things considered, been less gloomy than the preceding." Many Northern Protestants believed the progressive spiritual perfection of humankind required an end to slavery as a necessary preparation for the millennial advent. White Southern Protestants claimed that slavery was ordained by God and therefore might possibly survive or even flourish in the millennium.[40]

Southern academics chastised their Northern counterparts who argued that slavery violated the will of God. They pointed to biblical sanctions for slavery in both the Old and New Testaments. They specifically attacked the theological antislavery arguments of the Baptist minister and utilitarian educator Francis Wayland, who believed in humankind's ability to discern God's "higher law" that existed independently of scriptural revelation and condemned slavery. That Southern students were exposed to Wayland's moral philosophy texts in Northern colleges especially irked Southern intellectuals.[41]

Many Southern academics and intellectuals viewed abolitionism and utilitarianism as symptoms of societal decay. Northern progressivists, such as Mann and Wayland, included abolition (which they considered to be moral progress) and technical development in their progressivist vision. Abolition required white Southerners to reject the idea of moral progress, which was an integral feature of Northern intellectuals' progressivist thought. Furthermore, change, or progress, created by rapid technological development and associated with utilitarianism, unsettled many in Southern academia because potentially it threatened to upset the South's social order.[42]

Not all Southern academics, intellectuals, and proponents of higher education fretted over what Hammond called "the grandest problems of Human progress."[43] Progressivists believed that technical change was inevitable and argued that the South must acquire the skills to develop its natural resources in order to promote agriculture and manufactures. They wanted Southern schools to offer technical subjects so that graduates would be capable of freeing the South from material dependence on the North. These proponents of physical progress either avoided the subject of slavery or argued that progress would enable the South better to defend the institution. Southern progressivists believed in the inevitability of progress, but they also concluded that people must choose to encourage and support the progressive developments around them. Otherwise, progress passed over those who failed to aid its advance. Faith in progress resembled the message of Protestant ministers, familiar to most Southerners, who taught the inevitability of the millennium, yet enjoined the faithful to prepare for the Second Coming lest they not share in God's glory. Progressivists argued that, unless Southerners worked for progress, they risked missing its blessings, while others more faithful—Yankees, in particular—received its rewards.

Progressivists wanted Southern institutions of higher learning to embrace utilitarian education, so that the South might thrive in a technologically progressive world. Alexander M. Clayton, president of the Board of Trustees of the University of Mississippi, warned in 1849 that Mississippi must educate its citizens if the state hoped to receive the benefits of progress. He noted that Massachusetts provided for public education, adding that that "cold, barren and inhospitable" state "reared a shrewd, hardy, ingenuous race of sons, often of capacious intellect and comprehensive knowledge." Massachusetts prospered as a result, largely at the expense of the South. The state's merchant ships and mills wrung the real wealth from Southern cotton. "The cause of all this," Clayton noted, "is the Yankee school house," in which the "enterprising Yankee" is "formed." Yankees, he charged, "out *calculate* us." Clayton warned that to "battle them successfully we must stand upon the same platform, and use the same weapons. We must build school-houses."[44]

Francis W. Keyes admonished the University of Mississippi's alumni association in 1859 that the "state which turns a listless eye upon the march of intellect, and withholds its fostering for the mental culture of its sons, impedes its own progress and tramples upon its own highest interest." Keyes also noted that expensive apparatus was required for Mississippi to provide citizens with useful scientific knowledge. Scientific education required larger funds than historically had been necessary to operate collegiate institutions, but Southern proponents like Keyes justified the expense. One Texas legislator defended the cost of building and outfitting the proposed University of Texas by calling it a "temple of futurity" necessary for the state's preservation. Nevertheless, the cost of purchasing and maintaining apparatus, farms, and laboratories for scientific subjects discouraged many administrators from promoting scientific education when confronted with budget difficulties.[45]

Walter Monteiro lauded "the bright destiny that awaits . . . all who devote themselves to science," claiming that those who pursued knowledge recognized the "eternal progress of human intellect and human freedom." Monteiro told students of Virginia's Hampton Academy to remedy the fact that the South claimed virtually no native scientific talent and depended on the North for advances in industry. It distressed him that, in science, the South boasted no Franklin or Morse. Monteiro believed the region needed to support its own scholars financially, so as to refute the abolitionist charge that slavery yielded a backward and cruel Southern civilization.[46]

VMI's superintendent, Francis Henney Smith, argued that instruction in applied science promised to resurrect the fortunes of a declining state, enabling the latter, in effect, to escape or delay the cycle of decay expected to befall all societies. "The age we live in is one of progress," Smith observed, "especially physical progress." He asked rhetorically, "What is wanting in this great state [Virginia] to place her again in the lead of her sister states but the development of her immense physical resources?" If only Virginia embraced science and applied it to her resources, he claimed, the state soon would find greater prosperity.[47]

Progressivists like Smith wanted Southern institutions of higher learning to embrace utilitarian education so that the South could survive in a technologically progressive world. Yet Southern schools, notwithstanding the efforts of a few reformers, remained wedded to traditional approaches to higher education. William Mitchell, chair of the Board of Trustees' Prudential Committee, led the movement for reform at the University of Georgia in the mid-1850s. Mitchell wanted the school to offer a modern course of study. He complained that Southern colleges depended on the North "frequently for the men and always for the education." Mitchell wanted Georgia to establish two schools of applied science: one in the industrial arts and another in agriculture. He hoped that these schools would train engineers, artisans, manufacturers, agriculturists, chemists, and miners. The state, however, failed to provide funds for curricular expansion, despite the recommendations of Mitchell and his committee.[48]

Reform also failed at the University of North Carolina. Although the university established a "School for the Application of Science to the Arts" in

1852 that offered a few scientific courses, the school's focus remained firmly on the classics. The professor of mathematics emphasized pure rather than applied mathematics, and engineering and geology matriculants studied in the field only once or twice a year. John Kimberly, who replaced Hedrick as professor of agriculture and chemistry, found upon his arrival that the laboratory consisted of inoperable equipment and the floor was covered with broken glass. He complained that the laboratory contained no materials and that he had no textbooks for students. When Kimberly, a graduate of Harvard's Lawrence Scientific School, asked President David L. Swain how he should teach without apparatus, the classicist replied, "Lecture, lecture . . . no matter about what."[49]

The University of Alabama opened in 1831 and adhered to the traditional curriculum throughout the antebellum period. The school's Baptist president, the Reverend Basil Manly, issued an unreserved defense of classical instruction to the Board of Trustees in 1852. Manly claimed that colleges cannot "comprise every actual trade, business, calling and profession, in full and successful experiment," because too little capital and time was available to provide such a broad education. Furthermore, he contended that every effort in the United States that had abandoned classical studies for courses in applied science had proven "an utter failure."[50]

The other southwestern state university, the University of Mississippi, also engaged in little academic innovation before the Civil War. George Frederick Holmes served as the school's first president upon its opening in 1848. The twenty-eight-year-old defender of classical education previously had taught ancient languages at the University of Richmond and political economy at the College of William and Mary. Holmes dabbled in the positivist thought of Auguste Comte. He was attracted to the French philosopher's belief that order and progress complemented, rather than contradicted, each other. He eventually discarded Comtean philosophy because it rejected the necessity of Christianity for progress. Holmes opposed curricular innovation and considered practical studies a "lower order of education." He accomplished little at the University of Mississippi and abandoned the school four months after it commenced operation because of administrative difficulties, discipline problems, and poor health. The trustees replaced Holmes with Augustus Longstreet, who formerly had served as president of Emory. Although Longstreet had advocated instruction in applied science and manual labor at Emory, he demonstrated little interest in inaugurating such programs at Mississippi. The university's curriculum heavily emphasized the classics, and the responsibility for teaching botany, chemistry, geology, mineralogy, and physics resided in a single professor.[51]

Longstreet remained at the University of Mississippi for seven years. Upon Longstreet's resignation in 1856, the trustees appointed Frederick A. P. Barnard president. A native of Massachusetts who had been educated at Yale, Barnard tinkered in astronomy, photography, and surveying. Prior to his appointment, he had taught mathematics, chemistry, and physics at the University of Alabama. Despite Barnard's scientific reputation, he attempted no curricular innovations at the University of Mississippi. Previously, he had opposed the moderate elective system put into place during his tenure at Alabama. Barnard also rejected utilitarian studies and believed that pure research was the proper sphere of a university. He vigorously defended the classics and claimed that collegiate courses in the physical sciences, modern languages, and civil engineering "must be pronounced to be uncalled for and unnecessary" from an "educational point of view." Three-quarters of a century later, William Faulkner accurately described the university attended by his characters Charles Bon and Henry Sutpen—Barnard's university—as no more than a "small new provincial college" in "the Mississippi hinterland."[52]

South Carolina College also failed to catch the progressivist spirit. Longstreet obtained the presidency of that college in 1857 and spent most of his time there enforcing discipline, defending slavery, and campaigning for secession. He replaced Charles F. McCay, a professor of mathematics, who previously had taught at the University of Georgia. Born in Pennsylvania, McCay followed James Thornwell, a classicist, as president of South Carolina College and created a curricular controversy when he convinced that college's Board of Trustees to lessen its emphasis on the classics by eliminating the chair of belles lettres. Opposition from classical professors and riotous behavior by students quickly forced McCay from office. Upon Longstreet's accession to the presidency, the school returned to its traditional curriculum, despite the presence on his faculty of the celebrated scientists John LeConte and Joseph LeConte. Although the LeConte brothers enhanced South Carolina's scientific instruction, they initiated no curricular reformation. Like Barnard, Joseph LeConte preferred pure to applied research.[53]

Curricular reform efforts and the manual labor school movement failed to transform Southern higher education. Most Southern institutions remained under the control of classicists who were uninspired by the idea that their schools' graduates might aid the South in achieving greater scientific and spiritual progress. Most Southern schools demonstrated this dearth of inspiration through their commitment to the classics and their defense of slavery. Only when confronted by war would classicists finally start to surrender to progressivists some of their control over Southern academia.

Chapter 2

A Separate Education and the Lesson of Civil War

"In these troublous and disloyal times, we can render our mother State no better service," Francis Smith told the cadets of the Virginia Military Institute (VMI) in the late summer of 1856, "than by making her *independent*—by affording a home education for all her sons—and her daughters too." Smith believed that the specter of disunion generated by the abolitionist doctrines of that "most disloyal State of Massachusetts" demanded that Virginia prepare for any threat. Smith announced that VMI stood ready to do its part in the state's hour of need and reminded the cadets of the benefits the institution had provided for two of the state's most important interests—namely, "her internal improvements and her military defenses." Southern progressivist academics, like Smith, took advantage of the sectional crisis and the following civil war to propagandize the benefits of utilitarian studies through the "home education" and military school movements.[1]

Southern academics and their supporters deplored the fact that parents who deemed Northern schools superior to those in the South sent their sons north for collegiate instruction. Proponents of Southern education appealed to state and sectional pride in an effort to encourage parents to keep their children at "home" and to build Southern institutions. Furthermore, the influence of abolitionist professors upon Southern youth worried the South's intellectuals and provided another argument in favor of "home education." Prominent Georgia lawyer William H. Stiles told a Cherokee Baptist College (Georgia) commencement audience that "the injury to Southern youth from a Northern education would not only unfit them for their native institutions but at the same time implant in them a deadly hostility to the institution which nothing but its destruction could possibly appease."[2]

The fear of "foreign" education began with the birth of the Republic. Thomas Jefferson warned in 1785 that the young man who attended college in Europe learned drinking and gambling and acquired a taste for European "luxury and dissipation" that threatened his virtue. The student returned to his native country, Jefferson charged, a foreigner. Ironically, John Adams warned Jefferson (who ignored the New Englander's advice) not to employ foreign professors at the University of Virginia, lest they subvert the republican natures of their students.[3]

Prior to the intensification of the sectional crisis in the late 1850s, proponents of home education in the South tended to advocate a national and republican education. Rev. William A. Scott told a New Orleans school board in 1845, "We want a thorough Home Education," one that emphasized American and not European values. Public education, Scott argued, promised to help secure the perpetuity of the Union. By the end of the 1850s, however, Southern educators had transformed the term "home education" to mean a separate Southern, and not an American, education.[4]

Secession eventually provided the home education movement with its ultimate justification: Yankee education indeed equaled foreign education. After the outbreak of civil war, the Mercer University catalogue admonished parents not to send their sons north to school "in *a foreign nation.*" The South's separation from the idea of a national education, like its withdrawal from national politics and national religious denominations, represented another step toward the dissolution of the bonds that tied the Southern states to the Union.[5]

The hostility of home educators to Yankee letters extended beyond their opposition to Northern colleges. Proponents of home education also feared the influence of textbooks written and manufactured in the North and widely used in all types of Southern schools. They worried that abolitionist messages contained in the texts threatened to undermine the support of Southern students for slavery. They wanted texts that extolled the benefits and virtues of slavery and that promoted positive images of the South to the rest of the nation.[6]

Home educators also condemned Southern schools that hired professors from nonslaveholding states. Advocates of home education believed that professors and teachers held the power to form and shape youthful opinions, and they feared that abolitionism infected Southern classrooms. J. S. B. Thacher proposed that Mississippi establish normal schools, because he claimed that some Northern instructors teaching in Natchez's public schools inclined toward abolitionism. "Which if indulged in," he observed, "we may presume they are not slow to impart to their pupils." Suspicion of Northern educators extended even to Frederick Barnard, whose twenty-two-year professorial career in the South failed to protect him from accusations that he harbored abolitionist sympathies. While he was chancellor of the University of Mississippi, the Board of Trustees tried Barnard on charges that he accepted the testimony of a slave against that of a student, held "unsound" beliefs on the "slavery question," and arranged unnecessarily to have university documents printed in the North. The board ultimately acquitted Barnard, a slaveholder, and tendered him its vote of confidence. Nevertheless, Barnard's presence forced the university to endure allegations that it served as "an hot-bed of Abolitionism" and a "nursery of Yankeeism."[7]

Proponents of scientific instruction attempted to use the home education movement to their advantage. In his unsuccessful appeal for expanded scientific education at the University of Georgia, William Mitchell lamented "the necessity of sending our Southern sons to Massachusetts" for technical instruction. He also complained of Georgia's dependence on Northerners for the operation of its railroads, factories, and mines. A school of applied science in Athens, Mitchell argued, would give Georgia natives the practical training needed to conduct and develop industries that required scientific knowledge.[8]

The *Louisiana Democrat* applauded the Dolbear Commercial College in New Orleans for its plan to establish an agricultural and mechanical department. The program promised to alleviate the necessity for students to leave the South to secure a technical education. A Southern school of applied science, the newspaper noted, allowed youth to receive utilitarian instruction without imbibing the "poison of opposing sentiments" taught in Northern schools.[9]

Mercer University, shortly after it established a three-year "Scientific Course," added another "new feature" to its instruction: "a special study of the subject of slavery." The course offered "every argument on both sides logically tested, in order that our young men may be qualified to defend the institutions of their country." Apparently, the outcome of the "logical" debate never would be in doubt.[10]

Southern Episcopalians attempted the most ambitious effort to fulfill the demand for home education at the university level. Led by the Bishop of Louisiana, Leonidas Polk, Episcopal clerics raised funds to establish what they hoped would develop into the South's preeminent university. The proposed University of the South, located at Sewanee, Tennessee, promised to offer every classical and scientific course of study. The Board of Trustees planned thirty-two schools in all, including nine schools of ancient and modern languages, and schools of agriculture, commerce, fine arts, and mining. Polk explained to the bishops of nine slave states that the proposed university would offer an education comparable to that provided in the North. He claimed that the poor quality of Southern higher education required that "our children [be] expatriated or sent off to an inconvenient distance, beyond the reach of our supervision or parental influence, exposed to the rigors of an unfriendly climate, to say nothing of other influences not calculated . . . to promote their happiness or ours." The laying of the university's cornerstone occurred on October 10, 1860, amid great fanfare, with Frederick Barnard and the oceanographer Matthew F. Maury as featured speakers. Efforts to open the university, however, ceased following the outbreak of sectional hostilities and did not resume until after the Civil War.[11]

Another failed attempt to establish a preeminent Southern university occurred at the University of Louisiana in New Orleans. Claudius W. Sears, a graduate of West Point, the dean of the collegiate faculty, and professor of mathematics and natural philosophy, claimed that he had discovered Louisiana students in all of the Northern colleges. Sears complained that "long and freely have we been giving of our wealth to those who now scornfully taunt us with our dependence and our inferiority in the progress of civilization." Sears argued for expansion of his school's scientific offerings, as a means of rectifying Louisiana's technical inferiority in agriculture and industry. He believed that, if applied science could be taught adequately at the university, no reason would exist to send Louisiana students north, where they absorbed the spirit of abolitionism along with scientific knowledge.[12]

Sears's views on scientific education agreed with those of a curricular committee established by the university's Board of Administrators. In its report, the committee applauded colleges that, over the previous twenty years, had added new scientific courses of study to their predominantly classical programs. The committee recommended that the Board of Administrators establish a school of natural sciences that would include chemistry, geology, mineralogy, mechanics, agriculture, and natural philosophy. Despite the efforts of Sears and the committee, the proposed expansion failed for lack of financial support and students. Although a state university, it received little legislative patronage, and private donations failed to keep the school in operation past the start of the Civil War.[13]

The failure of state universities in Louisiana and other slaveholding states to adopt utilitarian curricula led some proponents of applied science to look instead to the South's growing desire for military education as a means of promoting their program. The military school movement started in earnest in the late 1830s and continued through the secession crisis. Public demand on the frontier that states provide the militia with qualified officers in case of conflict with Native Americans, the instillation of discipline in youths, and a love of things military—all these have been offered as explanations for the establishment of private and state military academies in the South during the 1830s and 1840s. Advocates of martial education also organized private military academies north of the Ohio River. The military school movement in the South, however, included the establishment of state military schools which represented a movement separate from the national effort. As sectional tensions intensified, increasing numbers of Southerners supported the creation of public military colleges, ostensibly to provide graduates capable of combating slave revolts. Northern critics charged that proponents wanted the schools to train graduates who could help the South militarily to resist federal authority.[14]

Many of those responsible for organizing Southern military schools wanted to instruct youth in applied science, as well as drill and tactics. Supporters of this type of education concerned themselves less with the development of martial skills than with the production of technical talent capable of freeing their section from its dependence on Northern manufacturers. That some Southerners looked to military schools to help remedy this situation is not surprising; historically, martial and scientific education are connected. Applied mathematics, chemistry, mechanics, mineralogy, and other technical sciences have military applications. The United States Military Academy at West Point, New York, proved the most significant scientific institution in the antebellum period and served as the model for utilitarian reformers. The academy, supported by Jefferson while he was president of the United States and established by Congress in 1802, served as the nation's first school of applied science. Strongly influenced by the École Polytechnique in Paris, the academy's course of study also emphasized natural science. The school excluded ancient languages and literature, as well as "pure" (as opposed to "applied") sciences. The academy initially focused on military engineering but quickly came to include civil engineering in its course of study.

Engineering carries military connotations, and the term "civil engineer" gained popularity in the eighteenth and nineteenth centuries as a means of discriminating between civilian and military engineers. Both types engaged in similar activities, particularly the design and oversight of the construction of bridges and roads. Supporters of West Point expected the institution's graduates to apply their skills to civilian works after their discharge from the army. By the mid-1820s, the academy's regulations required cadets to study public works. Many officers fulfilled the hopes of proponents of the U.S. Military Academy when they left the army and found employment as civilian engineers and worked on canal or railroad projects. Well over one hundred academy graduates worked as civilian engineers by the end of the 1830s.[15]

Some Southern educators understood that military institutions provided graduates who pursued industrial and technical occupations in the domestic economy. The South's first public military academy, the Virginia Military Institute (VMI), vigorously embraced applied science. Founded in 1839 at Lexington, VMI's curriculum and organization were fashioned after those of the U.S. Military Academy. VMI quickly developed the strongest scientific program in the South. Proponents of VMI's curriculum emphasized the industrial, scientific, and technical aspects of the instruction and the pragmatic benefits the school offered Virginians, rather than the military value of the education. VMI's governing board wanted the school to "do for Virginia what West Point has done for the United States" by giving students the "very best training in the scientific and industrial pursuits." The institute, its proponents believed, would enable Virginia to keep pace with national progress. The president of VMI's Board of Visitors, Philip St. George Cocke, claimed that it "is scarcely possible that in this country of progress, and in this age of physical progress, such a school will not at all times be crowded." At VMI, he added, "our young men . . . will come out learned in science, skillful in practice, with power to wield all the laws of nature in behalf of the physical, intellectual, and moral progress of their country." Cocke boasted in

1850 that, throughout the entire South, only his school provided thorough and exclusive instruction in the physical sciences.[16]

The institute's superintendent, Francis Henney Smith, argued that Virginia's future prosperity depended upon the institution's success in the graduation of scientifically trained alumni. Smith claimed a dual role for his school: to help Virginia adjust to industrial change and compete in the national economy. First, he noted, VMI provided the state with engineers to build railroads, geologists to exploit mineral resources, and agronomists to improve agriculture. Smith boasted in 1857 that, over VMI's first eighteen years of operation, the institute had graduated fifty students who found employment as engineers on state internal improvement projects. Second, Smith wanted VMI to serve the state in more direct ways. He offered the services of the institute's professor of chemistry to analyze soils and fertilizers for farmers and planters. This would furnish them with information capable of improving the quality of their crops and the quantity of their yields. Smith also encouraged the legislature to commission VMI professors to conduct an exhaustive geological survey of the state, identifying various types of natural resources. He also emphasized that VMI, as a scientific institution, aided the development of the state's commercial and manufacturing interests.[17]

Despite the accomplishments he credited to VMI, Smith believed the state legislature failed to provide the school with adequate appropriations. The superintendent claimed in 1856 that the U.S. Military Academy band received more funds annually than the support received by VMI. Smith wanted his institution to become the "great scientific school of the South," and he believed that accomplishing this task required more legislative funding. The institute depended upon interest from a legislative endowment, various building and operational appropriations, tuition, and private gifts.[18]

Smith claimed that VMI "paved the way" for the introduction of modern scientific curricula at other Virginia schools. He believed that VMI's reputation enabled West Point graduates like himself, Edward C. Courtnay at the University of Virginia, Benjamin Ewell at the College of William and Mary, and Daniel Harvey Hill at Davidson College in North Carolina to join academia and promote scientific education at their respective schools. Smith noted that his school, by the mid-1850s, provided the model for both operational and proposed public military schools in Arkansas, Georgia, Louisiana, Mississippi, and South Carolina. By the start of the Civil War, Alabama, Florida, and Tennessee also had taken steps toward establishing state military academies. At least two state schools, the Louisiana State Seminary of Learning and Military Academy in Pineville and the West Florida Seminary in Tallahassee, eagerly sought and employed VMI graduates as professors shortly before the Civil War.[19]

As the decade of the 1850s progressed, state legislatures intensified their efforts to establish state military schools and lent support to extant private academies. By the eve of the Civil War, all the states that joined the Confederacy, with the exception of North Carolina and Texas, directly sup-ported military education in some form. These schools joined the multitude of private military academies that emerged throughout the South in the decade before the Civil War. Many of the schools especially touted the practical nature of their courses of study. At least two schools incorporated the word *polytechnic* in their names, announcing clearly to prospective students the nature of the instruction. The term *polytechnic, De Bow's Review* explained, "derived from two Greek words signifying 'many arts,'" and polytechnic education referred to education that provided training in the "industrial professions," particularly chemistry, engineering, manufacturing, architecture, and metallurgy. The journal also reported that polytechnic instruction remained closely identified with military instruction, as both originally had been provided by the École Polytechnique, "the military school of the first Napoleon." One new Napoleonic school avoided any confusion that the Greek-derived word might create. It simply identified itself as a "military and scientific school," emphasizing that it provided instruction in machinery, geology, mineralogy, and scientific agriculture.[20]

The argument that the scientific nature of military instruction would enable the South to develop its own industrial talent appeared with increased frequency as the prospect of violent sectional conflict heightened. *De Bow's Review* claimed in 1859 that it "becomes those of us who are identified with great Southern educational movements to seek so to mould our system that it too shall bear upon the development of our industrial resources." The journal praised the Polytechnic School of Pennsylvania for its ability to aid that state's mining industry through its technically trained graduates and noted that the South needed similar scientific education in order to develop its "industrial resources." The journal hoped that the coming establishment of the Louisiana State Seminary of Learning, with its planned scientific and military organization (the Pennsylvania school lacked the latter), might provide similar benefits to Louisiana.[21]

George Mason Graham, who attended but did not graduate from West Point, served as vice-president of the Board of Supervisors of the Louisiana State Seminary of Learning. The post required him to attend to everyday problems concerning the seminary's organization. The board's primary job was to determine the school's course of study. Graham wanted to model the curriculum, organization, and system of discipline after those of VMI and the U.S. Military Academy. He especially wanted the seminary to give students a utilitarian education. Graham wrote to Louisiana's Gov. Thomas O. Moore that "there are plenty of other schools where those can go who desire to acquire a finished classical education," but there "is no school in the state, and but few out of it, of the utilitarian character that [the Board of Supervisors] desire[s] to give to this one, where those arts and sciences shall be taught which are of practical use in the every day employments of life." Moreover, Graham rejected any deviation from that purpose. He informed Governor Moore that he opposed the inclusion of Greek and Hebrew in the curriculum because "they take too much time from studies of greater utility." Graham won most of the board's support. The new school opened in January 1860 with a practical scientific orientation.[22]

Daniel Harvey Hill also greatly admired the scientific instruction offered at military schools such as West Point (his alma mater) and VMI. He encouraged the South to establish military academies that promised to provide the region with technical as well as military training. Furthermore, Hill wanted farmers to read agricultural journals. These, he believed, would convince farmers to embrace scientific agriculture. The native South Carolinian also advocated home education and wrote an algebra textbook with mathematical examples that chided Yankees for their alleged parsimony.[23]

Hill deplored the low esteem in which Southerners regarded scientists and their labors. Teachers of science, he complained, "rank, in the estimation of many, as first class *overseers*." Hill hoped, however, that attitudes toward science were changing. He believed that the internal improvements derived from applied science, including bridges, factories, and railroads, gradually convinced many people to reject the "foolish and anti-American notion" that the professions deserved higher status than "vulgar mechanics." He further praised West Point and the U.S. Naval Academy at Annapolis, Maryland, for the scientific education they bestowed upon their cadets. Graduates of these schools, Hill noted, easily found employment for their services as either engineers or teachers. He attacked as incompetent the 120 or so colleges in the United States that taught four years of ancient languages. "Where," asked the acerbic Hill, "is the body of accurate classical scholars to be found?"[24]

Hill personally attempted to help rectify the South's dearth of scientific institutions when he established the North Carolina Military Institute at Charlotte in 1859. The school, patterned after VMI and West Point, offered practical scientific, as well as military, instruction and, by the start of the Civil War, claimed 150 cadets. Only one cadet enrolled in an optional ancient languages course. When war came, a student remembered, Hill warned his excited charges that it would "last as long as the Revolutionary war and we would all get enough of it, [and] he mentioned the contrast of the resources of the North and the South, both in men and means and said many other things that pacified us at the time."[25]

The *Tuscaloosa (Ala.) Independent Monitor* called for the establishment of a publicly supported military academy, not simply to prepare Alabama for invasion, but also to provide training for "all the occupations of life, in which the exact sciences in their application to the arts are of the greatest usefulness." The newspaper praised West Point for the practical scientific instruction it offered the Southern cadets who attended that institution.[26]

Southern military institutions, their supporters argued, provided an additional benefit other than technical education. The South's military and scientific academies guaranteed that students would not be exposed to social ideas, particularly abolitionism, supposedly proffered in Northern schools. The military institutions' emphasis on discipline and order offered Southerners an opportunity to enjoy the benefits of physical progress without encountering the perils they associated with moral progress. VMI's Committee on Instruction in 1856 unanimously recommended a one-year extension of the institute's four-year curriculum, to create a five-year program. In part this action was designed to provide room for a course on the "principles of slavery, as expounded by the textbook of Professor [Thomas R.] Dew."[27]

As the sectional conflict intensified through the 1850s, the prospect of disunion, combined with John Brown's failed slave insurrection in October 1859, convinced many Southerners of the need for military education. The authors of a report on military education for the University of Alabama claimed that "the abolition raid of 1859 into the borders of Virginia opened the eyes of the Slave States" to the need for military schools. Paul O. Hebert, former governor of Louisiana and a graduate of West Point, wrote to George Mason Graham: "Whether it be the result of natural martial spirit, or a foresight anticipating coming domestic troubles, it is nevertheless true that schools with military discipline and instruction have been within a few years established in nearly all the Southern States." He added, "To foster and increase these is as an act of wisdom. What the pregnant womb of time may bring forth we cannot tell—yet we should be prepared for the worst."[28]

William T. Sherman superintendent of the Louisiana State Seminary of Learning, noted in a letter to his wife late in October 1859 that he heard "a good deal" of talk that the Southern states, by establishing military schools, "were looking to the dissolution of the Union." Two months later, Sherman, a native of Ohio, reported that Southerners might be designing "these military colleges as a part of some ulterior design, but in my case I do not think such to be the case." Instead, he believed the Louisiana State Seminary's Board of Supervisors adopted a military organization "because it was represented that southern gentlemen would submit rather to the showy discipline of arms than to the less ostentatious government of the faculty."[29]

Critics of martial discipline, such as the Reverend Simeon Colton, president of Mississippi College, observed that in military institutions "men are usually kept in subordination through fear"; however, "in a literary institution, we suppose that there is an elevation of character that will secure obedience through good principle." Student rebellions and riots occurred often in the antebellum South, however, and many friends of military instruction argued effectively that youths required martial discipline to maintain good conduct on collegiate campuses.[30]

Not all backers of martial discipline concerned themselves with student rebellion. Landon C. Garland, who obtained the presidency of the University of Alabama in 1855, publicly touted other benefits that the adoption of a military organization offered at his school. He claimed that military discipline and exercises would improve the young men's manners and physical health. Privately, Garland thought the conversion of the university into a military school would provide the state valuable service when Alabama left the Union. He overcame the opposition of many legislators, parents, and faculty members to convince the legislature to transform the university into a military institution. In 1860, he toured and reported favorably on the military academies in Charleston, Nashville, Lexington, and West Point. VMI particularly impressed Garland. Partly as a result of John Brown's raid, legislative and public support allowed for the conversion of the University of Alabama into a military school that same year. The primary change in the curriculum consisted of the addition of military engineering to a fledgling civil engineering course taught by a VMI graduate, James T. Murfee.[31]

Like Garland, West Florida Seminary's president, D. McNeill Turner, wanted to turn his classical school into a military institution. He toured various military academies in the summer of 1859 and met with Daniel Harvey Hill at his North Carolina Military Institute, where the two men discussed the advantages of martial instruction. The editor of the *Floridian and Journal* advised the school to proceed with caution in its effort to convert the three-year-old West Florida Seminary into a military institution. The process, the editor argued, must "be very gradual and only so much of it at a time as circumstances may render expedient." The conversion, however, occurred very quickly, perhaps hastened by news of John Brown's raid in October. The following summer the seminary's cadets paraded before the public at the Fourth of July celebration in Tallahassee.[32]

Not all collegiate administrations eagerly supported or implemented military programs. James Thornwell opposed the South Carolina legislature's establishment of public military academies at Columbia and Charleston. He claimed they lacked defined educational goals and therefore served no academic purpose. Thornwell, who resisted implementation of utilitarian instruction at South Carolina College, suggested that the legislature convert the academies into true scientific schools to enhance their usefulness.[33]

The administration of the state university in Mississippi proved quite reluctant to convert that institution into a military school. The Board of

Trustees resisted public pressure to change the organization of the university until after the state had seceded. The subject of military instruction first officially appeared before the board in June 1861, but the trustees took no action on the matter. Instead, they sent Chancellor Barnard on a tour of Southern military academies to report on the best martial organization applicable to Mississippi's state university. Barnard opposed any change in organization. He criticized VMI's curriculum because it included military science and tactics. The chancellor also asserted that the University of Mississippi did not require military regulations to maintain student discipline, since the school seldom suffered from riotous behavior. Barnard believed that the recent reorganization of the University of Alabama, which incorporated liberal, as well as military, studies into its curriculum, required more time in operation before the board could properly consider whether that school ought to serve as a model for the University of Mississippi.[34]

The Board of Trustees, confronted by legislative and public pressure, moved ahead and established a military department at the university, despite its members' own and Barnard's misgivings. The trustees shortly thereafter ordered that "present exigencies"—in other words, civil war—required that they declare vacant the chairs of governmental science and law, Greek, pure mathematics, English literature, and ethics. They voted to continue mathematics, mineralogy, and the new chair of military studies. The board also decided to continue a recently inaugurated civil engineering course. The trustees, owing to a shortage of funds, subsequently suspended the engineering program, along with a new course in agricultural chemistry, both of which the board acknowledged the South especially needed.[35]

Despite attempts to keep the University of Mississippi open, faculty and students quickly abandoned the school so as to participate in the war effort. The departures forced the institution to close before the end of 1861. Barnard opposed disunion but maintained his post at the university until it officially closed. The Board of Trustees claimed that the chancellor's resignation allowed him to consider a government position offered by Confederate President Jefferson Davis. Barnard's "vast scientific knowledge," the trustees offered, "may prove of eminent service to the government during the war." Barnard, however, had no intention of serving the Confederacy and wanted to return to the North.[36]

While a professor at the University of Alabama, Barnard had warned the citizens of Tuscaloosa of the consequences Southerners would face if they ever attempted to dissolve the Union. Although they prided themselves on their agricultural prowess, Barnard observed, Southerners depended upon the manufactured goods produced by "their more progressive neighbors" in the North. He told them that the labor of a single artisan produced two or three times as much as that of a farmer. Consequently, he declared, "the wealth of the progressive [Northern] people has become double or triple of what it was at first." Barnard believed that manufacturing and science held the keys to human progress. A manufacturing nation, he observed, enjoyed everything "invented for the promotion of human happiness; and is rapidly multiplying new comforts and new luxuries as time goes on." If the South seceded from the Union, Barnard believed that there existed little chance it might win its independence, because "the army, the navy, all the stores and munitions of war, the custom-houses of the great seaports, and more than all, the immense superiority of numbers, will remain on the side of the [Union]."[37]

Barnard's Unionism and his prophetic insight into the demise of the Confederacy convinced him not to help the South's war effort. He met with Jefferson Davis, who wanted the former university chancellor to conduct scientific work on behalf of the Southern cause. Barnard wanted safe passage out of the Confederacy. Nearly ten years before the secession crisis, Davis had expressed concern over the lack of college graduates in the South capable of constructing bridges, dams, roads, and mining operations. He doubted that Southern higher education had directed and properly prepared students to engage in utilitarian pursuits. Davis had feared that, if the national government ever reached the point where it provoked a conflict with the slave states, the South would need scientific education to develop the industrial capacity to defend itself. As Confederate commander-in-chief, Davis needed to find as much scientific talent as possible to help forge the industrial means to wage war. Thus, the Confederate government denied Barnard's request to cross into Union lines. Barnard stayed in Alexandria, Virginia, where he was liberated by federal forces capturing the town on May 10, 1862.[38]

Like Barnard, another Northern educator and Unionist in the Deep South doubted the Confederacy's ability to wage a successful war for independence. William T. Sherman told David French Boyd, professor of ancient languages at Louisiana State Seminary and Military Academy, that "the Northern people not only greatly outnumber the whites at the South, but they are a mechanical people, with manufacturers of every kind, while you are only agriculturists." Southerners, Sherman argued, could not manufacture for themselves steam engines or rails and could barely make a yard of cloth or a pair of shoes. "In all history no nation of mere agriculturists ever made successful war against a nation of mechanics," Sherman warned. "Yet you are rushing into war with one of the most powerful, ingeniously mechanical and determined people on earth—right at your doors. You are bound to fail." Sherman remained at the school until February 1861, when, shortly after Louisiana's secession, he resigned and headed north to join the Union army.[39]

President David Swain, despite public pressure, prevented the University of

North Carolina's transformation into a military school. Even so, the state did not lack schools featuring martial pomp. In addition to Daniel Harvey Hill's North Carolina Military Institute, two other schools established in 1859, the Hillsborough Military Academy and North Carolina College, offered military instruction. The latter institution added the "military feature" to its classical curriculum in its second year, in light of "the political condition of the country." Perhaps in order not to scare off parents of students with Unionist sympathies, the college's catalogue added that "secondly, and more especially," martial instruction offered to improve "the health and physical development of the students by a regular and systematic course of exercise."[40]

Although occasionally greeted with skepticism and suspicion within and outside the academy, both the home education and the military education crusades ultimately succeeded in keeping the South's youth in the region. The number of Southern students who went North for higher education increased threefold in the decade between 1840 and 1850 but remained static thereafter, while enrollment in the South's collegiate schools increased. Many of these young men chose to attend military academies.

The Civil War, when it came, almost destroyed Southern higher education. Only two state schools, the universities of North Carolina and Virginia, remained open for the duration of the war. The overwhelming majority of the region's private colleges also closed. Students and faculty alike abandoned their schools to join the Confederate cause in either a military or political capacity. Some schools attempted to remain open by lowering age requirements and establishing new preparatory departments for students too young to fight.[41]

Initially, secession and war, like the sectional conflict that preceded them, appeared to provide other opportunities for progressivist academics and their supporters to shift Southern higher education away from classical and ornamental studies toward scientific and utilitarian instruction. "There is something radically wrong in the system of education heretofore pursued," a contributor to *De Bow's Review* noted in the winter of 1862. The progress of civilization required that Southern schools dispense with the classics in favor of scientific studies. The writer believed that "the only hope for the country . . . is to force scientific education upon the whole people." The writer further proposed creating a national university consisting of the most able group of practical scientists that could be found. This university would serve as the "corner stone" of the new nation. "Our salvation is in the Lord," the contributor admonished the journal's readers, "and He is in the corner stone."[42]

Confederates frequently appealed to Divine sanction as justification for secession and slavery. Invocations of the Divinity appeared on behalf of a revolution in education as well. Edward S. Joynes, professor of Greek literature at the College of William and Mary, equated the South's drive for independence with the Apostle Paul's description of the newly saved Christian. "For this people," Joynes claimed, "'old things have passed away, and all things have become new.'" Southerners "stand, indeed, on the threshold of a new civilization." Joynes declared that the Union robbed the South of its commercial and industrial independence. More importantly, he deplored the South's antebellum dependence on the North for teachers and textbooks; "had these influences not been happily arrested, they would have undermined our opinions, our politics, our institutions . . . rendering their dominion complete, and revolution for us impossible."[43]

Joynes envisioned teachers, trained in newly established normal departments in Southern colleges and universities, leading the revolution in Confederate education that would transform Southern society. "This is an age of mighty activity—of wondrous thought—of new and teeming ideas," Joynes claimed, and "it will soon be an age of mighty progress." He believed that the Civil War offered an opportunity to lay the foundations for future material prosperity through the establishment of publicly supported programs to train teachers. Since so many Southern young men served in the army, these programs would have to enroll women, who would become the teachers of the postbellum Confederacy. The war promised to disturb the ratio of females to males and create a postbellum increase in unmarried women who would need economic support. They could work as teachers. Joynes postulated that "woman's sphere" safely could be enlarged to include the educational training of the next generation of Southern youth.

Antebellum Southern women's institutions had been the first in the nation to award women collegiate degrees, and the war even gave women's higher education in the South a temporary boost. Until the conflict forced most schools to close, many families sent their daughters out of the way of battling armies to the relative safety of collegiate institutions, swelling their enrollments.[44]

Another admirer of progress and a contributor to the March 1861 issue of *De Bow's Review* observed that a "hundred years ago the dead languages were properly considered a part of every polite education, for there was little else to teach." Presently, however, the writer noted the emergence of botany, chemistry, engineering, geology, mechanics, mineralogy, scientific agriculture, and other nascent sciences, all of which entailed many years of study for mastery. Farmers, engineers, merchants, manufacturers, sailors, miners, and soldiers, the author claimed, needed a scientific education. Furthermore, the very prosperity of the Confederacy depended upon advances in science. The article warned, "Where there is no progress, there is sure to be retrogression."[45]

For this contributor—as for other progressivists in the Confederacy—

progress no longer meant movement to the next cyclical stage, which classical republicans believed resulted in societal decay. On the contrary, stagnation led to the decline of civilization. Confederate schools must serve as vehicles to move the South forward economically, industrially, and scientifically.

Both this contributor to *De Bow's Review* and Edward Joynes shared the anxiety of antebellum republicans that the materialism and utilitarianism associated with progress threatened to undermine the morals, and therefore the virtue, of Southern youth. To combat this threat, both commentators found a vital place for traditional studies in Southern education. The contributor to *De Bow's Review* called for a dual system of higher education, in which some students would attend only progressive scientific classes, while others enrolled only in conservative classical courses. The scheme promised to keep the negative aspects of each type of education in check. Those persons educated in utilitarian pursuits would provide Southern society with physical progress, while classically educated students would give the South its moral and political leadership. Joynes, likewise, worried that the war would give Southerners an "extreme predilection for the so-called *practical* studies to the exclusion of those that are more purely intellectual and moral, and therefore better fitted for purposes of discipline and culture." Joynes wanted Southern higher education to continue to emphasize literary studies after the war.[46]

Most educators and their supporters remained sanguine about the revolutionary potential for progress the Confederacy offered Southerners. They believed that educational autonomy would ensure the South's political sovereignty and also promise the Confederacy its economic and industrial independence. They vigorously defended slavery as the safeguard of not only Southern, but also human, progress; and they believed that the war ultimately would demonstrate the superiority of the Southern labor system over all others by defeating the abolitionist army of the United States. A group of North Carolina academics proclaimed: "We will carry on this war in the pulpit, in the school-room, at the fireside, and at every other point where we are assailed by the great enemy of human progress."[47]

While academics generally supported the Confederate cause, many nevertheless resisted the conscription of their students and the impressment of university property for military use by Confederate authorities. Landon Garland, president of the University of Alabama, is perhaps the best example of an administrator who placed the needs of his school above those of the Confederacy. The university served as a state military post, and Garland took his command and his rank of colonel seriously. He accused of desertion students who left the university for the Confederate army. Garland vehemently opposed conscription and eagerly followed the orders of Alabama's governor not to allow Confederate induction officers onto campus. As a result, the university quickly developed a reputation as a refuge for shirkers. Although Garland recognized that many people had this view of his school, he nevertheless believed that the military education and training provided by the university served the defense of Alabama better than sending untrained youth into the Confederate army. Garland justified his unpatriotic conduct by declaring that the "allegiance I owe to the Confederate Government is *under* that I owe first to Alabama."[48]

In the spring of 1863, a rumor spread through the university that Union troops had besieged the nearby town of Elyton. The report offered Garland an opportunity to lead his cadets, most of them under the age of eighteen, into battle and to prove the value of his school's military instruction. In a military operation akin to that depicted in Samuel Clemens's tale, "The Private History of a Campaign That Failed" (though with less tragic results), Garland ordered his boys to march six or seven miles east of the university to search for Union raiders. The cadets found no enemy troops, and a frustrated Garland demanded that the governor grant him the right to impress horses so that his corps might respond more quickly to future threats, imagined or real. Union troops found the university nearly two years later, however, and torched the campus.[49]

The inclination of Confederate academics away from the fighting to obstruct the war effort occurred because the most enthusiastic and able-bodied faculty members quickly had obtained leaves of absence or resigned their posts to support the South's bid to win its independence. With their departure, those left behind were largely the aged, clergy, the physically unfit, foreigners, academic ideologues (who valued their institutions more than the Confederacy), and closet Unionists. While all academics in the Confederacy were protected by state and national laws that exempted them from conscription, such statutes benefited those men who felt little inclination to aid the Confederate cause militarily. At the Louisiana State Seminary and Military Academy, the wartime faculty consisted of a cleric and two foreigners, one of whom nearby residents accused of swearing loyalty to the United States government when federal troops later occupied the school.[50]

Despite the fact that Southern academics frequently voiced opposition to conscription officers and other military measures, the common characterization of Southern academia as a hindrance to the war effort is inaccurate. Academia provided the Confederacy with capable men who flocked from the schools into military and political positions. Many of those who remained behind, however, feared wholesale abandonment of Southern higher education. They sought to find a role for themselves and their institutions in the cause of Southern independence. Collegiate personnel wanted to accommodate Confederate authorities who sought to use their institutions as barracks, headquarters, and hospitals. However, these functions threatened to disrupt what they viewed as their academic contributions to the war effort. Higher educators, especially those at military academies and at schools with newly added military departments, attempted to convince Confederate authorities of the folly of sending uneducated and untrained boys into battle. Most, they believed, would die for want of training, and thus the "seed corn" of the Confederacy's future would be lost.[51]

Some advocates of utilitarian education saw the war as an excellent opportunity to convert classical schools into scientific institutions. They argued that practical science courses that trained men in chemistry and engineering—talents in short supply in the Confederacy—served as the most effective justification for keeping their schools open and in full operation. The close association of legislatures with state schools enabled them (unlike their privately supported counterparts) to seek public funds by claiming that new expenditures would help the Confederate military. Such support, however, rarely was forthcoming.

After the commencement of hostilities, the new chancellor of the University of Georgia, Andrew A. Lipscomb, claimed that "a new Era must soon begin in the history of Southern education, and I therefore think we should keep the University progressing, so as to avail ourselves promptly of any advantage [the war] may offer." Lipscomb especially wanted the Board of Trustees to start a school of engineering. The Methodist minister argued that the Confederacy's industrial needs required an unusual number of engineers. Lipscomb also contended that engineering instruction promised to provide the basis for the future development of Georgia's industry. The board approved the proposal, and Lipscomb found an engineering professor. However, the university's financial straits, due to inflation and a decline in students, prevented the school from hiring him. The university suspended classes early in 1864 and remained closed through the rest of the war.[52]

The Board of Visitors of the University of Virginia also embraced utilitarianism in an effort to continue operating. They organized a school of military science and civil engineering in May 1861. Like the University of Georgia, the Virginia school's dismal financial position forced the board abruptly to stop the experiment within a few months of its inauguration.[53] Landon Garland justified the continued maintenance of his University of Alabama and the state military academies of South Carolina, Georgia, and Virginia by emphasizing the skilled engineers they provided the Confederate armies. Francis Henney Smith also stressed the importance of military schools to the war effort and opposed the conscription of his cadets at VMI. The death of Gen. Thomas J. ("Stonewall") Jackson, the former professor of natural philosophy at VMI and a Confederate hero, provided Smith with an opportunity to propagandize concerning the importance of scientific instruction. He claimed that public opinion prior to the war turned against VMI's scientific curriculum and put pressure on the Virginia legislature to transform the course of study into that of an "ordinary college." Smith observed that the outbreak of war, however, had necessitated that the institute strictly adhere to its scientific course of instruction, "which the experience of the last four years has shown to have been most effective for the cause of our oppressed country." The implication was clear: the instruction at VMI promised to provide the Confederacy with scientifically trained future "Stonewall" Jacksons. The quality of VMI's education manifested itself, Smith noted, in the officers it provided for the army and the contribution of its corps of cadets to the Confederate victory at New Market, Virginia, in May 1864. When federal troops burned the institute one month after that battle, Smith successfully argued for its re-establishment at a new campus in Richmond.[54]

The need for scientifically trained officers quickly manifested itself. At the outbreak of the war, a contributor to *De Bow's Review* observed that the Confederacy's vast territory lacked fortifications. Construction of these required engineering skill. The writer lauded Robert E. Lee's appointment as a general officer, because he "is a practical and scientific soldier, and his services are absolutely needed to direct the general course of defence or invasion, and to devise plans for the many fortifications we shall need." Burwell Boykin Lewis, a twenty-four-year-old lieutenant in the Second Alabama Cavalry, noted in January 1863 the military qualifications of Northern-born Confederate generals, Gustavus W. Smith and John C. Pemberton, both of whom had been educated at West Point. "These men," Lewis observed happily, "are scientific generals" of the type the Confederacy needed so desperately.[55]

War quickly demonstrated to the Confederate government the importance of locating men with scientific knowledge, men capable of operating munitions factories, maintaining railroad lines, constructing fortifications, and building gunboats. The Confederacy's various colleges, institutes, and universities, however, failed to supply the demand. The Confederate Ordnance Department, which required technically trained officers, initiated examinations to eliminate the large numbers of unqualified applicants for commissioning as captains and lieutenants in the fall of 1862. The department inaugurated the tests at the suggestion of Maj. William LeRoy Broun, a former professor of mathematics at the University of Georgia. The examinations, administered by a committee chaired by Broun, revealed the inadequacy of antebellum Southern higher education in the preparation of students for scientific and technical subjects. Josiah Gorgas, chief of Confederate ordnance, noted that, of the more than five hundred initial applicants, fewer than one hundred attempted the examinations, and only forty or fifty managed to pass. The tests required that the applicant demonstrate an understanding of algebra, chemistry, physics, and trigonometry. Gorgas noted that the captaincy examination in effect required that the applicant previously have passed a college mathematics course. The only candidates with the mathematical skill to pass this test, Gorgas observed, graduated from the University of Virginia. The Ordnance Department awarded commissions for the rank of lieutenant to applicants who basically demonstrated a secondary school level of education.[56]

The effort by progressivist academics to use the home education and military school movements to foster scientific curricula accomplished little that proved of benefit to the Confederacy. The improvement in Southern scientific academic programs that resulted from these educational crusades appeared too late to help the South win its independence. Southern academia and state legislatures did not begin to acquiesce to the demands of a smattering of progressivist educators and start serious efforts to improve or implement scientific courses until the late 1850s. Too few students capable of building the industrial base necessary for the Confederacy to compete materially with the Union's highly industrialized military effort had graduated from these programs. Furthermore, the destruction of collegiate buildings and scientific apparatus during the war by both Union and Confederate forces wiped out the physical manifestations of progressivist educational reform.

The Confederacy relied heavily upon graduates of the United States military and naval academies, along with a handful of science professors, to build its military industrial structure. Gorgas, chief of Confederate ordnance, had graduated sixth in his class at West Point in 1841. Professor Broun commanded the vital Richmond arsenal. John W. Mallet, former professor of chemistry at the University of Alabama, directed the Confederate ordnance laboratories. John M. Brooke, a graduate of the U.S. Naval Academy, served as chief of naval ordnance. George Washington Rains, a graduate of West Point, commanded the powder works in Augusta, Georgia. South Carolina College professors John LeConte and Joseph LeConte worked for the Confederate Nitre and Mining Bureau. Other professors who labored in a scientific capacity for the Confederacy at one time or another include the University of North Carolina's professor of agricultural chemistry, John Kimberly, who attempted to manufacture sulfuric acid; and John Lee Buchanan, professor of mathematics at Emory and Henry College, who removed from caves the saltpeter necessary for the production of gunpowder.[57]

Although the Confederacy failed to develop anything that resembled industrial parity with the Union, the Confederate army's Ordnance Department managed, albeit with great difficulty, to sustain Southern troops throughout the war. The Confederacy built and operated various types of ordnance manufacturing works at Atlanta, Augusta, Charlotte, Columbia, Jackson, Knoxville, Richmond, and Selma. Such industrialization revolutionized Confederate society. It contributed to the establishment of a relatively strong central government in the South with a large measure of control over the economy. Heretofore unknown employment opportunities for women opened up in ordnance factories. Belatedly, consideration was given to emancipating African Americans who agreed to serve as Confederate soldiers. In essence, the Confederate revolution ended by violating everything its founders supposedly had set out to defend: states' rights, passive women, and slavery.[58]

Although Union troops destroyed the industrial infrastructure built by the Confederacy, they failed completely to eradicate the experience of industrialization. Like many Northerners who participated in the war effort, many Southerners learned from that revolutionary experience to appreciate what the combination of science, industry, and government could accomplish. Some eventually came to believe that women and African Americans might play an active role in the postbellum progress of their section. The Southern military officers most responsible for the effort to transform the Confederacy from an agrarian to a more industrial society—Brooke, Broun, Gorgas, Mallet, and Rains, among others—found employment in Southern higher education after the war. These and other officers carried into postbellum academia the experience of industrializing the Confederacy's war effort, which they accomplished through governmental initiative and the application of scientific knowledge to industrial problems. These men realized that their enormous effort at industrialization, while impressive, had proved too much to be accomplished in a short period of time.

The experience of Confederate field officers—including chronic food shortages, inadequate clothing, and confrontations with well-equipped Union soldiers—convinced those who later served as professors that the antebellum South's failure to embrace science and to industrialize had led to the Confederacy's defeat. Also, the handful of antebellum progressivists in Southern academia, such as Daniel Harvey Hill and Francis Henney Smith, believed that the region's destruction had vindicated their pleas for an industrial South. Other prewar academics like David Boyd, who had expressed little interest in the utilitarian value of science, returned to higher education after Confederate service changed and championed scientific education. They saw industrial science as the primary means of putting the South on the road to true progress.

These various postbellum academics concluded that progress demanded an economically independent but politically reconciled South, one integral to the progressivist destiny of the United States. They recognized the failure of antebellum Southern academics to establish a republic capable of embracing scientific progress and excluding the social progress associated with it, particularly abolition. After the war, progressivist educators were freed from the encumbrance of conservative charges that change threatened slavery. Thus they were able to lead the New South away from Old South education. For the men who entered postbellum Southern academia, the lesson of the Civil War was that the antebellum South had failed to measure up to the demands of progress. Confederate defeat, they concluded, demonstrated the value of science to society, and they believed that scientific education offered the means by which to obtain the benefits of progress. As postbellum academics, they promoted practical scientific higher education through research, teaching, and various propagandizing efforts. In the process, they kept the Confederate industrial and social revolutions flickering in Southern higher education.

Chapter 3

Progress and the Academic Origins of the New South

The Civil War devastated Southern higher education. Union and Confederate armies severely damaged collegiate campuses throughout the South. Federal troops often burned schools they suspected of aiding the Confederate effort and seized or destroyed university records. Both sides plundered campuses for apparatus, art, books, and furniture. The destruction levied against Southern schools prevented most from reopening quickly after the cessation of hostilities. Furthermore, many school administrations had invested their antebellum endowments in Confederate bonds, rendered worthless upon the Confederacy's defeat. This left completely destitute those colleges and universities which were dependent upon interest derived from that source.[1]

Southern colleges and universities lost the services of faculty who either died or were severely wounded in the war. Five members of the University of North Carolina faculty—one-third of the school's antebellum teaching staff—perished in the conflict. Institutions throughout the South suffered comparable losses. Southern schools also lost Northern-born or Unionist educators, such as Barnard, Sherman, Professor Robert Strong of the University of East Tennessee, and Professor E. C. Boynton of the University of Mississippi, who quit their institutions and headed north as a result of the war. After the conflict, many Southern academics left the region for higher salaries offered by more prosperous Northern and western schools. Prominent academics who deserted institutions in the former Confederate states for more profitable employment elsewhere included Eugene W. Hilgard of the University of Mississippi, who possessed a doctorate from the University of Heidelberg; Basil L. Gildersleeve, the University of Virginia's foremost classical scholar; and the LeConte brothers. Southern higher education also lost students who left school to join the army and, as a result of death, disability, or impoverishment, never returned to academic life.[2]

As part of their efforts to rebuild, Southern colleges and universities wanted former Confederate officers to serve as presidents and professors. In any case, with their faculty largely dead, maimed, or missing, most schools had little choice but to hire men with Confederate experience as administrators and teachers. Approximately 900,000 men and boys, well over half of Southern whites males of military age, had served in the Confederate military. Thousands of others had worked for the Rebel government in the civil service or in war industries. Those men with Confederate service who entered higher education brought with them ideas about how to build, within a reconciled Union, a progressive New South that nevertheless embodied the Lost Cause. Furthermore, for several years after the conflict ended, veterans made up a large part of the region's student body. This guaranteed that the pool of future administrators and faculty for a time would consist primarily of those with Confederate service.[3]

At least eleven former Confederate generals, two naval officers, three United States senators, and one congressman served as presidents of Southern colleges. Numerous junior officers also obtained such positions of leadership. State schools especially sought and attracted those who served the Confederacy. The vast majority of Southern state universities and agricultural and mechanical (A&M) colleges elected at least one president or faculty chair with Confederate service. Confederate veterans, primarily officers, dominated the administrations of most such institutions until the late 1890s.

It is instructive to study the presidencies and chancellorships of the fourteen Southern state universities and A&M colleges permanently established by 1890. Such an analysis reveals that, between the end of Reconstruction and the turn of the century, men with Confederate service led a combined 36 of 46 administrations (see table). From their establishment after the Civil War until the end of the century, Alabama A&M, Arkansas Industrial University, Mississippi A&M, and North Carolina A&M appointed only Confederate military or civilian personnel as presidents. Between 1880 and 1907, all five of Virginia A&M's presidents had participated in the Confederate war effort. A single Confederate general served Mississippi A&M from 1880 to 1899, as its first president. In addition, the University of Texas elected the head of the Confederate ordnance laboratories as its first faculty chair, and the chief of the Richmond arsenal as its second.[4]

Schools also hired Confederate veterans, particularly officers, in great numbers as faculty. The entire faculty of the Louisiana State Seminary upon its reopening in 1866 consisted of four Confederate field officers, a Confederate chaplain, and a Confederate surgeon. The school added three more veterans the following year. A majority of the faculty at the University of Mississippi consisted of Confederate veterans when it reopened during Reconstruction. Confederate veterans also figured prominently at the University of Virginia immediately following the war. By the end of Reconstruction, all of the state universities, agricultural and mechanical colleges, and military academies, as well as most private schools, employed men with Confederate service as professors.[5]

Veterans eagerly pursued both administrative and teaching positions in academia. Postbellum opportunities often failed to satisfy the expectations of men who believed that their stature entitled them to careers as planters, politicians, or professionals. These occupations proved either difficult to find in the economically devastated South, or, as in the case of political office, closed to most high-ranking Rebel officers during Reconstruction. These men used their status as heroes to gain employment in fields where their reputations served as a boon rather than a detriment. Former general officers often found employment on corporate boards and as representatives or sales agents in speculative enterprises, particularly with insurance companies, which hoped to use the veterans' reputations to attract customers and respectability. Academia provided similar opportunities for unemployed former Confederate officers to find acceptable professional positions. Schools used the reputations of these veterans to attract students and donations.[6]

The Confederacy's highest ranking and most celebrated general, Robert E. Lee, set a dignified precedent for others to follow by accepting the presidency of Washington College in Lexington, Virginia, shortly after the war's end. Quickly thereafter, the demand for prominent Confederates placed former officers in competition with each other for academic positions. Southern veterans sought letters of recommendation from Lee, whose endorsement impressed potential employers, including members of collegiate boards, and aided applicants in their efforts to obtain appointments.[7]

Veterans who entered academia brought not only their fame but also their wartime experience, which included a brief encounter with industrialization and the legacy of defeat. They drew upon their experience to reorient Southern higher education from a classical to a progressivist stance. Southerners did not doubt the appropriateness of placing former Confederates at the reins of Southern academia. As one commencement speaker at the University of Mississippi noted approvingly, the men of the Civil War generation "stand out in history as the sentinels of progress to mark the pathway of successive generations."[8]

Veterans, more than other Southerners, had witnessed and understood the magnitude of Confederate defeat. Atticus G. Haygood, president of Emory College and a former Confederate chaplain, called the South's defeat "utter and overwhelming." Other Confederate veterans who entered academia expressed similar sentiments. William Preston Johnston, former aide-de-camp to Jefferson Davis and president of Tulane University, told a commencement audience at the Alabama Polytechnic Institute in Auburn that the North had "overwhelmed" the Confederacy with "superior force." Therefore, he continued, "neither honor, nor common sense demanded that we should invite and endure further disaster." Johnston addressed the students at the invitation of the institute's president, William LeRoy Broun, who also understood the totality of the Confederacy's collapse. Broun remembered that, upon the

Chief Administrators at Fourteen Southern State Universities and Agricultural and Mechanical Colleges, 1878–1896

KEY

*	Confederate officer	^	Confederate scientist
**	Other Confederate veteran		(military rank, if any, uncertain)
***	Confederate congressman	>	Too young for Confederate service
~	Confederate chaplain	(2)	Multiple administrations

Alabama A&M College
Isaac Taylor Tichenor	1872–1882~
William LeRoy Broun (2)	1882–1883,* 1884–1902*
David French Boyd	1883–1884*

University of Alabama
Carlos G. Smith	1874–1878*
Josiah Gorgas	1878–1879*
Burwell Boykin Lewis	1880–1885*
Henry D. Clayton	1885–1889*
Richard C. Jones	1890–1897*

Arkansas Industrial University
Daniel Harvey Hill	1877–1884*
George M. Edgar	1884–1887*
Edward H. Murfee	1887–1894*
John Lee Buchanan	1894–1902 ^

Clemson A&M College
Henry Aubrey Strode	1890–1893*
John L. Idol, Jr.	1893–1897>

University of Georgia
Patrick H. Mell	1878–1888*
William. E. Boggs	1889–1899

Louisiana State University
David French Boyd (2)	1866–1880,* 1884–1886*
William Preston Johnston	1880–1883*
James W. Nicholson (2)	1883–1884,** 1887–1896**

Mississippi A&M College
Stephen D. Lee	1880–1899*

University of Mississippi
Alexander P. Stewart	1874–1886*
Edward Mayes	1886–1891**
Robert Fulton	1891–1906>

North Carolina A&M College
Alexander R. Holladay	1889–1899*

Chief Administrators at Fourteen Southern State Universities and Agricultural and Mechanical Colleges, 1878–1896 (cont.)

University of North Carolina

Kemp Plummer Battle	1876–1891
George T. Winston	1891–1896>

University of South Carolina

William P. Miles	1880–1883***
John M. McBryde	1883–1891**
James Woodrow	1891–1897 ^

University of Tennessee

Thomas W. Humes	1865–1883
Charles W. Dabney	1887–1904>

Texas A&M College

Thomas S. Gathright	1876–1878
John G. James	1878–1883*
Hardaway Hunt Dinwiddie	1883–1888*
L. L. McInnis	1888–1890>
Lawrence Sullivan Ross	1891–1898*

Virginia A&M College

Charles L. C. Minor	1872–1879
John Lee Buchanan (2)	1880, ^ 1881–1882 ^
W. W. Blackford	1880*
Thomas N. Conrad	1882–1886*
L. L. Lomax	1886–1891*
John M. McBryde	1891–1907**

Number of Schools 14
Number of Administrations 46
Administrations Headed by a Confederate Veteran   36 (78%)

SOURCES: Compiled from sources cited in chapter 3, note 4.

NOTE: Administrations that overlap the years 1878–96 are included. Prior to the end of Reconstruction, many schools experienced severe disruptions and multiple presidencies that often were held temporarily by Northerners or Southern Unionists. By the late 1890s, most Confederate veterans in higher education were either retired or deceased.

Confederate Congress's authorization to recruit black troops near the war's end, Southern lawmakers expected the Ordnance Department to furnish arms to an anticipated fifty thousand African American soldiers. As commander of the Richmond arsenal, however, Colonel Broun recognized that the destruction of Confederate resources by Union armies made arming so many men impossible. "I knew," he recalled, "we could not possibly arm five thousand."[9]

Veterans in academia often attributed the South's defeat to the North's superior material and technical resources. Former Gen. Daniel Harvey Hill, prior to becoming president of Arkansas Industrial University, repeatedly noted the South's inability to compete with Northern industry. "A state of war found [the Confederacy] without the machinery to make a single percussion cap for a soldier's rifle, or a single button for his jacket," Hill observed. The Confederate army, he claimed, lacked medical supplies, shoes, tents, wagons, and all manner of ordnance. The North, however, had "the best equipped . . . army in the world." David Boyd, who served as a Confederate engineering officer and after the war as superintendent and president of Louisiana State University (LSU), claimed that the power of Northern manufacturing forced the South to fight the equivalent of fourteen million more men than the Union actually put in the field. The outcome of the war, Boyd believed, demonstrated to the South that it stood "in need of *Mechanics*—mechanical education and the Mechanic Arts." A. J. Peeler, a member of the first Board of Trustees for Texas Agricultural and Mechanical College and a former Confederate captain, told a commencement audience that "during the late war we saw how helpless a country was that manufactured nothing at home."[10]

Southern academics who hoped to rectify the South's material and technological inferiority within the reconstructed Union believed that higher education eventually could transform the South into a dynamo of industry and science. Academics and others who wanted Southern higher education to embrace scientific and technical education pointed to the Confederate experiment as proof both of the efficacy of industrialization and of the South's ability to industrialize. The Confederacy, they argued, proved capable of holding off defeat for four years because of the immense industrial and technical efforts conducted by the Confederate Ordnance Department. Hill praised the industrial accomplishments of ordnance officers John Brooke, George Washington Rains, and others, for enabling the Confederacy to put up a good fight. William M. Burwell, a former editor of *De Bow's Review*, boasted to LSU faculty and students that, during the war, the Confederacy's "production of explosives and fixed ammunition was wonderful." Burwell also advocated the establishment of schools of applied science, which he believed necessary for the creation of a prosperous South.[11]

Samuel H. Lockett, a postbellum professor of engineering at LSU and the University of Tennessee, emphasized the importance of scientifically trained generals to the Confederate war effort. "At the beginning of the war there were many *legal, theological,* and *political* generals," observed Lockett, a former Confederate colonel of engineers, "but the last great battles were fought [by] men like Lee, Johnston, Bragg, Beauregard, Hood, and Hardee . . . all men who had received technical military educations." Lockett advocated the establishment of technical schools, similar to the Stevens Institute of Technology in Hoboken, New Jersey, and the Columbia School of Mines in New York City, to provide the South with mechanical engineers capable of rebuilding the region.[12]

Ultimately, the failures of Confederate industrialism proved more glaring than its successes, because the South lacked the industrial competence necessary to defeat the North. Veterans-turned-academics considered antebellum higher education largely responsible for that failure. Former Confederate Gen. Stephen D. Lee, who after the war served as president of Mississippi Agricultural and Mechanical College, noted the chronic shortage of skilled persons capable of working as telegraph operators in the Confederacy. Lee, who commanded troops at Vicksburg, credited the technical prowess of two operators with saving that city from Union forces in December 1862. Most of the operators in the South, Lee charged, were Northerners who headed home shortly after the war began. Armies needed such technically trained men, he explained, to fight a modern war successfully.[13]

David Boyd recalled Sherman's warning that the South's lack of industrial resources guaranteed its defeat. "I never saw our poor Southern boys half-naked and half-starved," Boyd remembered, "nor rode on a ri[c]kety train behind a broken-down, wheezing engine . . . but I thought of him." Lawrence Sullivan ("Sul") Ross, postbellum president of Texas Agricultural and Mechanical College, related a wartime experience which he believed exemplified the failures of antebellum Southern higher education. Ross, a Confederate cavalry officer, and his troops had captured a federal train that carried supplies which his men desperately needed. Fearing that enemy reinforcements would arrive shortly, Ross searched for someone in his command capable of operating the train to move it out of danger. An exasperated Ross found that none of his soldiers possessed the technical knowledge necessary to operate the engine. Superior numbers of federal troops soon arrived and forced Ross to abandon the train. Such experiences led men such as Lee, Boyd, and Ross to promote scientific education vigorously after the war.[14]

To a certain degree, the understanding that the Union had an enormous industrial advantage over the Confederacy relieved white Southerners of responsibility for defeat. Their recognition of the North's industrial superiority enabled former Rebels to argue that they had fought courageously, but that no amount of bravery or patriotism could have overcome their material disadvantage. Defeat, therefore, acquired an aura of inevitability that allowed rebellious Southerners to uphold their collective sense of honor by proudly pointing to the courage that they displayed and the feats that they accomplished in the face of overwhelming physical force. Southern academics who espoused this view argued that defeat also required the South to embrace science and industrialization, as a means of lifting the region out of poverty and economic dependence on the North. They believed that higher education offered Southerners the means to accomplish this task.

Daniel Harvey Hill specifically attributed the Confederacy's technical deficiency and its defeat to inadequate antebellum standards of higher education. Hill complained that dead languages, elocution, English classics, law, political economy, and rhetoric wasted the time and energy of Southern youths. As a consequence, these students failed to develop practical scientific skills comparable to those of Northerners, who he claimed eagerly had embraced technical education before the war. "Let the studies pursued when prosperity crowned the land," Hill pleaded, "be buried with that prosperity."[15]

Isaac Taylor Tichenor had received a classical education in his native Kentucky before moving to Alabama before the war. He served the Confederacy as a Baptist chaplain with the rank of captain in the 17th Alabama regiment. After the war, he became an ardent proponent of scientific utilitarian education and president of the Alabama Agricultural and Mechanical College. Although he praised the bravery and fighting ability of Confederate soldiers, Tichenor charged that the antebellum education they had received inadequately prepared them for war. He claimed that Southern politicians "never comprehended that steam engines and railroads, that looms and shuttles, that plows and hoes and reapers constituted a prime element of a nation's strength upon the field of battle. They knew not how to make these fight." Tichenor claimed that Alabama needed scientific instruction as a basis for the state's future agricultural and industrial prosperity.[16]

Antebellum proponents of scientific and technical education, such as Francis Smith and Daniel Harvey Hill, believed themselves vindicated by the outcome of the war. "It is not necessary that I should dwell . . . on the importance of the scientific course that claims the attention of this school," Smith told VMI's cadets in 1866. "The events of the last few years, and the circumstances of the country at this time, fully vindicated the policy which has regulated the educational system from the [school's] beginning." Hill believed that defeat had taught Southerners that they needed to revolutionize their entire system of education and that they must exchange aesthetic studies for scientific utilitarian education. In order to compete with the North economically, the South required engineers, machinists, manufacturers, miners, and scientific farmers to develop the region's natural resources. Hill looked to Southern higher education to provide courses in agricultural science, chemistry, geology, mineralogy, and meteorology. Only graduates thus prepared would be able to create the industries needed to lift the South out of its impoverished condition.[17]

Confederate veterans who entered academia believed that the South's defeat required them to embrace a new type of education. Edward Joynes asked Matthew Maury, formerly a commander in the Confederate navy, to address an 1869 meeting of the Virginia Educational Association on the topic "The Changes which the rapid progress and development of Physical discoveries, and the altered condition of our people, have made necessary, in the system of Southern education." Maury, at his inauguration as president of the University of Alabama in 1871, told the audience that great changes which had occurred throughout the South obligated the school to offer courses in the physical sciences. "In our mastery over these forces," he claimed, "consists the progress of the age, the greatness of nations and the prosperity of peoples. . . . This is what our university must do, and enable the South to take her true position in the onward and upward march of nations." John Mallet, professor of chemistry at the University of Virginia after the war, wrote that "weighty reasons of a special kind" existed for the South to embrace applied science instruction. Exhausted by war, its fields barren, its few manufacturers destroyed, the South, Mallet—former superintendent of the Confederacy's ordnance laboratories—believed, needed to look to technical education to "raise her from the dust."[18]

William Preston Johnston criticized the "ancient halls of learning" for perceiving too slowly the need for those arts and sciences that would fit young men "for eminence in the stations of life to which active civilization calls them." The courses the "ancient halls" needed to offer included the study of bridges, foundries, manufactures, mines, railroads, and sewerage. Robert E. Lee wrote to inventor Cyrus McCormick of the necessity of raising money to expand Washington College's curriculum to include a variety of scientific programs. "Such a course," Lee claimed, "is requisite to meet the present wants of the country [Virginia]." The inventor of the famed reaper responded by endowing the "McCormick Professorship of Experimental Philosophy and Practical Mechanics." The college appointed Richard Sears McCulloh to the position. McCulloh previously had served as a chemistry professor at New York's Columbia College (where he spied for the Confederacy until heading south in 1863) and as a scientist for the Confederate Nitre and Mining Bureau.[19]

The Baltimore-born McCulloh had developed a highly combustible material reputedly used by Rebel saboteurs in a conspiracy to burn New York and other Northern cities. He received a belated commission as a lieutenant colonel of engineers to protect him from summary execution for his espionage. Arrested by federal authorities at war's end for plotting acts of terrorism, he was confined in Richmond's Libby Prison until being paroled in March 1866. After his release, he obtained the McCormick professorship at Washington College and worked on plans to expand the school's scientific offerings.[20]

The idea that the South could build an industrial and prosperous society through education received confirmation in the minds of Confederate veterans in academia with Prussia's victory in the Franco-Prussian War of 1870–71. France's sudden defeat surprised many military men. Gen. Josiah Gorgas, a faculty member at the University of the South and former chief of the Confederate Ordnance Department, claimed that "nothing could be more astounding than the total and utter defeat of the French forces." The administrators and professors of the United States Military Academy, heavily influenced by French military thought before the war, afterwards placed greater emphasis on the Prussian experience.[21]

Confederate veterans who entered academia quickly overcame their astonishment at the war's outcome by comparing the French experience to their own. These veterans attributed Prussia's victory to its scientific and technical preeminence over France—their explanation, too, for the North's victory over the South. Southern academics especially credited Prussia's superior educational system with providing that nation with the industrial strength necessary to win the war. William LeRoy Broun claimed that scientific schools enabled Prussians "to display that skill and power which in a few months changed the map of Europe, and drew from the French an acknowledgment that their humiliation was due to [Prussia's] more general diffusion of scientific schools." William Preston Johnston observed that "Germany has tested and proved the theory that the best trained heads win the game of war." He also claimed that France, in the years following the conflict, "accepted and improved that lesson."[22]

Southerners, like the French, these veterans argued, needed to learn from their defeat and embrace science education so as to resurrect the South's fortunes. "As German universities conquered at Sedan," former Confederate congressman and cavalryman Jabez L. M. Curry told students at Alabama A&M, "so you are to win victories in broader and more useful spheres." The example of Prussia's victory over France and the lesson that it carried for the South—to embrace education, science, and technology—remained a favored subject for speakers at alumni society meetings, commencements, and other ceremonial occasions through the end of the century.[23]

Southern college students and graduates embraced the message they heard so often. The Reverend Robert Lewis Dabney, who feared that greed and moral degeneracy followed the unrestricted pursuit of material riches, complained at the 1882 commencement of Hampden-Sydney College that too frequently he heard the cry that "the North triumphed by its wealth" and that therefore Southerners ought to emulate Yankee ways. Dabney lamented, "I hear our young men quote to each other the advice of the wily diplomat Gorstchacoff, to the beaten French: 'Be strong.' They exclaim: Let us develop! [D]evelop! [D]evelop! Let us have, like our conquerors, great cities, great capitalists, great factories and commerce and great populations; then we shall cope with them [Northerners]."

Dabney's friend Daniel Harvey Hill, however, saw no reason why the South should not learn from the North. "It is lawful to be taught," Hill believed, "by those who have far excelled us in developing the resources of the country."

Johnston also wanted Southerners to learn from their Northern relations' superiority in the mechanic arts. "When in anything my brother is doing better than I am," Johnston claimed, "let me understand it and make myself his equal in that thing. It is an honest ambition."[24]

The idea that industrialization provided the key to both Union and Prussian victories allowed former Rebels, to a certain degree, to escape responsibility for their defeat. Confederate soldiers believed that they had fought bravely enough to more than satisfy the demands of honor, and that Southern civilians courageously had suffered the hardships placed upon them by an enormously powerful foe. Still, individual honor and courage had proven inadequate in the faceless reality of industrial war. It remained important, however, for former Confederates reared on these virtues to convince themselves, and others, that their actions had satisfied all the demands that honor and courage required. Long after the war, white Southerners remained sensitive to the charge that they had abandoned their cause before military necessity required them to do so. Confederate veterans, especially academics, seized public opportunities to laud their "feats of arms, which the world has never seen surpassed" and "skillful generals whose nobility won them the admiration of the world."[25]

Southern academics who embraced technical education denied individual responsibility for defeat by blaming antebellum education for the South's failure to industrialize. Former Confederates who entered academia further sought to evade personal accountability for the Confederacy's demise by eagerly embracing the idea that Providence had dictated the outcome of the war.

As most Southerners were raised in a Protestant tradition, they tended to accept the Christian notion that Providence—the implementation of God's predetermined will—controlled their destiny. Southern academics' belief that Northern industrialism had made the destruction of the Confederacy inevitable suggested that Providence had permitted an inevitable Union victory. The material advantages of Union troops, Daniel Harvey Hill told veterans of the Army of Northern Virginia, guaranteed Confederate soldiers "no hope of ultimate success." He noted, however, that his faith in God allowed him "to bow with adoring reverence to His decree which destroyed our hopes of Southern independence. I would not reverse that decree if I could do so." The dual forces of industrialization and Providence, equally mysterious, offered Southerners a rationale for accepting defeat and moving toward national reconciliation. Josiah Gorgas, confused by the Almighty's decision to allow Union victory, nevertheless advised conquered Southerners to "bow in submission and learn to curb our bitter thoughts."[26]

For white Southerners fully to accept the dictates of Providence, they needed to understand its purpose in their defeat. Gorgas lamented that nothing remained of the Confederacy after "the bitter end of four years of toil and sacrifices." He wondered, "Is it possible we were wrong?" Yet Gorgas, like most white Southerners, refused to believe that defeat had resulted from any moral failings with regard to slavery or secession. The conquered Southerners struggled to find in their defeat a greater meaning than simply that the North had overpowered the South.[27]

Confederate veterans in academia found an explanation that removed any need for guilt over defeat, secession, or slavery. They accepted the progressivist belief that Providence controlled human progress for a Divine purpose. Their faith in Providence allowed them to develop the idea that national progress had necessitated Confederate defeat so that the United States could resolve the problems of slavery and secession and fulfill its national destiny of achieving a perpetual republic. "In the wisdom of *Omniscient Providence,* the question of the Right of Secession, thus referred to the arbitration of the field, was decided . . . irrevocably and forever," Broun observed, "and what we now know to have been an element of division and weakness in our government, has been forever removed, and to-day we stand one people, one nation, under one flag, an indissoluble union of indestructible states." The end of debilitating sectionalism also required an end to slavery. "Providence wanted the Union," wrote David Boyd, "but He wanted the Union without slavery." Furthermore, progressivist academics argued, the South's retention of slavery had barred the region from embracing industrialization, granting dignity to labor, and pursuing science.[28]

Jabez Curry, who after the war served as a college president, English professor, and administrative agent for the Peabody Fund for Southern Education, called slavery "a great blunder" that had hindered the region's economic, political, and social progress. He claimed in 1882 that "the South rejoices that it is gone—irrevocably gone." Atticus Haygood expressed similar sentiments. Nevertheless, these academics refused to condemn slavery or secession in moral terms. They argued that slavery had brought civilization to African Americans and that secession had impressed upon all Americans the importance of self-government. The twin pillars of antebellum Southern politics, however, had ceased to serve the interests of the republic, and therefore Providence had removed them. Accordingly, individuals, who strove only to perform their appointed roles in the Divinely ordained human drama, need not bear any responsibility for the war or its outcome. (Even before the war ended, Northerners embraced the idea that Providence had preserved the Union and destroyed slavery. Perhaps the clearest expression of this faith is President Abraham Lincoln's Second Inaugural Address.)[29]

Progressivist academics interpreted their Confederate experiences as evidence of the antebellum South's failure to embrace progress. Burwell Boykin Lewis, president of the University of Alabama, claimed that the South had failed to win its independence because it had "failed to catch the great industrial spirit of the age." The former Confederate lieutenant believed that antebellum Southerners had rejected free labor, manufacturing, and physical science; and he argued that "no civilization can exist that antagonizes these fundamental ideas and tendencies of modern progress."

Veterans in academia wanted Southerners to learn from their defeat and build a stronger postbellum civilization. "The man trained by the world has the advantage of not having kind guides," William Preston Johnston claimed. "Defeat has been his most useful master. From defeat he has learned the best lesson we ever get here below." The destruction of slavery and the physical devastation suffered by the South convinced Johnston and other academics that Southerners needed to forget slavery and start a progressive "new era" by constructing a "new civilization" built upon industry and science.

The hope for a reborn South led quickly to the idea that a "New South" soon would appear. Col. Joseph W. Taylor of Alabama told the literary societies of the University of Mississippi in 1869 that "Providence has in reserve for this blasted and trampled land of ours a bright and prosperous future. From the mighty ruins of its past, from the blood of its martyred sons . . . there may arise . . . a New South of the future, grander and more beautiful than the Old."[30]

Confederate veterans associated with postbellum academia proved integral to the formulation and promotion of the New South ideology that developed after the Civil War. They joined an assortment of editors, industrialists, middle-class professionals, planters, and politicians who encouraged Southerners to build an industrial base, engage in diversified and scientific agriculture, and develop the South's raw materials. New South proponents urged Southerners to solicit immigration into the region to secure requisite capital and industrial skills to help accomplish these goals. They also cultivated an appreciation of the dignity of labor, in an effort to inspire white

Southerners to provide for themselves. Advocates of the New South called for national reconciliation and an end to the sectional political conflict that distracted Southerners from the work before them.[31]

Although the most conspicuous proponents of the New South creed outside academia ignored Southern education until after 1900,[32] New South academics of the Civil War generation created and advanced the ideology's tenets through classroom lectures, journal articles, institutional reports, and public addresses. They interpreted Confederate defeat as the result of the antebellum South's failure to embrace the cause of industrial and technical progress. In order to rectify this deficiency, they concluded that the "New South" demanded "a new education."[33]

The term "New South," in effect, served as a synonym for "progress." Academics and their supporters who embraced progress defined it as the predestined millennial march of civilization toward ever greater industrial, scientific, and social accomplishments. The idea of inevitable progress served Southern academics in two ways. First, it enabled them to escape blame for the South's defeat. Second, faith in progress provided them with hope that the South might regain its prosperity. New South academics believed that the North's industrially supported armies inescapably had brought devastation upon the South. Therefore, they reasoned, the progress that had destroyed the Confederacy ultimately would rebuild an even more prosperous postbellum South.

Southern progressivists subscribed to a faith in progress that can be termed "scientific millennialism." Reared in a Protestant tradition that taught of Christ's millennial return and the establishment of a paradisiacal kingdom, progressivist academics and their supporters easily fused this doctrine with a secular faith that inevitable scientific progress eventually would create a Southern paradise. The South, after suffering the death and destruction of the Civil War, could find resurrection and redemption through industry and science.

Those who believed that scientific education promised to raise up a New South frequently incorporated biblical language into their predictions of progress. The classically educated Confederate Gen. Jonathan T. Morgan assured the literary societies of the University of Alabama in 1875 that science guaranteed Alabama's future progress. "Alabama is a representative Southern State of the new era," Morgan claimed, "now just beginning to dawn after a long period of sad humiliation." He claimed that the future development of the state's natural resources would enable Alabamians to "behold with rapturous gaze the dawning revelations of her [Alabama's] coming glory and pray for lengths of days that we may be here to enjoy its effulgence with our children." Atticus Haygood urged Southerners to "press forward, following the pillar of cloud and fire always" toward the New South of free labor and industry. Joseph Taylor believed that university graduates would be "at the forefront of the march" in the imminent "industrial regeneration of the South." He claimed to "see them with banners" and hear their "jubilant shouts of victory" as they entered the promised land of "rich pastures and the flowing abundance of the New South of the future. Blessed and crowning consummation, let it come—let it come!"[34]

The rapid development of new technologies, which generated enormous material wealth in the nineteenth century, greatly impressed New South academia. Former Confederate Gen. Edmund Kirby Smith, professor of mathematics at the University of the South, expressed amazement at the scientific progress he witnessed around him. It led Smith to believe that humankind would "move onward, inevitably, the wave of progress until all that is great and good and godlike in the race shall have been evolved and developed."

A. G. Clopton, in his eulogy for Ashbel Smith, president of the Board of Regents of the University of Texas, asserted that "human progress is accelerated beyond anything the minds of our ancestors could conceive."

Broun attributed all the glory of nineteenth-century civilization to "progress in science." Southern academics, like their Northern brethren, marveled at the physical powers unleashed by engineers and scientists. "We live in an age of steel, steam, and electricity," Broun observed. "Never in the history of the human race was more activity manifested than in the present." Johnston echoed that science was able to "harness all the forces of nature as steeds of progress."[35]

The magnitude of material progress in the nineteenth century led New South academics and their supporters to abandon republican fears of societal decay and to embrace the idea of "permanent" or "perpetual" progress. They believed that the continued development of new technology would resurrect the fortunes of the South and enable American society to escape cyclical degradation. The idea that progress offered "permanent improvement," "permanent prosperity," and "permanent wealth" pervaded the discourse of New South academics. Technological achievements appeared immune from retrogression. As commencement speaker John Goode noted at the University of North Carolina in 1887, "The achievements of the inventor are permanent. They flow on in a perennial and an undying stream, and influence the most distant posterity."[36]

New South academics replaced the belief that progress through societal stages ultimately led to decay with the concept that progress prevented declension. Professor John Lee Buchanan, who returned to Emory and Henry College after the war, argued in 1874, that human progress need not know any limits. "God," Buchanan claimed, "hath not said to the nations as He has to the ocean, 'thus far shalt thou go and no farther. . . . ' Growth *or* decay

must be our history. Of most other nations it has been growth *and* decay."
The former Confederate scientist later would take his progressivist philosophy to Virginia A&M and Arkansas Industrial University, where he was to serve
as president.

Broun favorably quoted Francis Wayland's opinion that "God intended
us for progress, and we counteract his design when we deify antiquity and
bow down and worship an opinion, not because it is either wise or true, but
merely because it is ancient."[37]

Although progressivist academics embraced the idea of inevitable
human advancement, they warned that people must elect to embrace
progress, lest they be denied its blessings. Southerners readily could understand this concept, for it paralleled the Christian doctrine that, although the
Second Coming inevitably would occur, one must choose to accept Christ in
order to receive salvation. "The age is progressive," observed Joseph Taylor,
and, "as the car of improvement rushes on with lightning speed, laggards in
the race, whether they be individuals or communities, are left in the rear."

Boyd criticized the slow pace of Southern development after the war, as
he believed this "would seem to speak badly of our spirit of enterprise and
our progress as a people." In 1871, William Burwell warned the faculty and
students of LSU that "progress is a locomotive, you can either ride on or be
run-over by it at your option." Eugene Hilgard, professor of agricultural
chemistry at the University of Mississippi, criticized the South's slow development of scientific agriculture. "How much more ought *we* to do," the former
scientist for the Confederate Nitre Bureau charged, "with the additional
advantages given us by the gigantic progress of the arts and sciences,
advancing hand in hand so fast that but few of us are able to fully keep up
with their progress."[38]

Broun cautioned Southerners that they could no longer plant cotton,
debate politics, and ignore the social revolution wrought by the Civil War.
"We cannot stand still," he warned. "To stand still now is to lag behind. We
must go forward; we must keep pace of the age, we must diversify our
industries." For New South academia, stasis, not progress, brought eventual
societal decline. Burwell claimed that "the price of liberty is not," as traditional republicans believed, "eternal vigilance. It is perpetual progress."

Stephen Lee cast aside republican fears of excessive populations, when he
told a Mississippi audience not to worry about the *lack* of immigration into the
state. Immigrants would come, Lee assured his listeners, because Mississippi was
destined to acquire a dense population. Antebellum republicans had hoped to
discover a means by which societies could sustain the agricultural phase of social
development. Postbellum progressivist academics wanted to move society
forward to the industrial (and, they believed, the perpetual) stage.[39]

New South academics believed that the outcome of the Civil War demonstrated the inability of republican agrarianism to compete against modern industrialism, economically or militarily. "In our own country," Horace Harding, professor of engineering at the University of Alabama, observed in 1876, "compare in the past as well as in the present, the agricultural South, with the agricultural, commercial, and manufacturing North." Harding, who had managed the Mobile and Ohio Railroad for the Confederate government, believed that the South suffered in this comparison. Broun argued that Southerners needed to end their reliance on agricultural pursuits. "No nation of agriculturalists, ever in the history of the world, has successfully competed with a nation of mechanics," Broun claimed, employing words nearly identical to those that his friend David Boyd heard from Sherman. "Herein consisted, as past years demonstrated," Broun concluded, "the great weakness of the Southern States."[40]

New South academics and their supporters believed that Southerners, in order to wean themselves from their dependence on agriculture and develop new industries, needed to reconcile themselves with the Union. Progressivist educators asserted that reconciliation was an easy task. They pointed to the willingness expressed by most white Southerners to return to the Union as evidence that Providence intended the perpetual progress of the Republic. Dr. Bartholomew Egan, Louisiana's state chemist during the war and a member of the Louisiana State Seminary's Board of Supervisors, told a seminary audience in 1866 that Southerners presented a "spectacle unparalleled in the annals of nations. They accept with dignified submission inevitable results . . . [and] only ask . . . [that] they be permitted to aid in working out the great destinies ordained of God for this, the greatest Republic of all time."

A. J. Peeler told an audience at Texas A&M College that Americans would remember their civil war as "one of the most magnificent instances of faith in national unity and destiny, shining out from beneath the clouds of national adversity, the world has ever seen." William L. Bringhurst, a former Confederate ordnance officer and variously professor of English, history, and physics at Texas A&M, exulted, "Let us be glad and thank Heaven that the Union lives."[41]

Commencement speakers urged their young listeners to sustain the Union and lauded the material benefits that awaited a reconciled South. Confederate defeat, New South academics claimed, demonstrated Southerners' dependent circumstances. "Better a State in the Union, than a Cuba, Canada, or Algeria," Burwell warned. "You have only to look around and see every garment, implement, and weapon, imported in foreign vessels . . . to feel that a people so dependent could not maintain a position among independent nations of the Earth."

Similarly, Richard M. Venable, a former Confederate officer and a postbellum professor of engineering at the Louisiana State Seminary, wrote to Boyd that Louisiana, "if not tied to the U[nited] S[tates] . . . would sink to the level of the Central American States."[42]

Some Southern academics hoped to relieve the pecuniary needs of their institutions by cultivating reconciliatory sympathies. Benjamin Ewell, who had been adjutant general to Confederate Gen. Joseph E. Johnston, after the war repeatedly solicited the help of prominent Northerners, especially Union officers, to raise funds in the North for his beloved but destitute College of William and Mary. Henry Ward Beecher, Ulysses S. Grant, George B. McClellan, George G. Meade, and William T. Sherman, among others, responded favorably to Ewell's appeals. Possibly in gratitude to Grant for his efforts on behalf of the college, Ewell publicly supported the former Union general in his reelection campaign for the presidency in 1872.[43]

Shortly after the end of Reconstruction in Louisiana, David Boyd demonstrated that he harbored no resentment against the North by encouraging Northern parents to send their children to the financially strapped Louisiana State University. There, Boyd added enticingly, they "will be welcome—well taught and well treated by kind generous Southern people." There is little doubt as to the sincerity of Boyd's reconciliatory attitude. Only four years after war's end, Boyd praised his friend Sherman at the school's commencement as "one of the great captains of the age, [who] as a reward for his brilliant services, now commands the armies of the Union." Boyd's son Leroy remembered that, after the war, his father cheerfully entertained numerous Union officers in his home, including Grant, David Farragut, Winfield Hancock, George H. Thomas, and Sherman.

Tichenor wanted Alabama A&M's Board of Directors to provide funds to send the college's eighty-eight students to Philadelphia to the national exposition celebrating the Union's centennial. Hoping to encourage capitalists to invest in Alabama, he asked the Board of Directors to mount an exhibit touting the state's industrial and natural resources.[44]

New South academics viewed their Northern counterparts as "men of science" whose interest in scientific curricula, support for public education, and faith in progress nearly approximated their own. Southern educators exploited informal friendships and formal contacts with Northern academics to solicit advice about curricular reform and university organization. They joined national education organizations. Southern collegiate presidents and faculty toured expensively equipped and well-funded Northern colleges and universities, examining and familiarizing themselves with new scientific apparatus and discussing the latest pedagogical methods. Both Northern and Southern educators publicly and privately noted the reconciliatory character of their encounters.[45]

The assassination of a Republican president, James A. Garfield, in 1881, offered New South academics a great opportunity publicly to display their reconciliatory sentiments. Garfield, a former mathematics professor and college president who could speak French and German, was shot by a disgruntled office seeker on July 2. The attack did not kill Garfield immediately, and it was believed that the president might recover.[46]

Southerners, like other Americans, demonstrated their outrage. Louisiana State University's president, William Preston Johnston, expressed his "profound regret at so horrible a crime" and offered Garfield and his family the "sincere sympathy" of Johnston and the Board of Supervisors, along with their hopes for the president's recovery. Former Confederate Col. Ashbel Smith, president of the Board of Regents of the University of Texas, joined in "the universal joy that the President's life was saved" and "rejoiced exceedingly at the manifestations by the whole South of our horror and indignation of the crime and of our sincere rejoicing at the failure [of] the pitiful assassin." Such displays from former Rebels, progressivist academics believed, augured well for the future of reconciliation.[47]

Garfield survived for more than two months before finally succumbing to his wounds on September 19. Upon his death, Daniel Harvey Hill, president of the Arkansas Industrial University, at the faculty's request agreed to deliver a memorial address on Garfield's behalf. Several years after the assassination, Johnston listed the dead president in the same company as Daniel Webster and John C. Calhoun, among the nation's most eminent statesmen.[48]

In an effort to ease the trauma of reconciliation and the shock of the South's defeat, New South proponents, including educators, joined their Northern counterparts in celebrating the "Cult of the Anglo-Saxon," which appeared with increasing frequency as the nineteenth century progressed. Antebellum advocates of Manifest Destiny, including Southerners, in the 1840s had advanced the idea of Anglo-Saxon superiority to justify national expansion across the North American continent at Mexico's expense. They viewed national advances in material progress as evidence that American civilization had surpassed all previous cultures. They claimed the material prosperity of the United States resulted from the intellectual superiority of the Anglo-Saxon "race," which had immigrated to North America from Great Britain. Occasionally, American intellectuals celebrated the fusion of Anglo-Saxon, German, Norman, or Celtic "races," which they believed had created a "conquering, world subduing race." They asserted that God's plan for Anglo-Saxons required their expansion to the Pacific in order to develop the resources of the entire continent.[49]

After the Civil War, New South academics minimized the importance of Confederate defeat and the apparent lack of technological progress in the

South by celebrating the material and moral accomplishments of "Anglo-Saxon," "Anglo-Norman," or "Teutonic" culture, in which Southerners claimed to share. "The history of the Teutonic Race is the history of man's highest achievements," declared Burwell Boykin Lewis. Southern academics used Anglo-Saxonism as a means of promoting sectional reconciliation by offering most white Americans a common heritage after a divisive war.

William Preston Johnston touted the racial progress and unity of Northerners and Southerners when he told a New York audience in 1892 that the "Southern people, like yourselves, are with few and inconsiderable exceptions of pure British origin . . . [and] are eminently a superior race, high in the peerage of nations. They are the elect of the same blood and lineage as yourselves, descendants of sires who were next of kin, indeed, to your own sturdy Dutch ancestors and Pilgrim fathers." Southern academics praised Anglo-Saxon family life, political skills, inventive genius, and language. They only occasionally asked themselves why the South appeared to trail the rest of the so-called Anglo-Saxon world in material progress.[50]

The glorification of Anglo-Saxon culture by American academics and intellectuals, North and South, stemmed from their celebration of progress. They embraced the Social Darwinist notion that competition generated material and moral progress. They also believed that racial superiority could be determined by measuring the progress of each race. American academics frequently cited the technological progress of the nineteenth century, which they credited almost entirely to Saxon ingenuity, as evidence of the racial superiority of Anglo-Saxons. In comparison, blacks, Social Darwinists charged, demonstrated little or no progress.[51]

Southern academics familiarized themselves with the evolutionary and progressivist ideas of Charles Darwin, Thomas Huxley, and Herbert Spencer. Most, at least publicly, rejected as blasphemous the concept that humankind evolved physically through competition and natural selection. The dramatic progress of physical science, however, convinced Southern academics to accept the idea that human capabilities evolved in this manner. They had little difficulty accepting the progressivist "science" which fit their racial and theological beliefs, and rejecting that which did not.

The New South academics of the Civil War generation, in particular, adopted the language of Social Darwinism because it helped them to understand the historical connection between conflict and progress. "The war and reconstruction left Southern society sadly seamed and scarred in diverse ways," observed Johnston in 1891, "but they sifted and winnowed the weak and base material and the South is to-day tougher, more self-contained, more versatile and better trained for the hard contest of modern civilization than ever before." The New South which emerged from this process, Johnston claimed, "is the direct evolution of the Old South."

Kemp P. Battle, professor of history at the University of North Carolina, believed that his academic field provided humankind with "a logical view of the great stream of human events and the evolution of races and nations."

U.S. Rep. Hilary Herbert of Alabama told the University of Virginia's alumni society in 1887 that technical education aided social evolution. The former Confederate colonel and future secretary of the United States Navy encouraged government to provide universities the resources for scientific research and training, whereupon "we shall have 'the survival of the fittest,' and great men in every branch of science."[52]

The belief maintained by academics and others that African Americans eventually would disappear or cease to work in the face of labor competition from whites also helped to foster Southern academia's acceptance of Social Darwinism. Some postbellum Southern academics embraced the racist fantasy that the destruction of slavery would result in the ultimate disappearance of African Americans from the South. "The negro," wrote Gorgas, "will disappear in any event before the moral and intellectual superiority of the whites." Southern academics claimed that African Americans lacked the supposed progressivist predisposition of Anglo-Saxons. Maury commented on the "constantly diminishing numbers" of African Americans after the war, which he attributed to "the proverbial improvidence of the race." Stephen Lee claimed that, from "a statistical standpoint, the outlook for the negro is not encouraging." He argued that, without the progressivist influence of whites, African Americans tended to "retrograde."[53]

Southern academics also believed that blacks would refuse to work without slavery. Robert A. Hardaway, who served as professor of engineering at Alabama A&M and the University of Alabama, advised Southern whites that "it is useless to be casting about for Sambo or Ah Sin to be a laborer for you." The former artillery officer in the Army of Northern Virginia observed: "When we laid down the musket at Appomattox we had to take up the shovel and hoe." Daniel Harvey Hill claimed that "the negro population . . . can no longer be classed as a laboring element." In order to compensate for the South's supposed labor shortage, progressivist academics claimed that scientific education would give white Southerners the ability to develop labor-saving machinery.[54]

Southern academia embraced Anglo-Saxonism because it gave white Southerners a role in generating progress. New South academics accepted Social Darwinism because it explained how progress occurred through competition and conflict. They turned to history to explain why progress had lagged in the South and why the Confederacy had lost the Civil War.

New South academics believed that they could understand progress through the scientific study of history. Faith in progress requires a conception of the past which recognizes developmental change in successive events and believes that this change accounts for the present and portends the future.

Progressivist Southern academics turned to their Calvinist understanding of the linear movement of history toward a Providential destiny to help them intellectually to accept national reunification. "We have a right to assume . . . that there is a Plan of Providence,—that a Divine law prevails in History as elsewhere," claimed Johnston while professor of history at Washington and Lee University. "To discover the workings of this law . . . to trace the development of man and society, to disclose order, adaptation, and causation in the progress of humanity," Johnston believed, "is the noble and fascinating province of the philosophy of History."[55]

Johnston and other academic proponents of the New South who had served in the Confederate military studied their region's recent past intently. These and other Confederate veterans looked to history to vindicate their reasons for fighting the war. Former officers especially wanted to use history to provide proof of their wartime prowess and defend themselves against charges of incompetence. Personal assertions of bravery and skill proved little amid the acrimony and recrimination prevalent among veterans. To escape public censure, they wrote addresses, articles, and letters defending their actions and blaming others for personal military failures.[56]

To justify their wartime actions and defend their personal honor, many Confederates, especially those in academia, gathered evidence in the form of battle reports, maps, orders, and remembrances of eyewitnesses. Confederate veterans who entered academia joined such Northern historians as Herbert Baxter Adams and Albert Bushnell Hart in embracing the idea that the "modern" study of history required that this "innovative" discipline be studied as a "science." William Preston Johnston believed that the study of history should be included with the new technical studies that increasingly appeared in college curricula after the Civil War. The accumulation and proper interpretation of factual evidence, Southern academics believed, could be used to justify personal and societal behavior alike. Former Confederates believed that historical documents, carefully and impartially collected, sifted, and examined, promised to demonstrate white Southerners' military ability and simultaneously explain why the Confederacy failed. Southern academics also believed that the scientific study of history offered them the opportunity to demonstrate the justness of their cause.[57]

Southern academics helped form and joined regional and state historical societies and memorial associations dedicated to defending the region's history and Confederate military feats against supposedly slanderous attacks by Yankee critics. The South must not, Daniel Harvey Hill wrote to Stephen Lee, "let the Yankee account of this struggle be transmitted to posterity." Hill hoped to use his journal, *The Land We Love*, to "vindicate the truth of history," as well as to promote technical education and the development of Southern resources.[58]

The Southern Historical Society, founded in New Orleans in 1869, counted Hill, who later served as president of Arkansas Industrial University, and Robert E. Lee, president of Washington College, among its vice-presidents. Upon the society's reorganization four years later, William Preston Johnston was elected to its executive committee. These educators, who promoted scientific and technical instruction as well as historical studies, wanted their society to collect, classify, preserve, and publish "all the documents and facts bearing upon the eventful history of the past few years." To accomplish this goal, Confederate veterans in academia frequently contributed to the society's *Papers*. William LeRoy Broun, Daniel Harvey Hill, Stephen Lee, John Mallet, and William Preston Johnston, among others, published articles or addresses in the periodical; all of these works concerned the Confederate war effort.[59]

The Southern Historical Society denied that it intended to cultivate a "purely sectional" or "partisan character." Like Daniel Harvey Hill, it desired only to "vindicate the truth of history." Johnston claimed that the organization wanted to prevent the perversion of "history—Northern and Southern," through the transmission of "*a true* record of the war." Such transmission required the preservation and unbiased evaluation of source materials necessary "to vindicate the truth of history."[60]

The organization's members clearly intended it to serve as a repository for evidence that they believed ultimately would justify the Southern rebellion against the national government. They also emphasized, however, the reconciliatory nature of their endeavor. The society's Official Circular stated that anything which related to "this critical period of our national history, pending the conflict, antecedent or subsequent to it, from the point of view of either, or both the contestants . . . is to be industriously collated and filed." The society's members believed that the accumulation of primary source material would lead future "disinterested," or objective, historians to find "the secret thread . . . running through all history, upon which its single facts crystallize in the unity of some great Providential plan."[61]

Former Confederates wanted an ideology capable of convincing themselves, and Northerners, that they warranted an active role in the reunited nation's future. If white Southerners remained wedded to archaic defenses of secession and slavery, they promised to contribute little to the nation's progress and to receive only continued disparagement and hostility from Northerners. Yet, for Confederate veterans to feel secure and confident about their role in a reconstructed Union, they needed to define their past in a manner that allowed them psychologically to embrace the future. This dilemma led New South academics to help create the linked ideologies of the "Old South" and the "Lost Cause."[62]

The men who entered Southern academia immediately after the war and espoused the New South had no intention of denigrating their past. On the contrary, they had a psychological stake in elevating it. New South academics turned to history to defend the antebellum South and the performance of Confederate soldiers in the war. They claimed that the Old South had raised up a race of men who brilliantly and gallantly had battled a foe possessed of overwhelming resources. Those men had staved off inevitable defeat for four years in their hopelessly "Lost Cause" of Southern independence.

The sources examined by Confederate veteran-historians proved to their satisfaction that the war had occurred because of a misunderstanding between the sections over Constitutional principles. The almost universal moral stigma that Western society attached to slavery in the nineteenth century, combined with the humiliation of Confederate defeat, discouraged most white Southerners from continuing to defend slavery. The South's amateur and professional historians claimed that both Southerners and Northerners maintained morally correct reasons for going to war. The South fought for states' rights and the defense of its property (which they claimed only incidentally included slaves), while Northerners engaged in the equally honorable task of forging a more democratic and centralized Union. Samuel Lockett observed that the purpose of the memorial celebration in Montgomery, Alabama, which he addressed in 1875, was to honor those "who sacrificed their lives for the 'Lost Cause.'" Nevertheless, he felt compelled to tell the audience that "I for one am perfectly willing to acknowledge that the masses of the Northern people were animated by pure and unselfish motives." He believed that "it was their most sacred duty to answer the call" to save the Union.[63]

New South academics recognized that Southern society had failed in its mission of defeating the North. Advocates of change sometimes found themselves under attack from white Southerners who heard praise for the New South as a denunciation of the Old South. Academics of the Civil War generation who promoted progress rejected that equation.[64]

Johnston promoted "the New South" but asked that, "before we part with the Old South[,] let us see what it was, and what it did for the national welfare and glory." He praised antebellum Southern political achievements and slavery's supposed civilizing influence upon African Americans. He claimed that Confederates had lost the war only because the Union's superior resources overwhelmed them. Johnston argued that the New South, one in which he believed commerce, sawmills, mines, manufacturers, and railroads flourished, drew its "sap and vitality from a taproot deep down in the strong soil of a distant past."[65]

Likewise, David Boyd—who late in life fondly reminisced about his wartime associations and experiences—noted that "we hear much of the *new* South. It is the same *old* South—risen Phoenix-like from the ashes . . .

[Southern] young men are the rich legacy of the *old* South to the *new* South. It is *old* wine in *new* bottles—strong bottles that will not burst." Daniel Harvey Hill asked young Southerners to "admire and imitate whatever was grand and noble" of the Old South and to "reject whatever was wrong and defective."[66]

Progressivist academics conceded that the antebellum South had failed to satisfy the demands of progress, because history had demonstrated the inadequacy of slavery as a labor system and the supremacy of the Union over the states. Former Confederates in academia yielded intellectually what they previously had surrendered on the battlefield—namely, they acknowledged the necessity of abolition and a perpetual Union. The lessons of history demanded that Southerners accept reconciliation and embrace science and technology in order to build a physically prosperous New South. Through the application of scientific methodology to both the South's history and its material resources, New South academics offered white Southerners both psychic justification for their past and material hope for their future. Unlike other veterans who embraced the Lost Cause but who viewed the New South as antithetical to the Old South,[67] New South academics developed a progressivist vision of history that interpreted the New South, the Old South, and the Lost Cause as three interdependent creeds.

The dogma of the Old South and the Lost Cause stressed both the nobility and the inevitable failure of Confederate independence, enabling the veterans to separate their conception of honor from that of victory. They sought to demonstrate their honor by developing a historical record of their courage, integrity, and military skill. They acknowledged, however, that the notion of an independent South truly was "lost." History demonstrated the impossibility of Southern independence, because the South's lack of material progress before the war had left the region incapable of defeating the industrial North. These New South academics looked to higher education to remedy this situation and allow Southerners to keep step with progress.

The first generation of New South academics, especially former Confederate officers, concluded that the Confederacy's failure demonstrated the necessity of abandoning the republican conception of progress, characterized by fears of cyclical societal decay, in favor of the modern idea of progress, which emphasized inevitable and unlimited improvement. These academics believed that utilitarian education promised to create a prosperous New South founded upon industry and technology. Their belief in inevitable defeat permitted Confederate veterans-turned-academics to cherish the antebellum South, honor the memory of the Confederacy, and reconcile with the North, while avoiding recriminations for their failure to win Southern independence.

Colleges and universities administered by progressivist academics served as the vehicles for their efforts to convince white Southerners to accept their past and look forward to the future. Students in their classrooms learned of the coming New South. Graduates, parents, students, and others in attendance at alumni society and commencement addresses listened to predictions that the South would rise from the ashes of its defeat and create a new, superior, industrial, and perpetually progressive civilization.[68] The New South academics of the Civil War generation strove to use technical education to turn their vision of a New South into reality. To accomplish this goal, however, progressivists needed to overcome the opposition of those who did not share their dreams.

Chapter 4

Obstacles to Progress

Progressivist academics believed that, in order to "meet the wants of the New South," they needed to control at least some of the region's colleges and universities.[1] The Confederacy's collapse appeared to justify their charge that Southern higher education had failed to provide the kind of instruction necessary to sustain a modern state. Defeat convinced many collegiate boards to employ personnel capable of organizing the scientific courses that promised to restore the South's prosperity. The persons hired to restructure the curriculum consisted primarily of men with Confederate service, but also included antebellum and wartime academics who had warned that Southern educational inadequacies might result in military disaster. These men gained control over a number of colleges and universities, including most state schools, which could with less difficulty afford the costly equipment required to teach scientific and technical courses. Nonetheless, opposition to the goals of progressivist educators and their New South strongholds emerged quickly on the part of politicians, clerics, classicists, and farmers.

Confederate veterans in the immediate postwar years frequently criticized the predilection of antebellum white Southerners to look to politics to solve the South's sectional problems. The failure of classically educated politicians to secure the South's independence and the political uncertainties whites faced with Congressional Reconstruction taught many Southerners to reject politics and turn to academia to find the means of restoring prosperity. David Boyd, for example, claimed that Southerners before the war had been too much engaged in politics and had exhibited too little enthusiasm for the mechanical arts. He urged LSU's graduating class of 1870 to reconstruct the state, but "not so much *political* reconstruction [as] moral, social, and material!"

Hardaway Hunt Dinwiddie, in his valedictory address to VMI's class of 1867, criticized those who failed to realize that academic programs which educated students for political careers needed to be abandoned. Instead, "necessity" required schools to introduce "practical training that leads to achievements in the boundless fields of mathematical and technical science." Dinwiddie, who had interrupted his education at VMI to fight for the Confederacy, later taught chemistry and physics at Texas A&M before becoming that school's faculty chair in 1883.[2]

Progressivist academics developed an almost unshakable faith that scientific and technical instruction would create a new South. "There is no progress in modern civilization," asserted William LeRoy Broun, "without technical education." With little capital and virtually no industrial base left in the South, education offered an attractive means for a defeated and depressed people to recover their prosperity and even perhaps to become self-reliant. Technical education promised to provide Southerners with the inventive genius and skilled labor necessary for industrial development. To obtain these assets, they turned to their colleges and universities.[3]

"The first step of upward progress," Benjamin H. Hill declared before the University of Georgia Alumni Society in 1871, "is to build up our universities." Hill, a former Confederate senator, wanted Southern schools to establish departments of agriculture, commerce, manufacturing, mining, and technology. Although the speech drew the ire of those who believed that his call for a New South disparaged the Old South, Hill's insistence that schools add to their curricula courses in applied science already had been heeded by many Southern colleges and universities. These schools, including the University of Georgia, wanted men who had put their scientific training to practical use—a criterion met by most Confederate officers during the war—to build their programs in applied science.[4]

The University of Georgia, under the threat of Union forces, suspended operations in early 1864 and remained closed until January 1866. Shortly after its reopening, Chancellor Andrew A. Lipscomb urged the Board of Trustees to add classes in applied science. "Education . . . feels the revolution through which we have passed," he observed, and "must be adjusted to the new order of things." On July 4, 1866, the university established a civil engineering school. It also added agricultural science to the duties of the professor of natural philosophy. The trustees hired William LeRoy Broun to fill that position and changed his title to "professor of chemistry, geology, and agriculture."[5]

Lipscomb found a friend and ally in Broun, who eagerly supported the chancellor's effort to reconstruct the university's curriculum. The week before Christmas, 1867, Broun delivered an address to the Georgia Teachers' Association, entitled "Improvements Required in Southern Colleges." In this talk he claimed that the "altered condition of the people of the South" necessitated that they adapt their system of higher education in ways capable of promoting prosperity. Broun called upon Southern colleges to adopt or expand technical studies (which, he noted, entailed the purchase of expensive equipment). He also recommended that the South's schools follow the example of his alma mater, the University of Virginia, by adopting the elective system, which would allow parents and students to choose their own courses of study. This plan would enable Southern youths to specialize, which he claimed was necessary for them to master specific, and increasingly complex, sciences. The traditional prescribed course of study, Broun complained, overemphasized ancient languages at the expense of technical studies. He argued that science education promised to give youth the skills to generate material prosperity, while antebellum classical educations had taught young Southerners only "to despise work and energy, and industry." To Broun, the fact that four-fifths of those who passed the examinations he prepared for the Confederate Ordnance Department graduated from the University of Virginia demonstrated the superiority of the elective system.[6]

Broun's speech pleased George Washington Rains, the University of Georgia's professor of chemistry and the former head of the Confederacy's powder works in Augusta. Rains's endorsement of Broun's views paralleled that of others who read the published version of the speech, which circulated among academics in both the North and the South. Broun quickly found himself recognized as one of the nation's foremost proponents of curricular reform.[7]

With Lipscomb's support, Broun proposed a reorganization and expansion of the University of Georgia that would put his reforms into action. The university's trustees adopted the elective system in 1869. Georgia was not alone in implementing optional courses. At least thirty-five Southern schools joined many of their Northern counterparts and adopted some aspects of the elective system in the two decades after the Civil War. In 1872, the University of Georgia also approved a plan to expand the school's scientific curriculum. This plan closely followed Broun's recommendations. The trustees wanted to establish a school of applied science that would teach all branches of engineering, metallurgy, and scientific agriculture. The plan also contemplated the establishment of professorships of "economic geology" and "industrial mechanics." The board ultimately adopted courses in bookkeeping, history, mechanics, and scientific agriculture.[8]

The importance of this training to the future prosperity of Georgia, Lipscomb believed, could not be overestimated. He believed that education would "prove itself a positive agency of Providence" by uniting the interests of planters with those of manufacturers. He wanted the university placed "in living condition with the industrial economy of Georgia" through its alumni, who would work the state's factories, foundries, laboratories, and mines. Ultimately, he hoped that they would enable Georgia to free itself from economic and industrial dependence upon "others."[9]

The most celebrated effort to rebuild the South through industrial education, however, occurred at Washington College in Lexington, Virginia. Edward S. Joynes, the professor of modern languages and a wartime advocate of educational reform, declined an offer from Broun to come to Georgia in

1868. As he put it, "We are in the midst here of a great undertaking—precisely that which you have set so dearly before yourself in Georgia—that of reformation and progress, in the organization and work of our institution." Broun and Joynes eventually did unite in 1875, to aid in the development of the curriculum at Vanderbilt University. In the interim, however, Joynes chose to remain at Washington College under its president, Robert E. Lee, who had embarked on a program to add applied sciences to the school's traditional classical courses. The trustees of the college had appointed Lee to the presidency less than four months after Appomattox, and they hoped that the general's fame would attract both contributors and students.[10]

Lee wanted Southern youths to learn how to apply scientific research to farming, manufacturing, and mining, in order to develop the region's natural resources. His efforts received the support of the board, which hoped to add classes in applied mathematics and physics. Lee and the trustees recognized, however, that expensive apparatus was required to teach applied science properly. The general complained to one potential contributor that, "while other colleges with enlarged means have been enabled to keep pace with the progress of science, civilization, and improvement," Washington College had "stood still." In an effort to secure the revenue necessary to expand the curriculum, Lee undertook an extensive fundraising campaign. In 1866, the college received contributions from two benefactors which alone totaled $25,000.

Lee's name attracted students, not only from all the former Confederate states but also from ten loyal states, including one student from Massachusetts, a state long despised in the South as a home of abolitionism. Enrollment increased from 146 students in 1866 to 348 students two years later, and the faculty grew from fourteen to nineteen during the same period. Lee's success at soliciting donations and luring paying students enabled the college to inaugurate departments of applied mathematics, civil engineering, and modern languages in his first year as president. The following year, the college added the departments of applied chemistry, geology, and history.[11]

Although many faculty members and trustees at Washington College helped to develop and promote reform, it was Lee's advocacy of utilitarian education that particularly heartened academic reformers—some of whom did not hesitate to draw upon the general's stature in propagandizing their own efforts. In Broun's endeavor to convince Southern colleges to offer alternatives to the classics, he noted that under Lee's leadership an elective system had been inaugurated at Washington College. After Lee's death in 1870, proponents of technical instruction attributed Washington College's reforms solely to the general and frequently associated him with their cause. In an address supporting technical instruction at South Carolina College, Kemp Battle praised "the warrior Lee" as "pre-eminent in science."[12]

Other Southern schools quickly adapted their curricula to meet what Socrates Maupin, chairman of the faculty at the University of Virginia, called the "requirements of the times," by hiring technically trained professors capable of offering new courses in applied science. "The changed condition of Southern society," Maupin wrote, compelled the school to add professorships in "applied mathematics" and "applied chemistry." The university appointed John Mallet to the latter position, and he hoped to use technical instruction to generate the capital, industry, and skilled labor necessary to return material prosperity to the South.[13]

The Virginia Military Institute continued to stress scientific education under Francis Henney Smith. The school added John M. Brooke to its faculty, and Smith used him to demonstrate the institute's commitment to utilitarian instruction. Smith lauded Brooke's ability as chair of the department of "Practical Engineering" by noting that his technical education had enabled the U.S. Naval Academy graduate to clothe "the steamer *Merrimac* with the iron armor of the *Virginia*." Smith's meaning was clear: proper scientific education could transform the agrarian Old South into an industrial New South.[14]

Two years after the war, the architect who planned the rebuilding of the University of Alabama, James T. Murfee, also proposed a scheme to reorganize the university's curriculum. Murfee, formerly the school's commandant of cadets, advocated establishing colleges of agriculture, commerce, and engineering, whose graduates he believed would develop the economic resources of the state. He criticized the traditional curriculum for its failure to equip students with a specialized education necessary for success in the postbellum South. "Under the system of slavery, ignorance and idleness might acquire and maintain wealth," Murfee acknowledged; but, "under free institutions, the individual must depend upon habits of order, system, self-reliance, and a disciplined mind, stored with knowledge pertaining to his special pursuit."

Reconstruction difficulties (particularly violent threats from conservative Democrats that chased several would-be Republican presidents from the university) not only prevented any serious efforts to implement Murfee's plan, but also threatened the school's very existence. Finally, in an effort to avoid closing the university altogether, the conservative alumni association and the Republican-controlled Board of Regents agreed in June 1871 to model the university on VMI and appoint Matthew Maury, a professor from that institution with impeccable Confederate credentials, as president. Not surprisingly, the plans of the former VMI professor resembled those of Murfee, a VMI alumnus. The university increased its faculty from five to twelve and added new professorships in applied mathematics, chemistry, geology and mineralogy, military engineering, and modern languages. Maury, however, feared that the university lacked the means to carry out his proposals to build a first-rate scientific institution (or even to pay him) and resigned less than four months after his election.[15]

The board replaced Maury with the professor of chemistry, Nathaniel T. Lupton. A native of Winchester, Virginia, Lupton had received his undergraduate degree at Dickinson College in Pennsylvania in 1849. He then returned south and worked as a chemistry professor at various small Methodist colleges. In 1859, he moved to Europe and studied under Robert Wilhelm Bunsen, the famed German scientist, at the University of Heidelberg. During the Civil War, he served as a chemist in the Confederacy's Nitre and Mining Bureau.[16]

As president of the University of Alabama, Lupton followed Maury's plans for the school. He tried to solve the university's pecuniary difficulties by securing Alabama's portion of the funds designated for agricultural and mechanical colleges by the federal Morrill Act. The legislature chose instead to establish a separate agricultural and mechanical college at Auburn. Despite this development, Lupton continued his efforts to provide utilitarian education. He left the university and returned to Heidelberg in 1874, where he spent another year studying under Bunsen. After returning to the United States, he received a professorship at Alabama A&M, where he worked until his death in 1893.[17]

Louisiana State Seminary, closed for much of the war, reopened in October 1865 under Superintendent David Boyd, with its curriculum focused upon technical instruction. After the Confederacy's defeat, Boyd became an avid supporter of applied scientific education. Much of what he knew about the subject he learned from his correspondence with William LeRoy Broun. Boyd hoped that the education provided at the school would enable graduates to "make a *new* Louisiana and a new South." The seminary offered a bachelor's degree in science and established a Special School of Engineering which awarded a degree in civil engineering. Boyd boasted that the seminary (renamed Louisiana State University in 1870) had put together a faculty dominated by scientifically trained graduates of VMI, the University of Virginia, and West Point. The teaching corps also consisted of Confederate veterans, many of whom had obtained practical technical experience in the field to complement their academic training. Superintendent Boyd; Edward Cunningham, Jr., professor of chemistry; Samuel Lockett and Richard Morton Venable, professors of engineering; and John A. A. West, professor of natural and experimental philosophy, all had served as engineering officers during the war. One Unionist critic of the seminary complained that having so many former Confederates on the faculty made it "a Confederate institution for Confederate purposes." One of those purposes was to give students a utilitarian rather than a traditional education.[18]

The University of Mississippi also added courses in applied science to its curriculum. In 1865, the school hired former Confederate Gen. Claudius W. Sears, the architect of the University of Louisiana's ambitious antebellum plan to organize a scientifically oriented curriculum, as vice-chancellor and professor of mathematics. The Board of Trustees also selected another Confederate general, the West Point graduate Francis Asbury Shoup, to serve as professor of physics, astronomy, and civil engineering. They joined Eugene Hilgard, a professor of experimental and agricultural chemistry, who previously had worked as a scientist for the Confederate nitre bureau. Hilgard would serve as the nucleus of the university's effort to provide technical education. He created a plan that would have established chairs in "Technology and the Mechanic Arts" and "Practical Agriculture." The South needed these kinds of courses, he claimed, because, throughout American history, Southern farmers repeatedly had cleared new land, exhausted the soil, and then moved farther into the frontier to repeat the cycle. He believed that farmers who remained in the South had "long passed this stage of development" and needed "to be looking forward to a state of things that can endure permanently." Hilgard claimed that industrial education and scientific agriculture offered Southerners the means to furnish their own material goods and replenish the soil, both of which he considered essential if the region's prosperity were to be restored.[19]

Although much of Hilgard's ambitious proposal remained unrealized, the university did add classes in agricultural chemistry, civil engineering, and geology. Further emphasizing its appreciation of scientific education, the university conferred honorary doctor of law degrees upon two ardent advocates of reform, John Mallet (1872) and William LeRoy Broun (1874). The school also appointed a graduate of West Point and former Confederate general, Alexander P. Stewart, as chancellor in 1874. Under Stewart, the university emphasized the importance of its scientific apparatus for the education of Mississippi's youth. His successor, Edward Mayes, who had served in the 4th Mississippi Cavalry during the war, reorganized the curriculum to strengthen the emphasis on scientific instruction. As part of his effort, Mayes attempted—but failed—to secure the services of William LeRoy Broun.[20]

Some former Confederate officers in academia attempted to organize their own scientific schools. Gen. Raleigh E. Colston, with the aid of two other former officers and VMI graduates, William A. Obenchain and D. Truehart, reopened the Hillsborough (North Carolina) Military Academy. The academy's founder, C. C. Tew, had been killed at Antietam. Colston hoped that the school would be a place where Southern students "may come to learn the Arts of Peace and of Science and Industry, which will yet make their beloved native land smile and blossom like a rose." The faculty designed a course of instruction that promised to enable the South's young men to develop the region agriculturally and industrially. The curriculum included classes in agricultural chemistry, engineering, geology, and industrial drawing. Heavy emphasis was placed upon mathematics.[21]

Edmund Kirby Smith opened the Western Military Academy in Henry County, Kentucky, in 1869. The school's curriculum included botany, engineering, geology, history, and mineralogy. In 1873, Samuel Lockett acquired Calhoun College at Jacksonville, Alabama. He transformed the school from a classical to a polytechnical institution. Lockett viewed himself as something of a missionary bringing progress and science to the unenlightened people of Alabama's Piedmont. "The sciences," he wrote to David Boyd, "have never been taught in these parts." This deficiency Lockett hoped his school would rectify.[22]

Despite the hopes of Colston, Smith, and Lockett, their enterprises failed, primarily because they lacked the financial resources to keep them in operation. The schools, like many private and public colleges in the South, depended heavily upon tuition. Few students, however, could afford the high fees required to cover professors' salaries and pay for expensive scientific equipment. The problem intensified during the nationwide depression of the early and middle 1870s, which both private and public collegiate administrators blamed for dwindling enrollments and decreasing funds.[23]

Not even Washington College proved immune to economic hardship. In 1869, flush with money and students, the school embraced an expensive plan created by a faculty committee that included William Preston Johnston, Richard Sears McCulloh, and William Allan (chief of ordnance for Thomas J. "Stonewall" Jackson's corps). Lee supported the proposal, which promised to expand the school's curriculum dramatically. The plan included the organization of new departments of agriculture, commerce, and mechanical and mining engineering. The aim was to prepare graduates capable of moving the South away from a labor-intensive plantation economy toward one founded upon scientific agriculture, business expertise, and industrial innovation. Students in the agricultural department would take "rural engineering" and study irrigation systems and mechanized agriculture. The commercial department promised to teach students how to administer various business enterprises, including banks, canals, and railroads. Mechanical engineering students would discover how to construct factories, steam engines, mills, and locomotives. In addition to learning to work mines and identify ores, mining students would study the manufacture of iron and steel. The ambitious plan was published in De Bow's Review, which claimed that, if Lee lived to see it succeed, "he will have won the Lost Cause in the freedom and happiness of the South, redeemed and perpetuated through the education of her sons."[24]

Before applied scientific instruction could salvage the Lost Cause, however, Southerners needed to pay for it. Following Lee's death in 1870, the trustees, in a bid to keep the institution connected with the lucrative Lee name, both replaced Lee with his son, Custis, and changed the name of the school to Washington and Lee University. The university also obtained the endorsement of thirteen former Confederate generals who supported expansion of the school's utilitarian programs. The board hired Col. Joseph W. Taylor of Alabama, an advocate of internal improvements, industrial diversification, and scientific agriculture, to stump the South raising money for the university's ambitious plans. For purposes of raising donations and attracting students, these strenuous efforts served as poor substitutes for the Confederacy's premier general. Economic depression, mismanagement, and the revered general's death led to a dramatic decline in contributions and enrollments during the 1870s, forcing the school virtually to abandon its applied science curriculum.[25]

The high cost of technical instruction convinced many progressivist academics and their supporters that state schools, which potentially could draw upon large public resources for support, were the proper vehicles for providing scientific education. Denominational colleges, the commonest type of private schools, received their support from a limited sectarian pool of contributors and students. Therefore, progressivists believed, these schools usually would lack the resources to acquire the equipment and faculty necessary for proper scientific instruction. Reformers contended that denominational colleges performed satisfactorily when furnishing low-cost classical education, but not when offering expensive scientific curricula. Even supporters of sectarian institutions, who feared competition from state-subsidized schools, occasionally acknowledged the importance of public universities' deepening "the springs of learning" through science, while denominational colleges supplied moral and religious instruction. Together, the sectarian and state schools promised to "harmonize in the one great work of advancing Christian civilization and learning."[26]

During Reconstruction, state universities often found their efforts disrupted, not by disputes over curricular reform but by political conflicts over who would control the schools and whether they would be racially integrated.

David Swain, president of the University of North Carolina, became less effective in convincing the public to support his institution after his daughter married a United States Army general in 1867. A new Board of Trustees, appointed in 1868 and dominated by Republicans, accepted Swain's resignation and vacated all the professorships, replacing the school's Democratic faculty with Republicans. This move interrupted the reform effort, led by a displaced trustee, Kemp Plummer Battle, to add courses in applied science and establish the elective system. Solomon Pool, the university's Republican president, continued reform, but whites' fears that the new administration would allow racial integration discouraged many parents from sending their children to the university, and enrollment declined. Although blacks never attended the university during Reconstruction, the lack of public support forced the school to suspend operations in 1871. Reconstruction in North Carolina ended that same year, but the university remained closed until 1875. Conservatives replaced the Republicans on the school's governing board, and in 1876 that body elevated Battle to the presidency, which he occupied for fifteen years. Battle, who during the war had served as president of a North Carolina railroad organized to haul coal from Chatham County to Confederate ordnance manufacturers, promptly resumed his efforts at curricular reform. He achieved some success, particularly in the field of engineering.[27]

In the months following the end of the Civil War, the trustees of South Carolina College temporarily transformed that institution into the University of South Carolina and embarked upon a program to add technical studies and adopt the elective system. The board hired a West Point graduate, former Confederate Gen. Edward Porter Alexander, to chair the school of mathematics, civil and military engineering, and construction. The LeContes returned to the university, where John chaired the school of natural and mechanical philosophy and astronomy, and Joseph directed the school of chemistry, pharmacy, mineralogy, and geology. The trio of professors gave the new university a solid basis for developing a strong program in scientific education. Their courses were immensely popular; and, with the elective system in place, they attracted considerably more enrollees than the university's four classically oriented schools.[28]

After the advent of Congressional Reconstruction in 1868, the university's focus shifted from its curricular reforms to integration. South Carolina's new state constitution mandated that the university be open to students of all races. Fears concerning integration led many white students to withdraw from the university and deterred others from attending. A decline in enrollment resulted. The possibility of desegregation ultimately led to the resignation of the entire faculty, as well as conservative trustees. The first black student finally entered the university in 1873, and two years later approximately half the student population of 166 consisted of African Americans. The new faculty and trustees curtailed the elective system but attempted to offer utilitarian courses. The restoration of conservative control over the state government in 1877 ended integration at the University of South Carolina. A new board suspended operations, and the school emerged three years later as the South Carolina College of Agriculture and Mechanics.[29]

The hostility of white Mississippians toward integration threatened academic reforms undertaken at the University of Mississippi, too. Chancellor John Waddel announced publicly in September 1870 that he and the entire faculty would resign if the Republican legislature forced the university to admit African Americans. Gov. James Alcorn, a Republican, averted the mass resignation by convincing the legislature to establish a separate black school, Alcorn University, and allowing the University of Mississippi to remain segregated.[30]

White fears over integration also endangered Louisiana State University. For eight years after the war, the school's superintendent, David Boyd, managed to keep the university operating successfully. Boyd's antebellum secessionist sympathies, his respectable military record, and his effort to place former Confederate officers in all the faculty positions satisfied conservatives as to his fitness to oversee the higher education of Louisiana's youth. At the same time, his outspoken support of reconciliation and his friendship with high-ranking United States officers, including Sherman, convinced Republicans that Boyd should remain as the university's superintendent. He successfully balanced the demands of conservatives and radicals until 1873, when the legislature directed LSU to integrate.[31]

Boyd personally believed there existed no academic reason why African Americans should not attend LSU. "I would no more deny access on account of race or color, to the temple of learning," he claimed, "than I would exclude one, on account of race, from the temple of faith. Who may be permitted to enter the kingdom of Heaven, let us not exclude from the Republic of Letters: let him enter our University." Boyd believed that racial conciliation ultimately led to material progress—a proposition he hinted that Europeans understood. "Try to conceive of the University of Paris or Berlin, or Oxford, refusing admission to an Indian, or Chinee [sic], or African," Boyd suggested. "How absurd. Such an idea enlightened Europe would not for a moment entertain; and such an idea we of the South must discard." He wanted Southern whites to set aside their racial prejudice and discard their common belief that blacks were incapable of benefiting from higher education. Providence linked the fates of Southern blacks and whites, Boyd argued; and their mutual prosperity depended upon instruction in the applied sciences. Louisiana required men, regardless of their race, trained in mechanical engineering and scientific agriculture, who efficiently could increase the productive power of the state.[32]

Although most Southern academics lacked Boyd's enthusiasm for integration, many progressivists did advocate providing at least some education for African Americans. The instruction they envisioned, however, usually differed from that which they proposed offering Caucasians. The higher education that academics planned for whites required them to obtain scientific knowledge and apply it to building an industrial South. White academics wanted the education of African Americans, however, limited largely to manual training schools where they might learn various trades. Southern academics claimed that the region still needed blacksmiths, carpenters, wheelwrights, and other types of artisans. This kind of education, they argued, would enable the freedmen to work and provide for their material needs. Academics, in effect, encouraged blacks to learn skills still utilized in agricultural pursuits and therefore valuable to landowners and planters, who presumably would benefit from having more highly skilled black field hands, sharecroppers, and tenant farmers. This type of employment also would enable African Americans to purchase goods produced in the New South, while limiting them to occupations peripheral in an industrializing society. J. L. M. Curry, chief administrator of the John F. Slater Fund, which provided money for black education, stressed manual training for African Americans and released funds only to those schools offering vocational training. His advocacy of trade schools for blacks received the enthusiastic support of the most prominent African American progressivist educator of the late nineteenth century, Booker T. Washington. Curry was one of the few Confederate veterans in academia who corresponded with Washington. Most expressed little interest in Washington's "Normal and Industrial Institute" for African Americans at Tuskegee, Alabama.[33]

By 1890, a majority of Southern states provided some support for public institutions of higher learning for blacks, usually either in agricultural and mechanical colleges or in normal schools. Initially, some of these schools provided advanced instruction that included botany, calculus, physics, and trigonometry. The dearth of public schools in the South, however, forced many of the collegiate institutions also to provide black youth with secondary, or even primary, education. Louisiana's Southern University in New Orleans, for instance, served as a college, normal school, manual training institute, high school, and grammar school. The propensity for Southern states to provide more funding for white schools than for their black counterparts encouraged the latter to consolidate their resources and embrace coeducation before most white state colleges and universities did so. Chronic funding shortages often prevented black colleges from purchasing the expensive equipment necessary consistently to provide applied scientific instruction. Furthermore, state education boards and legislatures often stipulated that black schools primarily teach vocational subjects. By the early twentieth century, most public African American colleges resembled trade schools that graduated carpenters, rather than colleges that graduated scientists.[34]

Progressivists not infrequently couched their concern for the education of the freedmen in paternalistic rhetoric, in an effort to shame whites into providing some public funding for black schools. A. J. Peeler, a member of the

Board of Directors of Texas's normal school for African Americans, claimed that duty required "the superior race" to do all in its power to "educate and elevate our colored citizens." Kemp Battle observed that the black man "is here, and he is here to stay. Educate him. . . . We are the superior race. Let us make him better."[35]

Prior to the mass disfranchisement of Southern African Americans in the 1890s, progressivists frequently claimed that educated blacks would not be swayed by the supposedly pernicious teachings of demagogues or vote for Republicans who threatened the political power of the South's conservatives. Education, however, failed to influence African Americans in the manner hoped for by white progressivists. After noting the work of Atticus Haygood, Curry's predecessor as agent for the Slater Fund, one Mississippi critic complained in 1889 that, despite the instruction given them, African Americans still advocated federal regulation of state elections and denounced segregationist legislation.[36]

Not all progressivist academics welcomed the idea of African Americans receiving even rudimentary industrial education. Lockett dismissed whites' notions concerning their inherent superiority and feared that an educated black race eventually might surpass the material progress of Caucasians. Lockett believed in the existence of an innate conflict between the races and perceived it in Social Darwinist terms. He insisted, "There is a fierce struggle for supremacy going on in our Southern states between the two races." Lockett warned Southern whites not to neglect their schools, because, "just as sure as fate, if we of the white race retrograde in our educational attainment, the black race will become our superiors. We may talk of their lack of capacity and inability to go beyond a certain point in intellectual improvement as much as we please and console ourselves with our assertions, but the truth is the negroes are making rapid strides in self advancement." These gains Lockett attributed to the African Americans' desire for education (which he believed surpassed that of whites), to private donations given to black schools by Northern "negrophilists," and to public funding provided by the Southern states.[37]

Even David Boyd's support for black education, and especially for integrated programming, proved lukewarm. He backed conservative efforts to prevent integration at LSU, because he feared that whites would not attend or support a biracial school. Ultimately, he believed that the school needed the support of Democratic voters and their legislators to guarantee its public funding and its success. In 1873, Louisiana's Republican legislature discontinued state appropriations to LSU because of its refusal to desegregate. The loss of state funds, fear of integration, and the economic depression resulted in a dramatic decline in faculty and students. The campus population decreased from 175 students and 15 faculty for the 1871–72 session to 4 enrollees and 3 professors at the end of the 1874–75 term. Despite the university's difficulties, Boyd kept the school open but closed to blacks. The 1877 return of control over the state government to conservatives ended any consideration of integration at LSU for more than seventy years.[38]

Arkansas Industrial University in Fayetteville, established in 1872, suffered few problems directly related to Reconstruction. The university's first board, established by a Republican legislature, consisted primarily of Northerners, including eight Union veterans. Although initially the university could not legally exclude African Americans, the school admitted only two or three black students during Reconstruction. The university's acting president, Noah P. Gates, segregated these from the rest of the students and personally taught them. His successor, former Union Gen. Albert W. Bishop, who served as president of the university in 1874–1875, embarked on a plan to organize the school's curriculum around scientific instruction in agriculture, engineering, and the natural sciences. During Bishop's tenure, conservatives gained control of the legislature and established a new Board of Trustees encompassing both Union and Confederate veterans. Shortly thereafter, Bishop resigned, but he claimed that no acrimony existed between himself and the new trustees. Gates briefly returned as acting president. After a failed attempt to obtain former Confederate Gen. Joseph E. Johnston, the trustees secured Daniel Harvey Hill for the presidency. Hill largely continued Bishop's program.[39]

In Tennessee, Virginia, and Georgia, adroit leadership and the swift return of conservative rule enabled universities to avoid the political and racial conflicts that disrupted education elsewhere during Reconstruction. Even after the restoration of conservative state governments, obstacles to the implementation of applied scientific instruction in Southern state schools nonetheless remained. Supporters of denominational colleges opposed public funding for higher education. They claimed that government subsidies unfairly provided state colleges and universities with a secure source of income unavailable to private schools. Efforts by administrators of public institutions to obtain tuition waivers from state legislatures for some or all of their students further alienated proponents of sectarian education.[40]

Advocates of denominational colleges often hoped to undermine popular support for public higher education by repeating charges, first made in the antebellum period, that professors at state schools encouraged their students in religious apostasy. Advances in the natural sciences, especially biology and geology, had created doubts among many academics as to the accuracy of the biblical account of the Creation. Proponents of sectarian education criticized the study of these sciences outside of denominational colleges, which, prior to the Civil War, had started to furnish countervailing interpretations of scientific evidence in apologetics courses. Proper religious instruction offered students explanations, such as one provided by Rev. S. A. Goodwin, for apparent contradictions between Scripture and science. Goodwin admonished, "Ye followers of Darwin, and Tyndal[l], and Huxley . . . hide your faces in shame!" for inaccurately interpreting scientific evidence and spreading superstition. Goodwin exemplified the errors of these "proud boasters of reason" by claiming they had miscalculated the age of the Earth. Proper interpretation of the geological record, he declared, transformed geology from a "carping infidelity," used by atheistic academics to repudiate the Mosaic cosmogony, into a "handmaiden of religion" that ultimately proved the accuracy of Genesis by demonstrating the occurrence of the Great Flood.[41]

Progressivist educators responded to such attacks by attempting to minimize or reconcile apparent contradictions between Christianity and science. Burwell Boykin Lewis, who advanced scientific and technical instruction at the University of Alabama, maintained that "the destruction of faith by science on the part of so many intelligent people, is merely temporary; and, as science becomes broader and religion more fully transcribes the true spirit and methods of Christ, all conflict will cease, and one become the complement of the other." George Soule, a former Confederate colonel who operated a commercial college in New Orleans, defended evolution, a favorite target of religious educators. Soule declared that "evolution . . . with his torch of progress," far from being antithetical to Christianity, as sectarians charged, served as "God's master-workman" in shaping the world humans inhabited.[42]

F. Henry Smith, professor of natural philosophy at the University of Virginia, called Darwin's work "brilliant" and claimed that the study of the Bible, like biology and geology, was an imperfect science. Biblical scholars, Smith asserted "must concede the existence and value of another 'revelation'—that of material nature. . . . The Biblical student cannot be indifferent to those conclusions of physical science which bear upon the Bible." The former commissioner of weights and measures for the Confederacy encouraged exegesis and cautioned both natural and scriptural scientists from rashly proclaiming contradictions between—or harmonies among—the two "modern sciences." History demonstrated that both biblical interpretation and scientific theories underwent continuous transformation; therefore the conciliation of Scripture and physical science in one era might turn into discord in the next, or vice versa. Smith encouraged practitioners of biblical and physical science honestly to pursue their work and to let time, perhaps as much as a thousand years, reveal the truthful nature of both.[43]

Progressivist academics found their institutions, and occasionally themselves, under attack by religious critics. Prominent Methodists in Alabama charged David Boyd, while president of the state agricultural and mechanical college, with agnosticism and atheism for endeavoring to implement a plan proposed by his friend and predecessor, William LeRoy Broun, expanding the school's scientific instruction. Boyd, who belonged to no church, defended his efforts by telling the commencement audience of 1884 that "science and Scripture both tell us there is a survival of the fittest." Boyd resigned from the college shortly thereafter and returned to serve as president of LSU following a four-year absence.

Broun, after leaving Auburn for a more lucrative post at the new University of Texas (where the administration of Ashbel Smith sought to build a scientific reputation), resumed the presidency of Alabama A&M after Boyd's departure. As the price he exacted for his return, the Board of Directors agreed to allow Broun, who had helped Boyd obtain the presidency, further to develop the scientific curriculum. Broun remained as president until his death in 1902.[44]

William Preston Johnston left Lexington in 1880 for Louisiana, to become president of LSU. The *Louisiana Capitolian* hailed his arrival in the state, asserting that people like Johnston were "to lead in the march toward progress and enlightenment." In early 1883, Johnston resigned from LSU to accept the presidency of the inchoate Tulane University in New Orleans. He anticipated criticism as he planned to implement a scientific curriculum there. Johnston assured the Board of Administrators of the orthodoxy of his proposed curriculum by quoting Yale's president Noah Porter, who claimed that the sciences "not one or all together have made Atheism intellectually more attractive, or the denial of Providence more rational." The endowment provided by Northern industrialist Paul Tulane enabled the university to become one of the few private universities in the South that was able to purchase the equipment and hire the faculty necessary to offer extensive courses in the applied sciences.[45]

Clerical criticism also concerned George M. Edgar, a former Confederate colonel who in 1884 succeeded Hill as president of Arkansas Industrial University. Edgar spent some of his time writing histories of Civil War battles and fantasizing about Southern independence. His imagined Confederacy embraced progress and paralleled the New South. Confederate defeat, however, had not left Edgar in complete despair. He transferred his vision of an industrialized Confederacy to Arkansas and attempted to use his university to help that state win its economic independence from the North.

Edgar embarked upon a program to expand the school's curriculum to include courses in business, mechanical and mining engineering, and modern languages. He nevertheless felt compelled to say that his efforts to improve Arkansas's material condition would not threaten the spiritual welfare of students. The university's professors, Edgar claimed, "should be chosen from that class who are God-fearing, and who derive their notions of sociology from the teachings of God's Word."[46]

Sectarians criticized progressivist education—increasingly epitomized by public universities—for promoting crass materialism at the expense of spiritual enlightenment. Their fear that materialism undermined the spirituality of students paralleled the republican notion that luxury undermined the virtue of the Republic. Bishop William M. Green, chancellor of the Episcopal University of the South at Sewanee, Tennessee, assailed the materialism espoused by progressivists who "believe in Evolution, in Natural Selection, in a school without a Bible, in a self-made world, and in a universe that can take care of itself." If Americans followed these advocates of "Progress and Civilization," Green feared that the nation would suffer the fate of "prostrate Rome," corrupted by wealth, extravagance, factional strife, physical expansion, and foreign immigration.[47]

Progressivist educators denied that materialism contradicted Christianity or threatened the Republic; on the contrary, they argued, it coincided with the former and enhanced the latter. "We are invoking science to transmit, by its wondrous alchemy, the beaded drops that fall from the brow of honest labor, into large stores of golden grain," claimed Isaac Tichenor on behalf of the scientific goals pursued by the faculty at Alabama A&M. "We are working for humanity," he continued, "for the children of our common Father."

Lockett told medical students at the University of Tennessee that the work of Darwin, Huxley, and Tyndall would aid physicians in their inevitable victory over pestilence and disease. Medical advances during the century, Lockett claimed, gave "good ground for hope that the day of deliverance is not in the very distant future."

Broun forthrightly acknowledged the materialistic bent of progressivist academics. "While we adopt Kant's definition that 'the duty of education is to reveal to our consciousness—to evolve—the inherent ideal of divinity in man,'" Broun claimed, "we must say with Herbert Spencer, the important question for us, is 'how to live.'"[48]

The Board of Directors of Texas A&M College claimed that industrial education was necessary to protect a nation's economic security. They credited the work of Spencer, Huxley, and others, on behalf of industrial education, for saving the British textile industry from the depredations of Continental manufacturers. The directors argued that Americans' support for technical education in other states had proven at least as successful in protecting their economic interests. The board urged Texans to support their A&M college so that it, likewise, might produce scientifically trained graduates capable of improving the state's economic health and security.[49]

Bishop Green's vitriolic outburst against materialism may have been prompted by his own school's financial inability to provide effective utilitarian instruction. The university opened several years after the war and attempted

to offer extensive scientific courses, as envisioned by its antebellum origina-
tors. The Board of Trustees sought notable Confederates to serve as the vice-
chancellor, the school's chief administrative post, in an effort to attract
benefactors and students. Robert E. Lee and Matthew Maury both declined
the honor, after which the board settled for another scientifically trained and
experienced Confederate officer, Josiah Gorgas. The former chief of Confederate ordnance arrived at the school in 1868, following the financial collapse of
a foundry he jointly owned and operated with his friend John Mallet at
Brierfield, Alabama. The trustees also appointed Francis Shoup and Edmund
Kirby Smith, both West Point graduates and former Confederate generals, to
the faculty. The vice-chancellor wanted the University of the South to move
away from classical instruction and embrace more practical studies. By the
mid-1870s, the curriculum included chemistry, engineering, and physics.[50]

Unfortunately for Gorgas, the untimely economic depression saw enrollment decline. Fundraising, too, was severely impaired, hampering efforts to
provide expensive scientific instruction. Conflict also appears to have developed
between the graduates of West Point on the faculty, who advocated a scientific
curriculum, and classicists who feared that practical instruction would undermine
the virtue of students by encouraging materialism. Dissatisfaction with the
school's administration and its poor financial condition led the trustees to
terminate Gorgas's tenure at the end of 1878, by declaring that only a cleric
(which Gorgas was not) could hold the vice-chancellorship.

The appointment of ministers as presidents was a common practice at
denominational colleges, and these men generally took a more conservative
approach to education than their secular counterparts. At Sewanee, the
appointment of a minister to the vice-chancellorship effectively halted the
university's efforts to provide technical instruction. The problems facing
progressivist education at the University of the South typified those at other
denominational schools. Most such institutions were unable because of cost,
or unwilling because of orthodoxy, to embrace scientific studies. After his
termination, Gorgas briefly considered starting his own military and scientific
school, but instead he accepted the presidency of the University of Alabama,
which also wanted him to head the engineering department.[51]

The administrators of state universities took measures to defend their
schools from clerical charges that they taught heresy. Arkansas Industrial University, the University of Mississippi, and the University of South Carolina offered
classes in "Evidences of Christianity." Under Hill's administration, the Arkansas
school also required students to attend religious services every morning and
Bible class on Sundays. Under Lipscomb's successor, Rev. Henry H. Tucker, the
University of Georgia's trustees authorized the chancellor to teach "Evidences of
the Christian Religion." The University of North Carolina continued the

antebellum practice of presenting Bibles to graduating classes into the twentieth century, with, according to Battle, "not a word of opposition . . . uttered by educational or religious critics."[52]

Progressivist academics also faced the opposition of many classical educators who feared that the elective system and technical courses threatened to diminish the number of students they received. Many classicists also equated technical education with apprentice or vocational instruction, which they considered beneath the dignity of the collegiate curriculum. At several public universities, including Texas A&M, the University of Tennessee, and the University of Georgia, classicists mustered significant opposition to applied science.[53]

Experienced pedagogue Thomas S. Gathright in 1876 became the first head of Texas A&M College. In this post, he advanced classical education to the exclusion of agricultural and mechanical studies. The school's board wanted the college to offer courses in agriculture and mechanics and replaced Gathright (who scrupulously had avoided Confederate service) with John Garland James, a former Confederate officer. James moved to reorganize the curriculum along more practical lines.[54]

The University of Tennessee's president, Rev. Thomas W. Humes, a Unionist during the Civil War and a committed classicist, consistently fought reform efforts from his election in 1865 until his resignation eighteen years later. Humes barely survived a challenge to his leadership in 1877, when fifteen trustees voted to elect the progressivist David Boyd president, but they fell two votes short of a majority. Nevertheless, Humes had to contend with progressivists on his faculty, including Edward Joynes, the reform-minded professor of elocution; John McBryde, professor of agriculture and former Confederate cavalryman and civil servant; and Samuel Lockett, professor of mathematics. All these professors fought to advance the school's utilitarian curriculum. Dissatisfaction with Humes contributed to the resignations of both Joynes and McBryde, who accepted posts at South Carolina College in 1882. Humes's resignation in 1883 finally allowed reformers fully to implement a course of study containing classes in applied science. Ironically, McBryde turned down an offer to return to Tennessee as president, instead assuming the presidency of South Carolina College and embarking upon the organization of its scientific curriculum.[55]

Reformers also suffered under classical leadership at the University of Georgia. The depression of the 1870s put a severe financial strain on the institution and crippled its effort to provide expensive technical instruction. After Lipscomb's resignation as chancellor in 1874, the trustees appointed Henry Tucker, a Baptist minister and dedicated classicist who both lacked a Confederate service record and opposed the elective system and costly applied scientific courses. Tucker's efforts to increase the importance of classical instruction succeeded largely because financial difficulties hobbled development of the scientific curriculum. Tucker's administration also ended Lipscomb's open elective system in favor of a curriculum of multiple courses with fixed criteria. Tucker's outspoken opposition to utilitarian science, however, ultimately led to his removal by reform-minded trustees in 1878. They replaced him with another minister, Patrick H. Mell; but Mell had served as a Confederate field officer.[56]

Although annoyed by obstructionist clerics and classicists (particularly non-Confederate veterans like Gathright, Humes, and Tucker), progressivists viewed the public as the biggest hindrance to the fulfillment of their educational goals. After Reconstruction, Southern state legislatures generally balked at the large expenditures required to provide utilitarian scientific instruction at state universities. The legislators' parsimony may have rendered particularly attractive the comparatively low expenditures needed for classical instruction, or the zero costs to the public purse occasioned by denominational colleges. Yet progressivists at state schools rarely criticized the legislative bodies that controlled the fate of public higher education. They preferred instead to blame the South's white "masses" for their disinterest in education and their wish for low taxes. Progressivists aimed to educate the public, especially the "working classes," concerning the importance of offering scientific instruction in state schools. Ultimately, progressivists hoped that enlightened popular opinion would force legislatures to provide state colleges and universities with ample funds.[57]

Higher educators faced a difficult task in convincing the public to supply them with comfortable salaries and modern facilities. While touring Louisiana to promote LSU in 1883, President James W. Nicholson discovered that the university went largely unnoticed by the public. The school's chronic economic difficulties, the Confederate veteran believed, stemmed directly from the fact that "our people [are] not sufficiently alive to the importance of education." Battle attributed the unwillingness of the masses to support higher education to their failure to appreciate the growing importance for Southern society of technical "specialists," and to the costs involved in educating them. Progressivists also credited the persistence of the popular conviction that state universities provided education for elites at the expense of the masses with undermining efforts to raise money for public institutions. Furthermore, proponents of state schools rejected their opponents' claims that Southern states needed to focus public expenditures on scarce primary or secondary schools before spending money on higher education. Public universities, their advocates insisted, provided the teachers for the public schools. The difficulties progressivists faced in arousing popular support led some to attribute such intransigence to ignorance. "The uneducated," Curry commented, "do not appreciate the import and value of education."[58]

Progressivist educators and their adherents appealed to state pride in an effort to win public support for higher education. "We appeal to the patriotism of our fellow citizens," pleaded the trustees of Arkansas Industrial University in 1887, "to insist upon appropriations of money enough to make the University what it ought to be but cannot be without much more money." Progressivists argued that Southerners must educate their own architects, chemists, engineers, industrialists, and miners, or otherwise have educated Northerners and foreigners reap the profits derived from rebuilding the South. Proponents of public higher education also begged Southern parents not to resume the antebellum practice of educating their children outside the region. "Shall we admit that we must send our young men to the schools of science and technology, north and elsewhere to familiarize themselves with the demands of modern progress?" asked a contributor to the *Knoxville Daily Tribune*.[59]

In an effort to attract patronage, progressivist academics sought to forge connections between themselves and the public. Academics canvassed their states, urging people to support public higher education and explaining the benefits of scientific instruction. Professors also delivered public lectures on issues they believed to be of general interest. Lectures at the University of Texas for 1886–87 included "Food and Its Adulterations," "Private Corporations," "The Progress of Engineering," and "Frictional Electricity."

Additionally, state schools opened various types of museums, in part to provide learning materials for their students, but also as a ploy to attract public patronage. David Boyd appealed to Louisiana's manufacturers, mechanics, and merchants to provide material for "a good Industrial Museum," particularly model bridges or steam engines. Arkansas Industrial University boasted over five hundred mineralogical and zoological specimens, and its science departments welcomed public donations in the form of fossils and Native American artifacts. Although the contributions university museums received—such as birds' nests, rabbit skins, even a "hair ball from the stomach of a steer"—usually were of little academic or monetary value, administrators believed they helped foster good will among donors.[60]

Academics attempted to ally themselves with manufacturers by explaining to them the benefits they believed technically trained graduates offered to industry. To accomplish this task, progressivist educators joined Southern industrial associations and cultivated contacts with manufacturing interests. Tichenor represented his state's agricultural and mechanical college at the organizational meeting of the Alabama Industrial Association in September 1877. Boyd served on a committee of the Baton Rouge Industrial Association. Eugene A. Smith, a Confederate lieutenant and professor of mineralogy and geology at the University of Alabama, helped found the Alabama Industrial and Scientific Society in 1891. The organization proposed to facilitate contacts between "scientific and practical men, for mutual help and inter-change of experience," which, the founders noted, "has always proved of great material advantage." Lipscomb urged the University of Georgia's faculty to create ties with industry by connecting "your classes more closely with workshops, mines, and factories."[61]

Progressivist academics, however, had very limited success in approaching industry. Nascent Southern industrialists lacked either the inclination or the means to provide much material or political help to progressivist educators. The South's businessmen frequently viewed struggling academic institutions, with their relatively few technically trained professors and often ill-equipped laborato-ries and shops, as poor investments. Business interests believed that attracting capital and cheap labor to the region were more effective methods of developing the New South than expending resources on higher education. In addition, the business community was concerned more with lobbying state legislatures for tax exemptions than for appropriations for state colleges and universities (which might result in higher taxes for business).[62]

Academics placed their hopes of winning significant political support in another group. "It is of prime importance," wrote Francis Henney Smith to Matthew Maury, "that we ally ourselves closely with the *Agriculturists.*" Progressivist academics—especially those at A&M colleges—believed that, in a region dominated by agriculture, the patronage of farmers was essential if scientific education at state schools was to succeed. Professors of science attempted to teach farmers basic principles of scientific agriculture at Farmers' Institutes sponsored by schools at various locations throughout their respective states. These institutes promised to gain the confidence and support of "intelligent and progressive farmers." Administrators at A&M colleges invited members of the Grange and Farmers' Alliance to examine their scientific facilities and hold annual meetings on their campuses. Profes-sors from both state universities and A&M colleges spoke at meetings of agricultural societies to stress the importance of their schools to farmers.[63]

Progressivists, however, faced a difficult task convincing many farmers that public money spent on higher education benefited agriculture. Many farmers frequently associated collegiate education negatively with classical instruction and the training of preachers, lawyers, and physicians. Farmers often feared that children educated at college would lose interest in agricul-ture and abandon it in favor of the professions. Proponents of utilitarian science endeavored to convince farmers that higher education stood to benefit them and not wean their sons away from the farm. "Farming is a science. It is the highest and noblest of sciences," Daniel Harvey Hill told the Orange (North Carolina) County Grange, and future farmers "must know chemistry, geology, botany mineralogy, zoology and etc."[64]

Leaders of farm organizations, especially state granges, acknowledged the importance of applied science for agricultural pursuits. They feared that many farmers failed to understand the impact of industrialization upon society. Recurring economic depressions and chronically depressed prices for crops in the last quarter of the nineteenth century confronted many farmers with bankruptcy or other financial hardships. Distressed farmers often blamed their misfortunes on the owners of banks, corporations, trusts, and railroads, who farmers believed benefited from discriminatory laws and superior educations. Some leaders of the Grange, encouraged by progressivist academics, believed that technical education offered farmers the scientific means to increase production, decrease labor costs, and effectively compete with their enemies. "In the march of progress the farmer has been forced out of the beaten tracks almost in spite of himself," remarked a Granger from Mississippi. "Knowledge adapted to farming fifty years ago will not suffice . . . hence, from the necessity of the case, agricultural colleges have been established."[65]

The Morrill Act of 1862 offered Grange leaders and progressivist academics some financial means to advance technical education, as well as an opportunity to demonstrate to farmers how higher education might benefit them. The act granted to each state thirty thousand acres of federal land, or compensatory scrip, for every senator and representative a state had in Congress. The federal government required legislatures that accepted the grant to use funds derived from the sale of land or scrip to endow "at least one college where the leading object shall be, without excluding other scientific and classical studies, and including military tactics, to teach such branches of learning as are related to agriculture and the mechanic arts." The law specifically prohibited states from using the grant to construct educational facilities; thus, state legislatures that accepted the offer needed to provide the buildings. The act allowed legislatures to designate either an established or a new school to receive the endowment. States in rebellion initially were ineligible, but subsequent legislation after the war allowed them to apply for the grant.[66]

The law intentionally left undefined how and how much the agricultural and mechanical arts were to be taught, which quickly gave rise to disagreements among academics and farmers. Some farmers opposed agricultural colleges because they feared traditionalists would attempt to turn the schools into classical institutions (as occurred at Alabama A&M before William LeRoy Broun's return). Other farmers opposed them because they thought the colleges intended to teach routine agricultural procedures, such as harvesting or plowing, that could be learned more readily and less expensively on the farm. Academic proponents of A&M colleges generally did not want the land grants used to advance primarily classical studies, although many disagreed with farmers who wanted such studies excluded altogether. Furthermore, while some academic supporters of A&M colleges advocated teaching manual labor skills, most wanted the schools to teach complex mathematics and sciences and apply them to agriculture. Broun advised parents who wanted a son "to learn how to plow" to place him on a farm or plantation. However, if they wanted him to "learn *why* to plow," they should "send him to a good science college."[67]

Academics themselves divided nationally over whether the colleges should teach a new generation of farmers how to use scientific knowledge on their own farms; or if instead they should train a class of specialists to work at A&M schools, state agricultural bureaus, and experiment stations, who would then instruct farmers on how to improve the production of crops scientifically. The latter option required that farmers themselves learn little science; they need only follow directions provided by agricultural experts. Others argued for both scientifically educated farmers and specialists. In any case, William LeRoy Broun doubted that scientific agriculture would enable many young Southerners to return to the farm. Broun told the Association of American Agricultural Colleges and Experiment Stations in 1892 that college graduates "can not engage in farming without a farm, and this, as a rule, they do not possess; hence they must begin as wage earners, as teachers, engineers, chemists, or in whatever capacity their education and environment render possible." Nearly eight years earlier, he told former Confederate Gen. Henry D. Clayton—a supporter of utilitarian education who later would serve as president of the University of Alabama—that Southern youths needed "a scientific or technical education in mechanics" that would give them "wage-earning power." Broun countered the republican notion of those who feared that scientifically trained but dependent employees would succumb to materialism and vice. Successful farming, he believed, depended largely on good land and favorable market conditions. The latter, he understood, was a circumstance unlikely during the agricultural depression rampant in the late nineteenth century.[68]

Although academics had varying objectives for rural education, they consistently exaggerated the immediate benefits of scientific agriculture, in an effort to win the support of farmers. The imprudent rhetoric of progressivists led farmers to expect college graduates who would return to their farms, perform a few scientific miracles that improved the quality and yield of their crops, and lift their parents out of debt. When these things failed to happen to any significant degree, farmers—suspicious of publicly supported colleges to begin with—turned against the administrators and faculties of these institutions. The failure of agricultural science to meet farmers' expectations did not lead them to blame progress or science. Instead, they demanded either the replacement of a school's administration or the establishment of an agricultural school separate from the state university, where presumably classicists could not influence the curriculum.[69]

The most notable case in which farmers demanded a separate institution occurred at South Carolina College. During the 1880s, President John McBryde and his administration came under attack from farmers led by "Pitchfork" Ben Tillman, who charged that the college, akin to classical institutions, taught only theoretical, or pure, science and failed to teach practical, or applied, science that graduates could use on the farm. Tillman insisted that the legislature remove the school's Morrill grant and use the funds to establish a separate A&M college.[70]

Ironically, McBryde was a widely known and dedicated advocate of scientific agriculture. Educated at South Carolina College and the University of Virginia, he conducted "practical" scientific experiments on farms in Virginia in the years after the war and avidly promoted the application of theoretical science to agriculture. He wanted first, however, to familiarize students with the theoretical principles of biology, botany, and other sciences related to agriculture, before teaching them to how to apply these through experiments. McBryde believed that agricultural progress occurred slowly, through painstaking experimentation performed by qualified personnel trained in scientific agriculture. He did not believe that large numbers of college graduates, trained scientifically or not, would return to the farm; in this he differed with Tillman.[71]

During McBryde's administration, South Carolina College once again became a "University." McBryde helped to organize a school of scientific agriculture and two schools of engineering, but his efforts at reform were short-lived. McBryde resigned from the college in 1891 and accepted the presidency of Virginia A&M shortly after the South Carolina legislature, with Tillman as governor, removed the school's Morrill money and granted it to the newly established Clemson Agricultural and Mechanical College. Ironically, Clemson took over and implemented most of McBryde's technical program. The University of South Carolina once again became South Carolina College and temporarily became a classical institution. Nevertheless, its new president, James Woodrow, a noted Darwinian and former head of the Confederate chemical laboratory, moved once again to broaden the curriculum to include more science instruction. Likewise, although farmers' organizations successfully pressured the legislatures of Mississippi (1880) and North Carolina (1889) to establish separate agricultural and mechanical colleges, after originally awarding the Morrill grant to existing state universities, those schools endeavored to offer scientific and technical instruction.[72]

Disgruntled farmers in Arkansas who believed that the technical education provided by the state university was too theoretical, passed legislation in 1887 that created a new Board of Trustees, required students to do actual farm work, and lowered the president's salary. These actions prompted President Edgar, who supported scientific agricultural studies, to resign. He blamed the high cost of equipment and low legislative appropriations for the university's failure to conduct extensive agricultural experiments and provide students with practical training. The new board replaced Edgar with another Confederate veteran, Edward H. Murfee, a professor of mathematics and brother of James T. Murfee. The new faculty president, armed with an increase in funds provided by the legislature, continued Edgar's efforts at progressivist education. To ward off continued opposition from farmers, however, Murfee's administration strategically added a couple of two-year "short" courses in practical agriculture and mechanics.[73]

Progressivist academics readily turned to each other for help in devising strategies to overcome the obstacles they faced—integrationist Republicans and segregationist conservatives, faithful sectarians, fearful classicists, parsimonious legislators, and impatient farmers—in building the institutions they believed would create a New South. To fulfill this mission, progressivists relied upon old friendships (many established during the war) and cultivated new ones through frequent correspondence and occasional meetings in which they swapped catalogues, shared trustees reports, and discussed curricula.[74]

In the years following the war, progressivist academics (particularly Confederate veterans) took operational control of most of the region's public collegiate institutions. By the mid-1880s, former Confederate soldiers—Boyd, Broun, Dinwiddie, Edgar, Stephen Lee, Lewis, McBryde, and Stewart—contemporaneously served as presidents of Southern state universities and agricultural and mechanical colleges. These and other educators who shared the Confederate experience advanced curricular reformation in their schools. Indeed, when opposition to reform arose at such schools, it occurred during times when they were *not* under the control of administrators with Confederate service.

Although progressivist educators changed the orientation of the curriculum, they often lacked the financial resources to implement their programs adequately. A study near the end of the century found that the scientific equipment at nine Northern schools averaged a value of $211,000 per institution, while nine comparable Southern institutions averaged only $41,587. The lack of resources guaranteed their failure to create a New South in their lifetime, yet progressivist academics would pass their vision of progress on to a second generation of postbellum academics.[75]

Chapter 5

Legacy of Progress

"**N**o sort of education but a 'practical education' will enable our young men and their children's children to retrieve the fortunes of the South," Matthew Maury wrote to Francis Henney Smith in 1867. "The task must be handed down to them," Maury continued, "for we shall never finish it."[1] Progressivist academics believed they needed to impart their faith in progress and technology to the first postwar generation of students if white Southerners ever were to escape the devastating physical and psychological impact of the Civil War and work for a New South.

This endeavor required Southern youth to forego the battles over slavery and states' rights that their parents already had fought and lost. For the wartime generation to transmit a legacy of progress, not guilt, though, young Southerners needed to respect the sacrifices of their elders. In an effort to accomplish these dual goals, progressivist academics taught their students reverence for the past through military instruction and the study of history, and confidence in the future through mechanical instruction and the study of science. Academic reformers also taught Southern youth to embrace governmental activism and social change as part of their effort to build a prosperous future. While these men failed to create the New South in their lifetimes, they successfully passed on their progressivist vision, spawned by the Confederate revolution, to students who became the next generation of Southern academics.

The "teachers and students" of Washington College, claimed a contributor to the *Virginia Gazette,* "have been the soldiers and orphans of the Confederacy." The same could be said of faculty and students at most postbellum Southern institutions of higher learning. There, in addition to being taught by many veterans, "orphans" studied alongside others. The University of Mississippi estimated that, in the years immediately following the war, as many as half of its students consisted of Confederate veterans. Even before the Civil War ended, the University of Virginia offered maimed Confederate veterans free tuition and board. Georgia lawmakers passed legislation that paid for wounded veterans to attend either the University of Georgia, Mercer University, Oglethorpe University, Emory College, or Bowdon College. The program, which operated between 1866 and 1868, provided those schools with badly needed revenues. The veterans who attended the University of Georgia reminded one observer of life in the Confederate military. A student remarked that the veterans at the university created the atmosphere of a military camp.[2]

The presence of disabled soldiers on campuses demonstrated to students the sacrifices—and the defeat—that these former Confederates had endured. Veterans who worked as administrators and professors were determined that those who had been too young to fight would have the intellectual skills necessary to escape the degradation suffered by the wartime generation.

Former Confederate soldiers who entered academia, and especially those trained at military academies with a historical connection between martial and scientific training, endeavored to give that type of instruction to their students. The Morrill Act reinforced the association between applied science and military instruction by requiring schools that accepted the grant to teach "military tactics" as well as agricultural and mechanical arts. The Confederacy's devastating defeat had not soured Southern schools on military instruction. Communities and schools throughout the Southern states competed vigorously to obtain the Morrill funds. As one Tennessee observer noted, the South desperately needed these funds for the promotion of its "industrial progress." Most colleges that succeeded in securing the grant did not hesitate to organize military departments. Furthermore, the South Carolina and Virginia legislatures continued to support the South Carolina Military Academy and Virginia Military Institute, respectively. Southern state universities in Alabama and Louisiana also quickly resumed their antebellum and wartime efforts to supply students with military instruction.[3]

Southern schools almost invariably adopted gray as the color of their cadets' uniforms. Ostensibly patterned after uniforms worn at West Point or at Southern military academies before the war, they were suspiciously similar to the attire worn by Confederate officers. During the 1870s, administrators at the University of Alabama, the Arkansas Industrial University, and the University of East Tennessee sought to arm their cadets and asked the United States War Department to provide them with weapons. The department instructed the presidents of those schools to have the governors of their respective states petition the Secretary of War for weapons made available to state militias under a congressional act. Upon receiving the federal arms, state authorities could designate collegiate corps of cadets as state militia and provide them with the weapons. Mississippi A&M, under the leadership of Stephen D. Lee, received 150 rifles and 2 rifled cannon from the federal government in 1885.[4]

The United States Army and Navy provided many A&M colleges, including a number of Southern schools, with commissioned officers to serve as commandants and instructors in fields including engineering and physics. The federal government in 1886 even provided Louisiana State University with a new campus, giving the school the former site of the United States Army garrison at Baton Rouge. The grant included over two hundred acres of land and buildings valued at $150,000.[5]

Students born too late to fight in the war thus were exposed to a complex array of influences on Southern campuses. They attended classes taught by former Confederate officers and had veterans as fellow students.[6] Those who enrolled learned applied science to prepare them for the future, along with military skills that taught them to remember the past. At federally provided A&M colleges, gray-clad cadets drilled under United States military officers with weapons provided by the national government. The exposure to veterans, science, drill, and the obvious authority of the federal government impressed upon students the need to honor the past, prepare for the future, and accept national reconciliation.

Not all Southerners approved of military instruction. Kemp Plummer Battle noted that the University of North Carolina, despite initially receiving the state's share of the Morrill grant, repeatedly postponed implementing federally mandated military instruction because "our people were so sick of war and all likeness to it that there was no demand for military teaching." Critics charged that administrators at A&M colleges overemphasized military studies, at the expense of technical instruction in agriculture and mechanics. William LeRoy Broun's son, Roy, a professor of chemistry at LSU, noted in 1884 that the military department there was "the only thing that . . . is in any way developed." He also observed, however, that the high cost of instruction prevented the school from adequately developing its scientific curriculum. Broun noted that the school's mechanical engineering professor maintained a metal lathe, but "that the castings cost so much that he rarely works it." The relatively low cost of drill and the study of military tactics frequently was covered by the federal government, making them an economical means of fulfilling at least one of the requirements of the Morrill Act.[7]

Critics of military instruction in South Carolina especially attacked the state military academy in Charleston, which they charged taught classics instead of science and spent too much time on ornamental drill and parade. "The war is over and we are whipped," read one letter to the *Charleston News and Courier.* "We need anything, everything, more than we do soldiers." Another opponent of the institution charged that South Carolina wasted $20,000 a year "to keep a few young men in brass button and gold lace" while the school's scientific studies "languished."[8]

Proponents of military instruction claimed that it improved the discipline of students and provided them with healthy exercise and manly dignity. Gradually, the association between applied science and military science weakened, and even some progressivist educators expressed concern that military drill interfered with their students' work in laboratories and at other scientific studies. At the urging of faculty and students in the South and the rest of the nation, optional physical education programs and intercollegiate sports increasingly replaced military drill. These developments satisfied the concerns of those Victorian educators who insisted that students have an opportunity, which military drill had provided, physically to maintain and display their masculinity.[9]

In addition to military instruction, academics endeavored to educate Southern youth about their past through historical study. After the Civil War, schools throughout the South implemented new chairs, courses, and departments in history, or "historical science." Progressivist academics taught their students to understand the discipline as the record of an evolutionary and inevitable series of human events best understood scientifically through the objective interpretation of primary sources. Former Confederate Col. James Reid Cole, professor of English language, literature, and history at Texas A&M College, told the school's Board of Directors that he intended to present history to his students "as a picture of the march of the human race—advancing from darkness to light, from the fogs of antiquity to the civilization of the present age."[10]

Former Confederate veterans in academia hoped to use history to convey to the subsequent generation of Southerners that they need not feel ashamed of their parents' supposedly treasonable behavior and failure. Robert E. Lee quickly undertook efforts to obtain an endowment for a chair of history at Washington College. He succeeded, and the school appointed William Preston Johnston as professor. Johnston claimed that, if historians were to understand the plan that Providence possessed for "the progress of humanity," they must follow "methods strictly scientific and historical." History, like science, he believed, needed to be useful, and historians "must reject whatever cannot be used as an element in the development of society or of man." Johnston urged Southern teachers of history, "As you tell the contemporary story of our unmerited though inevitable overthrow to the offspring of heroes," to "draw from your knowledge of the past a multitude of precedents teaching patience, fortitude, moderation and magnanimity."[11]

Lee himself maintained a special interest in the study of history. He believed that all should attempt "to collect and disseminate the truth, in the hope that it may find a place in history." The former general sought materials that would enable him to write a history of his campaigns, so that the "world shall know what my poor boys, with their small numbers and scant resources, succeeded in accomplishing." The idea that future generations might deem the participants in the South's war for independence as "rebels" and "traitors" driven by "an insurrectionary spirit," and not as defenders of Constitutional principles, worried Lee.[12]

Veterans in academia did not rely solely upon classroom instruction to teach history. Progressivist educators used the United Confederate Veterans (UCV), organized in 1889, to guarantee what they considered to be the proper telling of their story to subsequent generations of Southerners. Edmund Kirby Smith chaired the UCV's first history commission, and other veterans and academics who served on the committee included James Nicholson and Stephen D. Lee. William Preston Johnston assisted the commission in achieving its primary goal of approving historical texts for Southern schools that provided "proper" interpretations of the War Between the States. The commission condemned works suggesting that secession equaled treason or that white Southerners fought for slavery instead of fighting to preserve Constitutional principles and drive out Yankee invaders.[13]

After Smith's death in 1893, Stephen Lee succeeded him as the commission's chairman. An ardent proponent of industrial education, Lee also took a serious interest in Southern history. He insisted that history textbooks recognize the "fighting qualities and exalted motive" of the Confederate veteran. Yet Lee wanted to instill in young Southerners not only pride in their parents' efforts at independence, but also patriotic devotion to the United States. He consistently encouraged white Southerners to embrace national reconciliation and praised the bravery of Union soldiers. Lee argued against the commission's employing as reviewers of school texts persons biased in favor of the Confederacy. "To select those, which are partisan to the South," he claimed, "would be as objectionable as those which are partisan to the North." Still, Lee believed that any "fair history" based on the "facts" would exonerate white Southerners for attempting to leave the Union. Conversely, he thought that any history that criticized the heroism or motives of Southern secessionists necessarily was biased and based upon falsehoods. Lee and the other members of the commission failed to recognize (publicly at least) that their own preconceived conclusions tainted the accuracy of their historical analyses.[14]

Stephen Lee, with his love of the Lost Cause, his desire for national reconciliation, and his zealous promotion of utilitarian education for the New South, embodied the progressivist creed as proclaimed on the masthead of the UCV's official organ, the *Confederate Veteran*: "Fidelity—Patriotism—Progress." Lee ultimately rose to the rank of commander-in-chief of the UCV in 1904.[15]

In addition to guiding the historical activities of the UCV, academics participated in the founding and activities of regional and state historical societies. Stephen Lee served as president of the Mississippi Historical Society. Kemp Battle helped organize the North Carolina Historical Society, which operated on the campus of the state university, where he also wanted to establish a museum of science and history. Eugene Smith labored on the executive committee of Alabama's historical society. Southern historical organizations urged members to search for primary materials, particularly diaries, military journals, and letters, in an effort to help historians chronicle Southerners' contributions to the nation's welfare and their exploits during the Civil War.[16]

Veterans in higher education further expressed their historical interests by writing articles for various periodicals, such as the Southern Historical Society's *Papers* and *Century Magazine*. Not all submissions met the scientific standard suggested by Johnston. An assistant editor for *Century,* in rejecting a submission by Daniel Harvey Hill, claimed that it was "entirely proper to refuse to print a communication which would increase, rather than lighten, our responsibility for imperfect history already printed in our magazine." Nevertheless, *Century* accepted other submissions from Hill, as well articles from Johnston, Stephen Lee, Samuel Lockett, Edmund Kirby Smith, and Raleigh Colston.[17]

Some veterans in academia sought to tell their stories through books. Curry chronicled the difficulties of the Davis administration in his *Civil History of the Government of the Confederate States.* Others, such as former Confederate Gen. Lunsford Lindsay Lomax, found official capacities in which to make their contributions to historical understanding. Lomax, after his retirement from the presidency of Virginia A&M, in 1899 joined the staff at the War Department in Washington, which compiled the *Official Records of the War of the Rebellion.* Later, he served as a commissioner of Gettysburg National Park. President William McKinley appointed Stephen Lee as one of three commissioners to oversee the Vicksburg National Military Park. Lee also served as president of the Board of Trustees of the Mississippi Department of Archives and History. Four years after leaving the University of Mississippi, Alexander Stewart became a member of the Chickamauga and Chattanooga National Park Commission from 1890 until his death in 1908.[18]

These veterans-turned-academics focused on Southern history, especially the Confederacy, in part to redeem themselves in the eyes of Northerners and their fellow Southerners. They also wanted, however, to instill pride in their students and convince all Americans that the children of Confederates deserved a place in the reconstructed Union. To bolster the self-esteem of young white Southerners, progressivist academics aimed to initiate them into the cult of the Anglo-Saxon. J. L. M. Curry told an Alabama A&M commencement audience near the turn of the century that the school's Anglo-Saxon graduates belonged to a virile race, "progressive, enduring, pure of blood, inviting future boundless possibilities." Southern youth were quite familiar with such rhetoric. Over the last quarter of the nineteenth century, they increasingly had been taught that English grammar, literature, and history were indispensable to the advancement of civilization. Southern progressivists wanted teachers to be, in the words of William Preston Johnston, the "torch bearers of liberty," handing down to their students a legacy of British freedom "hardened in fire and blood by our English ancestors." Thomas Jefferson had insisted that a course in the Anglo-Saxon language be part of the curriculum at the University of Virginia. Similar programs rarely appeared elsewhere in the South until after the Civil War, when classes in the history and language of Anglo-Saxons, along with closely related Teutonic courses, proliferated rapidly.[19]

While the complexities of Saxon grammar may have escaped most Southern students, they nevertheless embraced the history and racism of Anglo-Saxon ideology. Student addresses on Anglo-Saxon themes frequently were featured at commencements and public exhibitions, bearing such titles as "A Plea for the Study of Anglo-Saxon," "The Manifest Destiny of the English Speaking Race," "Triumphs of the Aryan Race," and often simply "The Anglo-Saxon." The importance of an Anglo-Saxon heritage was not lost upon William Myers, a student at the University of Georgia during Reconstruction. Myers, painfully aware of the anti-Semitism that permeated Georgia, feared that people in Athens mistakenly would conclude from his last name and physical appearance that he was Jewish. In order that he "might have a little more Anglo Saxon look," Myers followed the suggestion of a fellow student and a future chancellor of the university, Walter Hill, and "shaved off his side whiskers."[20]

Progressivist academics looked to military, historical, and cultural education to teach students to have pride in their past, so that they might move confidently into the future. To complete this task, academic reformers believed Southern youth needed scientific training. Educators searched for pedagogical methods that would provide graduates with the skills they would need to industrialize and restore prosperity to the region.

"We must devise systematic plans for progress," observed William T. Sutherlin, a quartermaster in the Confederate army and an author of the applied science curriculum at the Virginia A&M College in Blacksburg. One of the most prominent plans endorsed by Sutherlin and other progressivists to rebuild the South through industrial education was the *Russian System of Instruction in Practical Mechanism,* named after the method of technical education developed by Moscow's Imperial Technical Institute in the late 1860s. The Russian system abandoned apprenticeship in favor of systematic instruction for transmitting industrial knowledge. Students methodically learned the forms and functions of various tools—such as files, squares, hammers, chisels, and planes—and practiced the uses of each instrument before attempting to construct a finished product. They also were taught basic mechanical skills and how to apply them to physical problems. Eventually students advanced to learning forging techniques, doing foundry work, using lathes, and designing and producing original models.[21]

The Imperial Technical Institute mounted a display at the Centennial Exhibition in Philadelphia, in which the system was introduced to the United States. The method especially attracted Southern academics, who believed that technical education could provide graduates capable of creating an industrial South. The region lacked the concentration of mechanics' shops, the large mechanized factories, and the skilled and semiskilled workers responsible for the development of Northern industry. Academic supporters of the Russian system hoped that they could substitute the school for the shop and thus disseminate technical knowledge throughout the South.[22]

Southern academics may have been attracted to the Russian system because of apparent similarities between the South and Russia. The termination of serfdom in that country in 1861 may have seemed analogous to Southerners' experiences with emancipation. Russia also trailed Western Europe's industrial development, much as the South lagged behind the North. In any case, both Russia and the South looked to education as a rapid means of industrialization.[23]

William LeRoy Broun admired Russia's efforts to establish "superior technical schools" and considered them "worthy of imitation." He introduced David Boyd to the Russian system, and Boyd promptly embraced the method. He intended to inaugurate the system at LSU, but the school lacked the financial means to implement it. Boyd's successor, William Preston Johnston, managed to introduce a mechanical course based on the systematic and progressive principles of the Russian system. The course instructed students in proper use of tools and from there advanced "step by step to the higher grades" of instruction, including construction of bridges and buildings. An avid proponent of the Russian system, Johnston also implemented the plan at Tulane.[24]

Robert Hardaway organized his mechanical engineering course at Alabama A&M around the Russian system in the late 1870s. He received the enthusiastic support of Isaac Tichenor, who secured one thousand dollars in gold to purchase models, foot motors, saws, and other equipment necessary to start the program. In 1882, Texas A&M also adopted the Russian system, three years after it initially was proposed by Alexander Hogg, the college's professor of mathematics. A classically educated Virginia native and a former Confederate cavalryman, Hogg believed that the South required an industrial education that would enable Southerners to inaugurate a "new era" in which they would build mills and foundries. "We lack the education," Hogg told the Centennial Bureau of Education in Philadelphia, "which produces 'producers.'" The Russian system, he believed, promised to rectify that problem.[25]

Progressivist academics recognized, however, that training graduates capable of rebuilding the South would require students to perform a certain degree of physical labor. These educators did not advocate mindless, repetitive work, but the physical application of knowledge to labor of the type necessary to survey roads, create fertilizers, and improve steam engines. F. Henry Smith noted that such intelligent labor served as "the universal adjunct of progress" and was necessary for the continued improvement of humankind. Nevertheless, progressivists believed that, in order to attract students into their schools, they needed to overcome the squeamishness of both parents and students toward labor. Advocates of utilitarian science, like their antebellum counterparts, blamed slavery for the negative attitudes many white Southerners held toward work. Progressivist educators hoped to use chemistry laboratories, engineering workshops, and experimental farms to inculcate in students a belief in the "dignity of labor."[26]

Postbellum progressivists also hoped that the destruction of slavery, by foes presumably scientifically educated and hardworking, provided evidence enough to convince skeptics that the South needed to change its attitudes toward labor. Certainly Southern universities and colleges, Kemp Battle noted, no longer would manifest a hostile attitude toward labor. "The war," he claimed, "has beaten such notions out of our heads." Nor, Isaac Tichenor warned, could Southern elites ignore their changed circumstances. "The time has come," he observed, "when we can no longer remit our agricultural interests to our overseers and our slaves."

George Edgar concurred. He told the trustees of the Arkansas Industrial University that all of his students should be required to do some form of physical labor, so that they would "learn *to do* as well as direct how to do what will contribute to [the] material comfort and the growth of the industries of life." Academics no longer believed that they needed to separate science from labor, as William Gilham had advocated prior to the Civil War, to convey to their audience the importance of scientific study.[27]

Although progressivists wanted students to be taught agricultural and mechanical science, to conduct experiments, and to undergo manual training so as to cultivate a positive attitude toward labor, collegiate administrators often had difficulty finding qualified teachers. To alleviate the shortage, many school presidents and trustees turned to Northerners who had graduated from schools outside the South. A substantial number of Northerners served on Southern faculties between the end of Reconstruction and 1900. Alabama A&M, Arkansas, Georgia, North Carolina, Mississippi A&M, South Carolina, Texas A&M, Tulane, and Virginia all hired nonsoutherners to establish or join various engineering and science departments. Texas A&M employed enough Northerners to enable critics to charge that "imported Yankee Republicans" dominated the faculty.[28]

The administrators who appointed Northerners to their faculties did so primarily because there were too few qualified Southerners to fill technical positions. However, the hiring of Yankees by Southern administrators also reflected their reconciliatory attitudes toward the North and indicated their willingness to allow the South's youth to learn from their conquerors.

Complicating the effort by Southern academics to find qualified personnel to teach applied science, progressivist educators had to compete with well-funded Northern schools which offered prospective professors higher salaries and better equipped facilities. The South's academics blamed much of this difficulty on the parallelism that continued to afflict Southern higher education after the war. Competition for federal, state, and private funds among colleges, normal schools, and universities produced duplicate academic programs throughout the United States, but especially in the South. During the 1880s, Southern states maintained more colleges and universities than the New England and mid-Atlantic states combined. Tennessee alone counted a total of thirty-seven male colleges and female seminaries. Furthermore, the overall economic condition of Southern schools compared unfavorably with that of their Northern counterparts. Sixteen New England schools in 1881 had a combined income of $1,024,563 and a total of 720,187 volumes in their libraries. In contrast, 123 Southern colleges and universities counted a total income of $1,089,187 and owned fewer than 669,000 library volumes. One Southern critic believed that the South had three times as many institutions as it could support properly.[29]

The main objection to parallel academic institutions concerned the growing cost of collegiate education. Eugene Hilgard wrote to Boyd in 1874 that, in addition to the difficulties schools faced in providing costly laboratories, professors qualified to give practical scientific instruction were "notoriously few and far between as yet, and will necessarily command high salaries." Hilgard suggested uniting A&M colleges with state universities so as to avoid the duplication of apparatus and instruction. E. Kirby Smith agreed, claiming that the establishment of separate A&M colleges violated the "spirit of modern education," which, he claimed, "is concentration."[30]

Nevertheless, Alabama, Georgia, Mississippi, North Carolina, South Carolina, Texas, and Virginia established separate state technical schools and universities. These multiple state schools alarmed many academics who believed that legislatures had failed to provide adequate funds for even a single collegiate institution. By 1890, Georgia maintained six campuses throughout the state for its agriculture and mechanical arts college. A professor of law at the University of Texas and a former governor of Texas, Oran M. Roberts, complained to an Austin audience that, if lawmakers compared the curricula of the state agricultural and mechanical college, normal school, and university, they would find that the legislature "had allowed to be put up three universities, instead of one, for the general collegiate education of the youths of the state."[31]

Segregation compounded the economic woes of Southern higher education. A second Morrill Act, passed by Congress in 1890, reserved part of the revenues from federal land sales for A&M colleges. Under the act, the government added an additional one thousand dollars a year to a onetime appropriation of $15,000, until the subsidy reached a total of $25,000, at which time the amount of payment would remain permanently fixed. The law required states to use the funds only for appliances or instruction that promoted agricultural and mechanical education and the English language (which of course, included Anglo-Saxon). Unlike the first Morrill Act, the new legislation required states to use the money to educate both black and white students. States that refused to distribute the funds equitably forfeited them. The law did not insist upon integration, but it required states receiving the grant to offer public educational facilities to both races. Even so, despite the fact that dividing the money meant duplicating faculty and equipment, Southern states remained wedded to segregated agricultural and mechanical programs.[32]

Frustration with low budgets led some academics actively to embrace politics. In 1889, Stephen Lee launched a failed campaign for the governorship of Mississippi in which he promised, if elected, to lead "our citizens in one industrial progressive movement." Lee's platform included the establishment of a Board of Agriculture, prison reform, spending public funds to encourage immigration to Mississippi, and increased public aid for primary, secondary, and higher education. Lee joined the Farmers' Alliance and served as chairman of an Alliance committee that petitioned the state's 1890 constitutional convention to create a popularly elected railroad commission, maintain a public school system, and reject property and educational qualifications for suffrage. Lee eventually chaired the convention's education committee.[33]

Other progressivist educators eschewed direct politics but attempted to gain the political support of the public by magnifying the benefits of higher education. William Preston Johnston asserted that there could "be no progress without great intelligence in the leaders of a people; its statesmen, warriors, thinkers, jurists, mechanics, and merchants." He argued that higher education provided the means by which society obtained this intelligence. New South academics and their allies argued that science improved the daily quality of people's lives by increasing the production and quality of food, improving sanitation, making transportation easier and faster, and producing labor-saving conveniences. Furthermore, progressivists charged that the state had a duty to cultivate scientific discovery through colleges and universities. During an 1884 ceremony at the University of Texas, former Confederate Col. A. W. Terrell called for even further government subsidization of science when he demanded that the state establish "a scientific department of government" that would provide financial support for scientists.[34]

Progressivist academics claimed that physical progress led to moral or spiritual progress. Andrew Lipscomb complained that the public little recognized the positive relationship between the application of "the mind to physical circumstances and the marvelous developments of civilization." Such application moved society simultaneously "towards the material universe and towards human brotherhood."

Former Confederate Gen. Samuel Bell Maxey told the students of the University of Texas that "material progress, the logical outcome of intellectual expansion, moves the statesman, the philosopher, the philanthropist, the schools, and the man of business."

F. Henry Smith exulted that "scientific intelligence" brought countries closer together by transcending national borders and "welded all lands into one republic of science" where the "discoveries of one country soon become the common possession of all." Smith proclaimed the nineteenth century "the greatest in the Christian era." No nation had contributed to its progress more than the United States, this Southerner boasted.[35]

Despite such affirmations, Southern academics were disturbed by the immense political power achieved by industrialists during the 1880s and 1890s. That power was derived from the vast concentrations of wealth created in part by the technological improvements extolled by progressivists. Technology's promises—a virtually endless supply of inexpensive, high-quality, and safe products; and relief from arduous labor—appeared jeopardized by the greed that epitomized the Gilded Age. Johnston complained that Americans, in their "mad race for fortune," had allowed "unlimited power to be placed in the hands of a few men, leaders in business enterprises, and thereby tempt them to usurpation and dishonesty." He further chastised the nation for admiring and applauding those "who, by systemized breach of trust, watering stock, freezing out minorities, stifling competitive industries and oppressing labor, are, in a brief season, transformed from grubs to moths."[36]

Unlike nonsouthern academics and literati, such as Henry Adams and Samuel Clemens, who became disillusioned with progress and turned to medieval virgins for salvation, Southern progressivists, who looked to the state government to provide higher education, also looked to it to curb what they considered dangerous consolidations of power in society. "The least government possible," Johnston told a commencement audience, "now means all the government necessary for a denser population, an ignorant suffrage, and more complex civilization."[37]

Southern progressivist academics, who as part of their revolutionary experience had encountered the Confederate government's regulatory power over the South's wartime economy, broke with their New South counterparts in business, politics, and journalism, who preferred a laissez-faire approach to economic development. Progressivist educators anticipated the Southern Progressive movement by calling upon the state variously to protect people from adulterated food and water, to prohibit child labor, to prevent the leasing of convicts, to regulate railroads, to provide for public sanitation, to require mandatory and universal public schooling, and to limit work hours. Johnston embraced a broad program of reform that would have required the state to escheat watered stocks to the public treasury, levy income and inheritance taxes, and regulate the salaries of officials employed by public corporations. If these things were done, Johnston declared, "they would tend to prevent the aggregation of colossal fortunes" by financiers, who used their wealth to subvert the economic well-being of the mass of people. Johnston's respect for the South's states' rights position prevented him from looking to the federal government for reform. He also recognized that Southerners had little contact with government, and that any expansion of state—much less federal—authority would be opposed by many because it would violate the traditional power arrangements of their communities. Still, he called upon the states to pass legislation that would hold the strong in check, protect the weak, and advance the individual in the "line of progress" that led to "a higher plane of morality and intelligence."[38]

Academic progressivists also sympathized with the women's education and equal rights movements. Science, they believed, should be no less available or liberating to women than to men. "It is true that some walks of life are recognized as more suitable to woman than others," Samuel Lockett attested, "but if she chooses to fight the battles of life in the same ranks and on equal footing with her brothers, no one will say his nay." Lockett cited the work of the mathematician Mary Fairfax Sommerville, the novelist George Eliot, the historian Agnes Strickland, and the astronomer Maria Mitchell as evidence that women could succeed in academic fields as well as men.[39]

Progressivist academics understood that women had worked effectively in ordnance factories and in other capacities during the Confederate revolution. They also had anticipated that, after the war, many women, with their husbands dead or disabled, would have to work outside the home. Progressivists argued that, if women were going to acquire the skills required to provide adequately for themselves and their families, they needed more educational opportunities. Curry noted in 1899 that, in the past, women's ability to master collegiate studies had been disputed. "The *female* mind," Curry declared, "was condemned as unable to master pure mathematics and metaphysics, or to follow the inductions of scientific investigation. To-day, there is a truer conception of women's possibilities and rights, and eight-tenths of the colleges and universities are open to women students."[40]

While suspect among conservatives for its alleged potential to encourage debauchery, coeducation received the approval of progressivists. With the overwhelming support of his faculty, Tichenor during the 1870s appealed to the Board of Directors of Alabama A&M to allow female students, but to no avail. Hill, at the coeducational Arkansas Industrial University, wrote to Johnston in 1881, "Some of our brightest students are girls."

The University of Texas, like the Arkansas university, embraced coeducation from its inception in 1883. "Texas," Terrell claimed, "has recognized the fact that civilization cannot be advanced by man alone, and that the accomplished mother is a more potent instrument in stimulating the ambition and moulding the character of her boy, than the father can be." He believed that "custom and the unwise selfishness of her master, alike condemned woman to wait for the dawn of a more liberal spirit in the nineteenth century."[41]

Women's education thrived at state schools in Mississippi. The University of Mississippi, under the administration of Alexander Stewart, first accepted women in 1882 and graduated its first female students three years later. Mississippi A&M likewise allowed women to attend, and Stephen Lee wrote to George Edgar in 1885 that the school's "experiment" in coeducation "has worked well as far as tested." Lee believed that the recent establishment of the publicly supported Industrial Institute and College for the Education of White Girls of Mississippi in Columbus, however, would draw female students away from the Starkville school.[42]

Academic progressivists' concern for women's education stemmed not solely from an altruistic impulse, but from a realization that changes in society increasingly required families to have educated women. "In this world of change, when the rich of to-day may be the poor of to-morrow," noted A. J. Peeler, "it not infrequently happens that the educated daughter is able, by securing the position of a teacher, to keep from want and suffering an aged and dependent father and mother."

The *Jackson (Miss.) Clarion-Ledger* called upon all the nation's agricultural and mechanical colleges to accept women and to help them become "good farmers' wives." A knowledge of botany, chemistry, and geology, it argued, would allow women to "compound nutritious, appetizing, inexpensive viands" and enable them to more "fully fit the place of daughter, wife and mother."

The boon of coeducation caused Curry to wonder "what centers of culture, of power, of high influences, the homes of our land will be when presided over by women of purity and cultivated intellects?"

Edmund Kirby Smith claimed that the object of women's education "should be to make them useful laborers." Women ought not to remain idle,

Smith asserted, while "everything round breathes progress, advance." A woman who received a higher education and was prepared to do "professional work," he continued, enabled her to lighten the burden of a husband of little means.[43]

The type of "professional" or "industrial" labor progressivist academics had in mind was reflected in the course of study at Mississippi's industrial institute for women. It included bookkeeping, telegraphy, and typewriting. These skills were integral to the anticipated bureaucratized, corporate, and industrial society of the New South. Stephen Lee, who promoted coeducation, a propertied woman's right to vote, and equal pay for equal work, understood the impact that economic change in the late nineteenth century had had upon the role of women in society. "Present conditions," he observed, "have brought women to an extent hitherto unknown into industrial and educational occupations." This fact, he concluded, was "not due simply to her own volition, but to the logic of events which she is powerless to control."[44]

The recognition that progress meant change in traditional economic and social relationships, not only between the sexes, but also between Americans and their government, did not dampen the enthusiasm of Southern academics for the future. "Each cycling day," George Soule told his students, "brings with it something to be reformed, and for a brief time to be utilized for man's service, when it, too, will be replaced by new things, new thoughts, and new customs, each to serve a divine purpose in the never-ending changes of progress."

John McBryde, unable to put into his own words the joy and excitement he felt for the young men graduating from Virginia Polytechnic at the turn of the century, quoted a "brilliant novelist" who had declared, "To be twenty years of age in 1901, with the prospect of seeing 1950, if one lives the allotted span of three-score years and ten, is to be heir to an inheritance better and greater than the richest millionaire can leave behind him."[45]

Despite their efforts, the academic progressivists of the Civil War generation failed to create the New South through their institutions. They successfully transferred their vision of progress to the next generation of Southern academics, however. Progressivist educators accomplished this task through a curriculum of history and military drill, English language and literature, applied science and physical labor, that incorporated the trinity of the Lost Cause, the cult of the Anglo-Saxon, and the New South in an integrated ideology of progress.

Progressivists used colleges and universities such as the University of North Carolina, where white Southern youth could partake in the activities of a state historical association, a Shakespearean club, and a scientific society, to inculcate in students respect for their history, confidence in their culture, and faith in their future.[46] The aid for military, linguistic, and applied science instruction that Southern academics received from the two Morrill acts convinced the South's progressivists that the means they used to promote reconciliation and progress had received the support of the nation.

If some Southern students missed the message of progress propounded by their professors in class, progressivist academics sought celebrated New South spokesmen, such as journalists Henry Grady and Walter Hines Page, along with a host of lesser lights, to deliver it at commencements and other ceremonial occasions. Student addresses echoed those of their elders, toasting the "Character of Lee," boasting of the "Priceless Heritage of Our English Blood," calling for the "Cultivation of a National History," marveling at the "Colossal Power of the United States," tying the "progress of man" to the "Triumphs of Engineering," and predicting that the "South Will Live Again by the Aid of Her Industrial Institutions." Other popular subjects included inventors, the New South, and agricultural, mechanical, and scientific progress.[47]

Southern college students especially embraced the idea of evolutionary progress. They frequently put the word *evolution* in the titles of their addresses: "Evolution of Agriculture," "Evolution of Nations," and "Evolution of the Plow." One University of Georgia student, Glen Waters, whom a classmate described as "scientifically inclined" and having "the brightest mind in the class," delivered an 1887 senior oration on the subject of physical evolution—but only after the proposed speech had been censored somewhat by the faculty and trustees, who approved of the scholarship but feared the wrath of religious listeners. Evolution also recurred in articles in collegiate journals. One student at the Arkansas Industrial University hoped for "radical change" through "the natural process of social evolution," so that the people might regulate "the trusts and combinations."[48]

Like their professors, students applied the lessons of evolution to their own history, using the concept to explain their parents' defeat and to generate hope for a prosperous New South. "For six thousand years," observed a Mississippi A&M student,

> humanity has been struggling to elevate itself . . . recoiling before overwhelming forces of adversity, but only to be strengthened and begin with renewed vigor the march toward a higher prosperity and civilization. . . . So it is with our people. Only a quarter of a century ago . . . they the patriots of the South clashed arms . . . with their brothers, the heroes of the North. . . . We, as the next generation following that dismal period . . . are in the midst of . . . a new and different era. Our people have bowed with a noble submission to the decree of

fate, but with an unfailing courage and an unrelaxing energy they have evolved from the ruin of antebellum prosperity new industries that promise greater power and wealth than their fathers ever dreamed of.

Postbellum students, who by the mid-1880s had no personal experience with the Confederacy, easily accepted their teachers' promise of a prosperous New South that was to be part of a "great Republic" which would continue "to grow in influence and in power." They also readily accepted the idea that slavery had hindered Southern progress. J. T. Strayhorn, a senior at the University of North Carolina in 1881, confidently predicted that the abolition of slavery ultimately would allow the South vastly to increase its wealth.[49]

More than just to mimic their words concerning progress, academics of the Civil War generation wanted their students to create a New South. Many Southern students did enter scientific courses; between the end of the Civil War and 1900, the region's colleges and universities produced agricultural chemists; civil, electrical, and mechanical engineers; factory managers; geologists; and other technically skilled graduates. At A&M colleges, Southern students, like their Northern and western counterparts, preferred mechanical—or, to use another word, engineering—courses to agricultural studies. This circumstance concerned Grangers but not progressivist academics who believed that the South needed engineering skill to hasten industrialization.[50]

Southern schools produced far too few technically trained graduates of any kind to realize the progressivist academics' dream that their students would usher in a New South. Of nine graduates who received bachelor's degrees from Mississippi A&M in 1885, eight were still living in 1900. Of these, only two, both of whom became horticulturists, had entered technical occupations. Texas A&M graduated only eleven students in 1886, eight from its mechanical course and three from its agricultural course. Seven years later, three worked at the college, three had become engineers, and the others included a draughtsman, an assistant postman, a surgeon in the United States Army, and an assistant at the state agricultural experiment station. Robert Hardaway noted in 1888 that, in the six years he served as professor of engineering at the University of Alabama, twenty-seven of his thirty-nine engineering graduates (two were dead) found employment in technical pursuits. From 1869 through 1900, only forty-two LSU graduates received jobs in engineering-related fields. Between 1893 and 1899, North Carolina A&M graduated fifty-eight engineering students, or an average of just over eight a year; of these, three or four years after graduation, forty were working in technical occupations.[51]

Although these and other Southern schools produced graduates who entered technical fields, they nevertheless proved too few in number to build the economically independent and industrial New South envisioned by progressivist academics. The turn of the century found Curry wondering who would build the South's cities, commerce, factories, mills, and railroads. "There must be trained heads to do this work," he reasoned. "Will they be imported from the North and Europe, or shall we develop them here from among our own people?" By 1900, the South remained economically dependent on the North, lacked a diversified economy, continued to rely on unskilled labor, and remained the poorest region in the Republic.[52]

The problem was not necessarily too few graduates. No guarantee existed that, even if Southern schools doubled, tripled, or even quadrupled their annual output of scientifically trained graduates, the South would have industrialized any faster than it did. Progressivist educators operated from what well may have been a flawed premise: that, by itself, higher education could generate the skill and capital necessary to foster industrialization.

Northern industry, at least prior to the 1860s, developed rapidly without the aid of agricultural and mechanical colleges or state university graduates with bachelor of science degrees. Inventive Northern mechanics, trained largely through apprenticeship, created labor-saving devices that built industries and generated capital, much of which industrialists invested in developing new technologies. As part of their investment, Yankee manufacturers supported scientific education in the North, which produced chemists, mechanical engineers, and other skilled personnel for Northern factories. However, industry and capital initially stimulated applied science instruction in higher education, not vice versa.[53]

Although the academics of the Civil War generation failed to create a prosperous New South through their graduates, they did produce alumni who filled the ranks of Southern academia. The South's schools, whenever possible, appointed their own graduates or those from other Southern institutions to academic positions. Often these young educators had received postgraduate training at Northern schools, such as Cornell, Johns Hopkins, or Rensselaer, or, like other Americans, at German universities.[54] Although Southern students learned the more scientific aspects of their chosen fields, such as chemistry or history, at these schools, Northern and foreign professors did not need to introduce them to progressivist thought. Those persons who had been too young to fight in the Civil War and who entered academia prior to 1900, already had learned the lesson of Southern progress: the South's inevitable defeat, followed by national reconciliation, ultimately would lead to a prosperous future.

At a meeting of the New England Society held in New York City on December 22, 1906, University of Virginia President Edwin A. Alderman spoke on the subject of Northern and Southern sectionalism and American nationality. "Fate driven, these sections came to war, the New Englander fighting for the liberty of the individual . . . and the idea of union; the Southerner for the liberty of local self-government and the right of Englishmen to determine their affairs," Alderman told the audience. The war, he continued, "was not of conquest or glory. To call it rebellion is to speak ignorantly. To call it treason is to add viciousness to stupidity." The conflict, the 1882 graduate of the University of North Carolina assured his applauding listeners, had removed "the curse of slavery" from the South and established "the indestructibility of the Union." For New England, he continued, much of the nineteenth century had been a "Golden Age" of economic development and political freedom. As for the South, "rid of its economic misconceptions, and proven fine steel by the ordeal of fire, [having] spent forty-five years in courageous industrial and political adjustment to the modern world," Alderman enthusiastically predicted, its "Golden Age is yet to be." His address contained all the major elements of Southern progressivist thought: Providence, the Lost Cause, Anglo-Saxonism, national reconciliation, and the inevitable progress of the New South.[55]

Alderman, who previously had served as president of the University of North Carolina and Tulane, often is considered one of the Progressive educators who freed Southern higher education from academic conservatives. Such conservatives remained enamored with classics, resisted Yankee curricular innovations such as applied science courses, and waxed nostalgic about the Old South. He and other academics and their supporters who had been born too late to fight in the Civil War, such as Thomas D. Boyd (David Boyd's younger brother), Charles W. Dabney, Charles D. McIver, Edgar Gardner Murphy, Francis P. Venable, and George T. Winston, frequently are credited with helping to create a "great educational awakening" in the South after 1900. Such men are characterized as reconciled "apostles" of the New South.[56]

Particularly noted are the efforts of the Watauga Club, a group of young (all under thirty years of age) North Carolina Progressives including Dabney, McIver, Page, Josephus Daniels, and others. This group in 1884 launched a campaign from Raleigh to enlighten public opinion on the benefits of all levels of public education, farmers' institutes, scientific agriculture, and good roads. Their efforts are recognized as having started a broad educational reform movement in the South which helped to spur the Progressive crusades to use the power of government against child labor and hookworm. These Progressives also advocated the education of white women, who after the turn of the century increasingly entered state colleges and universities.[57]

The generation that followed the academics of the Civil War generation was composed largely of Southern Progressives and proponents of the New South. Their progressivist orientation was not spontaneous, however; it had been inherited from the first generation of postbellum academics. Like them, the subsequent generation took pride in the material progress of the United States, believed that education would create a New South, embraced the cult of the Anglo-Saxon, admired Herbert Spencer, espoused the study of scientific history, and attributed Prussia's victory over the French to superior schools.[58]

No one did more than Charles W. Dabney to enshrine the second generation of postwar educators as the saviors of Southern education. He was the son of Robert Lewis Dabney, the Presbyterian minister who served as Stonewall Jackson's chief of staff during the Civil War and later wrote a biography of the dead general. Like many clergymen, the elder Dabney remained resistant to reconciliation, feared that the progressivist orientation of the New South would undermine republican virtue, and defended academic conservatism. Charles Dabney, born on June 19, 1855, and therefore much too young to enlist in the ranks of the Confederacy, embraced reunion, the New South, and academic reform.[59]

In 1873, Dabney received a B.A. degree from Hampden-Sydney College, where he struggled with algebra, learned surveying, and studied the classics. He subsequently entered the University of Virginia, where he studied under John Mallet and F. Henry Smith. Dabney took a deep interest in the natural sciences, particularly applied chemistry, which he learned from Mallet. Beyond the importance of the applied sciences, the University of Virginia exposed him to other aspects of progressivist thought that predominated in the South's state universities: the idea of inevitable progress, the importance of national reconciliation, and the creation of a New South through education.[60]

When Dabney left the university in 1877, Emory and Henry College appointed him as its first professor of chemistry, mineralogy, and geology, following recommendations from Mallet and Smith. The college's dismal financial condition, Dabney believed, prevented him from acquiring the resources necessary to perform his professorial tasks adequately, and he resigned from the position a year later. Dabney left Virginia for the University of Göttingen in Germany, where, like his mentor John Mallet, he received a Ph.D. degree.[61]

After his return to the United States, Dabney briefly taught chemistry at the University of North Carolina in 1881 and subsequently served as the director of North Carolina's agricultural experiment station. He spent seven years in that state, and while there he joined the reformers of the Watauga Club. In 1887, Dabney took part in the successful effort, led by Leonidas L. Polk of the state's Grange, to establish in Raleigh an agricultural and mechanical college committed specifically to applied science instruction and separate from the state university.[62]

Dabney left North Carolina in 1887, after obtaining the presidency of the University of Tennessee, which he hoped would become "the great industrial school of the South." He worked there for the next seventeen years, attempting to accomplish that goal. Additionally, Dabney adopted and perpetuated a vision of progress created by former Confederates who entered academia after the Civil War. "The North conquered us, not because she had braver men, for there never were braver men than our own," Dabney wrote, "but because she had superior scientific, mechanical, and commercial resources, and so, greater wealth." He concluded that "our neglect of education and our ignorance of science, mechanical arts, industry and commerce, were what doomed us to defeat from the beginning. . . . These are the plain lessons of history." Nevertheless, Dabney asserted, Union victory destroyed slavery, which had made all "manual labor dishonorable, or at least disrespectable." This attitude, as "is universally acknowledged, retarded the general, scientific and educational development of the Southern people." Dabney believed that "social evolution like everything else in the universe is continuous. . . . [Southerners] speak of the civil war as revolution, and it was a complete revolution of our whole life, political, social and economic; but to the scientific student of history this great cataclysm was only a phase of the regular evolutionary process."[63]

An ardent nationalist, Dabney rejoiced in 1911 that, "after fifty years of complete or partial separation from the rest of the nation, the South had become fully re-nationalized." Commercial and industrial growth, he claimed, had restored the South to economic health and allowed it to share in the nation's prosperity. "More than any other influence," however, Dabney crowed, education "has changed the South from a conservative bulwark into an engine of progress in the nation." Education, he believed, acted not only as an instrument of physical progress, but as an "agency of social progress" that elevated public morality.[64]

Dabney and other Progressive educators appropriated as their own the progressivist vision—inevitable defeat, national reconciliation, and progress through education—forged by the Civil War generation. "With all respect for the fathers, we believe that men have to be educated for their period," Dabney opined concerning the education proffered by Confederate veterans. The "error of the fathers," he believed, "was that they persisted in trying to make the old education answer for the new times." But, Dabney claimed, "a new generation has entered [public] life, educated to think new thoughts and to do new deeds." Dabney perpetuated this interpretation of a progressive new generation overcoming the reactionary educational beliefs of the "fathers" in his two-volume work, *Universal Education in the South,* published in 1936. His interpretation rarely has been challenged.[65]

Southern Progressives mistakenly interpreted the musings of their

academic elders about the Lost Cause as yearnings for Southern independence and the Old South. The new generation of Southern educators failed to
realize that their predecessors, like themselves, viewed the Civil War as
another (albeit major) point on the road of Southern progress. Furthermore,
the "educational revival" in the South—which provided larger budgets for
white public schools of all levels and increased the size of enrollments,
faculty, and curricula—occurred after most of the older generation of academics had either died or retired. Dabney and other Progressive-era educators, who themselves had been crusading for these improvements since the
1870s and 1880s, lived to witness this fruition and received the credit for the
improvements in Southern education. Other than the occasional paean given
to Robert E. Lee for his work at Washington College, Progressive educators
and their supporters slighted the progressivist beliefs and efforts of their
predecessors and themselves took credit for the "educational awakening"
that occurred on their watch. Progressives, however, equated their teachers'
paltry results with their motives. Since the fathers had not brought about an
educational revival, Progressives reasoned, they must not have sought one in
the first place.[66]

Despite the enthusiasm of Progressives for the future of Southern
academia, troubling problems remained. Parallelism continued to plague
Southern higher education, as legislatures, well into the twentieth century,
continued to establish new and underfunded state universities, colleges,
industrial schools, and teachers' colleges. Progressive academics also believed
it necessary to continue to mollify religious denominations by praising
religious education and courting the support of sectarian colleges. More
troubling to those higher educators who prided themselves on supporting
objective and scientific inquiry, the public and trustees generally insisted
upon persecuting (and seeking the dismissal of) those few professors who
questioned white supremacy.[67]

Akin to the first generation of postbellum academics, Southern
Progressives could not agree on the type of academic training African Americans
should receive. Charles Dabney believed that Southern blacks needed to learn
only the skills necessary to know "how to work and labor" on a farm. Whites,
however, he wanted to be taught the scientific "arts of agriculture and industry."
Henry Clay White hoped to avoid the problem of African American higher
education altogether. Born in Baltimore in 1850, White studied at the University
of Virginia under Mallet in the 1870s and was elected professor of chemistry at
the University of Georgia during Lipscomb's tenure as chancellor. White also
served as president of Georgia's agricultural college from 1890 to 1907. An
admirer of Spencer and Darwin, White believed in "social evolution" and demonstrated his Progressivism through his support of the Lake Mohonk Conference on

International Arbitration, which promoted world peace. His attitude toward African American education was somewhat less progressive, however. He begrudged blacks their share of the 1890 Morrill grant and fretted to his friend William LeRoy Broun that his college would have "trouble" with "the Negro question . . . in educational matters."[68]

Another Progressive academic, Walter B. Hill, demonstrated more concern for the higher education of African Americans. Hill, born a decade before the start of the Civil War, attended the University of Georgia from 1868 to 1871. While there, he enjoyed Broun's experiments and lectures, private conversations with Andrew Lipscomb, and a friendship with fellow student Henry Grady. Hill also joined the university's branch of the Young Men's Christian Association, organized by Broun, and the students' Temperance Society. After graduation, Hill became an attorney and taught law at Mercer University. He also developed an interest in populist politics and avidly supported prohibition and universal education. The University of Georgia's trustees appointed him chancellor in 1899. Unlike Dabney and White, Hill believed that African Americans ought to have access to higher education. He worked for this goal while serving as a trustee for Paine College in Augusta, Georgia.[69]

Like their progressivist predecessors, Southern academics of the Progressive era and their supporters embraced, or at least accepted, segregated higher education. Ultimately, white legislators and education boards insured that African Americans at publicly supported schools received largely manual training. Furthermore, legislative spending on black colleges declined after 1900 in relation to funds spent on higher education for whites—a circumstance that Progressives largely left unchallenged.[70]

More troubling to Progressive academics than parallel institutions, religious opposition, and black education was the observation that, despite all their efforts, the South continued to demonstrate too little progress. Francis Venable, like Dabney and White, studied chemistry under Mallet at the University of Virginia in the 1870s. After graduation, he found employment as professor of general and industrial chemistry at the University of North Carolina. "We are falling behind in the world's progress," Venable warned in 1883, "and whatever of civilization and of knowledge we possess we tamely accept from others. This must not be." Twenty years later, Venable complained that, educationally, the South continued to trail the rest of the nation.[71]

The slow rate of Southern progress especially disturbed David Boyd's younger brother, Thomas. Too young to fight in the Civil War, Thomas Boyd had graduated from LSU in 1872, taught there intermittently, and served as the school's president from 1896 to 1928. He warned lagging Southerners in 1900 that they must advance, for "whatever does not progress has a retrograde movement."

Alderman likewise grew impatient. "The South must pass from an agricultural order, depressed by poverty and misrule," he insisted in 1908, "to an industrial democracy."

These men's concern about the South's relatively slow rate of progress stemmed in part from fears that the Southern public still failed to appreciate the benefits of education. Despite generally increased legislative appropriations after 1900—due more to the South's general economic recovery, perhaps, than to any increased desire on the part of the public to support higher education—Progressive academics lamented "the scant equipment" and "precarious incomes" that continued to plague public colleges and universities.[72]

Although academics recognized that the South had undergone considerable industrial growth in the decades after the Civil War, they also realized that the region had not closed the gap that existed between its wealth and that of the rest of nation. This circumstance led them to a dual conception of Southern progress. They appreciated the development that had occurred since the war and which allowed them to proclaim, as Henry Grady did, that the New South had arrived.[73] Still, Southerners remained largely rural and plagued by poverty, isolated from national politics, and excluded from the nation's general prosperity. The New South, therefore, also appeared to Progressive academics, just as it had to their predecessors, as a millennial expectation of a "Golden Age" yet to be fulfilled. The Progressives' New South—and any subsequent New South— thus resembled the Christian conception of the Kingdom of God:[74] already present and yet still in the future.

"To us the Confederate Veterans is due the resurrection called the New South," observed Stephen Lee, "which we bequeath as an inheritance to our sons."[75] There is considerable truth in Lee's assertion. Intellectually, Lee and other Confederate veterans who entered academia opened the way to the New South. They did this by transforming the Southern idea of progress. What had been viewed as a struggle to maintain an agrarian order in the face of endless republican cycles now entailed embracing infinite industrial growth. They also provided the subsequent generation of higher educators with the doctrinal tenets—the Lost Cause, national reconciliation, and the New South—of Southern progress. In turn, Progressive academics preached their faith to students in their classes and to the public in their addresses. It has been this perpetual hope of progress which has led Southerners—and historians—to believe in the promises of the first New South and to look always forward to another.[76]

Notes

Abbreviations

A&M	Agricultural and Mechanical
De Bow's Review	*Commercial Review of the South and West*
GPO	United States Government Printing Office, Washington, D.C.
LSU	Louisiana State University, Baton Rouge, Louisiana
NCDAH	North Carolina Department of Archives and History, Raleigh, North Carolina
RBVVMI	*Report of the Board of Visitors of the Virginia Military Institute, 1850–57.* VMI Archives, Lexington, Va.
Ser.	Series
Subser.	Subseries
SHC-UNC	Southern Historical Collection, Wilson Library, Univ. of North Carolina, Chapel Hill
SHSP	*Southern Historical Society Papers*
VMI	Virginia Military Institute, Lexington, Virginia

Introduction

1. A. D. Mayo, *The Training of Teachers in the South: A Paper Read Before the Normal Department, National Educational Association, Nashville, Tenn., July, 1889* (N.p.: [1889]), 2.

2. Anne Rivers Siddons, *Hill Towns: A Novel* (New York: Harper Collins Publishers, 1993), 6–7; Thomas G. Dyer, "Higher Education in the South Since the Civil War: Historiographical Issues and Trends," in *The Web of Southern Social Relations: Women, Family, and Education,* ed. Walter J. Fraser, Jr., and Jon L. Wakelyn (Athens: Univ. of Georgia Press, 1985), 127, 130; Rod Andrew, Jr., "Soldiers, Christians, and Patriots: The Lost Cause and Southern Military Schools, 1865–1915," *Journal of Southern History* 64 (Nov. 1998): 677–710; Frederick Rudolph, *The American College and University: A History* (New York: Knopf, 1962), 244; Allan M. Carter, "The Role of Higher Education in the Changing South," in *The South in Continuity and Change,* ed. John C. McKinney and Edgar T. Thompson (Durham, N.C.: Duke Univ. Press, 1965), 281–89; Joseph J. Mathews, "The Study of History in the South," *Journal of Southern History* 31 (Feb. 1965): 4; Joseph M. Stetar, "Development of Southern Higher Education, 1865–1910: Selected Case Studies of Six Colleges" (Ph.D. diss., State Univ. of New York at Buffalo, 1975); Joseph M. Stetar, "In Search of a Direction: Southern Higher Education after the Civil War," *History of Education Quarterly* 25 (Fall 1985): 343–57; Charles Reagan Wilson, *Baptized in Blood: The Religion of the Lost Cause, 1865–1920* (Athens: Univ. of Georgia Press, 1980), 68, 81–86, 139–60; Harvey Neufeldt and Clinton Allison, "*Education and the Rise of the New South*: An Historiographical Essay," in *Education and the Rise of the New South,* ed. Ronald K. Goodenow and Arthur O. White (Boston: G. K. Hall, 1981), 259; Charles W. Dabney, "The Progress of Renationalization of the South" [1911], typescript in folder 318, box 25, ser. 5, subser. 5.2, Charles W. Dabney Papers,

SHC-UNC. Among the very few who took exception to the view that Confederate veterans were academic conservatives lost in the Old South was William B. Hesseltine. In his undocumented *Confederate Leaders in the New South* (Baton Rouge: LSU Press, 1950), 77–92, Hesseltine asserted that Confederate veterans in academia embraced the New South.

3. J. B. Bury's often cited or summarized definition of the idea of progress remains among the clearest and most useful. He defines *progress* as the belief that "civilization has moved, is moving and will move in a desirable direction." There are differences among adherents as to the types of progress, however. For example, some differentiate spiritual and technological progress. Variations also exist regarding the movement of progress ("rectilinear" or "spiraliform"), the pace of progress (discontinuous or constant), and the agent of progress (Providence or nature). The amorphousness of the concept leads W. Warren Wagar to conclude that "the idea of progress is a thought-form, not a doctrine with a specific ideological context." J. B. Bury, *The Idea of Progress* (London: Macmillan, 1928), 2; John Andrew Bernstein, *Progress and the Quest for Meaning: A Philosophical and Historical Inquiry* (Rutherford, N.J.: Farleigh Dickinson Univ. Press, 1993), 17–18; Christopher Lasch, *The True and Only Heaven: Progress and Its Critics* (New York: Norton, 1991), 47; Roger Nisbet, *History of the Idea of Progress* (New York: Basic Books, 1980), 4–5; David Spadafora, *The Idea of Progress in 18th-Century Britain* (New Haven, Conn.: Yale Univ. Press, 1990), 4; W. Warren Wagar, *Good Tidings: The Belief in Progress from Darwin to Marcuse* (Bloomington: Indiana Univ. Press, 1972), 3–10. On the development of the idea of progress in Europe, see Ronald Victor Sampson, *Progress in the Age of Reason: The 17th Century to the Present Day* (Cambridge, Mass.: Harvard Univ. Press, 1956); and Jules Delvaille, *Essai sur l'Histoire de l'Idée de Progrès jusqu'à la Fin du XVIIIe Siècle* (1910; reprint, Geneva, Switzerland: Slatkine Reprints, 1969).

4. Emory M. Thomas, *The Confederacy as a Revolutionary Experience* (Englewood Cliffs, N.J.: Prentice-Hall, 1971), 87–99, 135–36. See also Raimondo Luraghi, "The Civil War and the Modernization of American Society: Social Structure and Industrial Revolution in the Old South Before and During the War," *Civil War History* 18 (Sept. 1972): 243–46; and Frank E. Vandiver, *Ploughshares into Swords: Josiah Gorgas and Confederate Ordnance* (Austin: Univ. of Texas Press, 1952).

5. To describe and refer to Southern academics who adhered to ideas of progress, I employ the adjective and noun *progressivist*, rather than *progressive*, to avoid confusion with the latter word's more typically understood historical connotations.

6. Nisbet, *History of the Idea*, 103. See also Madsen Pirie, *Trial and Error and the Idea of Progress* (London: Open Court, 1978), 10–12; and Wagar, *Good Tidings*, 6.

7. W. J. Cash, *The Mind of the South* (New York: Vintage Books, 1941), 141–45; James C. Cobb, "Does Mind No Longer Matter? The South, the Nation, and The Mind of the South, 1941–1991," *Journal of Southern History* 57 (Nov. 1991): 681–718; C. Vann Woodward, *Origins of the New South, 1877–1913* (Baton Rouge: LSU Press, with the Littlefield Fund for Southern History, Univ. of Texas, 1951; rev. ed. 1971), 436–46; Mark K. Bauman, "Confronting the New South Creed: The Genteel Conservative as Higher Educator," in *Education and the Rise of the New South*, ed. Ronald K. Goodenow and Arthur O. White (Boston: G. K. Hall, 1981), 109n.

Chapter 1. Progress and Academia in the Antebellum South

1. Robert Polk Thomson, "Colleges in the Revolutionary South: The Shaping of a Tradition," *History of Education Quarterly* 10 (Winter 1970): 399–412; Kemp Plummer Battle, *Sketches of the History of the Univ. of North Carolina, Together with a Catalogue of Officers and Students, 1789–1889* (N.p.: Univ. of North Carolina, 1889), 2, 39, 47–48; Henry McGilbert Wagstaff, *Impressions of Men and Movements at the Univ. of North Carolina* (Chapel Hill: Univ. of North Carolina Press, 1950), 5; Jurgen Herbst, "The 18th-Century Origins of the Split Between Private and Public Education in the U.S.," *History of Education Quarterly* 15 (Fall 1975): 277; Donald G. Tewksbury, *The Founding of American Colleges and Universities Before the Civil War: With Particular Reference to the Religious Influences Bearing Upon the College Movement* (New York: Columbia Univ. Press, 1932), 166–82; Alma Pauline Foerster, "The State University in the Old South: A Study of Social and Intellectual Influences in State University Education" (Ph.D. diss., Duke Univ., 1939), ch. 1; Thomas G. Dyer, *The Univ. of Georgia: A Bicentennial History, 1785–1985* (Athens: Univ. of Georgia Press, 1985), 3–21.

2. Kemp P. Battle, *History of the Univ. of North Carolina* (Raleigh, N.C.: Edwards and Broughton, 1907), 1:48–55, 1:98–99, 1:780; Archibald Henderson, *The Campus of the First State University* (Chapel Hill: Univ. of North Carolina Press, 1949), 107; Laurence R. Veysey, *The Emergence of the American University* (Chicago: Univ. of Chicago Press, 1965), 23–24, 121–26; Kemp Plummer Battle, *Memories of an Old Time Tar Heel,* ed. William James Battle (Chapel Hill: Univ. of North Carolina Press, 1945), 80–81; Thomas Dyer, *Univ. of Georgia,* 11–15, 21–26; Robert Preston Brooks, *The Univ. of Georgia Under 16 Administrations, 1785–1955* (Athens: Univ. of Georgia Press, 1956), 19–23; John S. Brubacher and Willis Rudy, *Higher Education in Transition: A History of American Colleges and Universities, 1636–1968* (New York: Harper and Row, 1968), 84; James Gregory McGivern, *First Hundred Years of Engineering Education in the U.S. (1807–1907)* (Spokane, Wash.: Gonzaga Univ. Press, 1960), 127; E. Merton Coulter, *College Life in the Old South* (Athens: Univ. of Georgia Press, 1951), 34–35; Maurice Kelley, "Additional Chapters on Thomas Cooper," *Univ. of Maine Studies* 33 (Aug. 1930): 10–25, 64–65; Thomas Cooper, *Address to the Graduates of the South Carolina College, Dec. 1821* (Columbia, S.C.: D. Faust, 1821), 6–15; M. LaBorde, *History of the South Carolina College* (Charleston, S.C.: Walker, Evans and Cogswell, 1874), 158–77; Daniel Walker Hollis, *Univ. of South Carolina* (Columbia: Univ. of South Carolina Press, 1951), 1:126–74; James Riley Montgomery, Stanley J. Folmsbee, and Lee Seifert Greene, *To Foster Knowledge: A History of the Univ. of Tennessee, 1794–1970* (Knoxville: Univ. of Tennessee Press, 1984), 15–35, 48–57.

3. Daniel J. Boorstin, *The Lost World of Thomas Jefferson* (Chicago: Univ. of Chicago Press, 1948, 1981), 213–25; Thomas Jefferson to Thomas Cooper, 25 Aug. 1814, in Thomas Jefferson, *The Writings of Thomas Jefferson,* ed. Albert Ellery Bergh (Washington, D.C.: Thomas Jefferson Memorial Association, 1907), 14:123–25; Thomas Jefferson to Thomas Cooper, 10 July 1812, in Thomas Jefferson, *The Writings of Thomas Jefferson,* ed. H. A. Washington (Washington, D.C.: Taylor and Maury, 1854), 6:72–74; Thomas Jefferson to David Williams, 14 Nov. 1803, in Jefferson, *Writings,* ed. Bergh, 10:428–30.

4. Stow Persons, "The Cyclical Theory of History in 18th-Century America,"

American Quarterly 6 (Summer 1954): 147–63; J. G. A. Pocock, *The Machiavellian Moment: Florentine Political Thought and the Atlantic Republican Tradition* (Princeton, N.J.: Princeton Univ. Press, 1975), 333–552; Lance Banning, *The Jeffersonian Persuasion: Evolution of a Party Ideology* (Ithaca, N.Y.: Cornell Univ. Press, 1978), 42–69, 126–60; Drew McCoy, *The Elusive Republic: Political Economy in Jeffersonian America* (New York: Norton, 1980), 13–119.

5. McCoy, *Elusive Republic,* 105–19, 166–235; John F. Kasson, *Civilizing the Machine: Technology and Republican Values in America, 1776–1900* (New York: Grossman, 1976), 3–51.

6. Harold Hellenbrand, *The Unfinished Revolution: Education and Politics in the Thought of Thomas Jefferson* (Newark, N.J.: Univ. of Delaware Press, 1990), 136–40; Jefferson quoted in Roy J. Honeywell, *The Educational Work of Thomas Jefferson* (New York: Russell and Russell, 1964), 225.

7. Honeywell, *Educational Work of Jefferson,* 250–51; Thomas Jefferson to Josiah Meigs, 20 May 1803, quoted in William M. Meigs, *Life of Josiah Meigs* (Philadelphia: n.p., 1887), Appendix D, p. 125.

8. Arthur Alphonse Ekirch, Jr., *The Idea of Progress in America, 1815–1860* (New York: Columbia Univ. Press, 1944), 31–32; Persons, "Cyclical Theory," 161; Kasson, *Civilizing the Machine,* 38; Jefferson, quoted in Honeywell, *Educational Work of Jefferson,* 251.

9. Thomas Jefferson to John Adams, 15 June 1813, in Jefferson, *Writings,* ed. Bergh, 13:252–56; Thomas Jefferson to John Adams, 12 Sept. 1821, in *The Adams-Jefferson Letters: The Complete Correspondence Between Thomas Jefferson and Abigail and John Adams,* ed. Lester J. Cappon (Chapel Hill, N.C.: Institute of Early American History and Culture, 1959), 2:575. See also Thomas Cooper, *Address to the Graduates of the South Carolina College, at the Public Commencement, 1830* (Columbia, S.C.: S. J. M. Morris, 1831), 10.

10. Thomas Jefferson to Cornelius Camden Blatchly, 21 Oct. 1822, in Jefferson, *Writings,* ed. Bergh, 15:399–400; Honeywell, *Educational Work of Jefferson,* 251; Thomas Jefferson to John Holmes, 22 Apr. 1820, in Thomas Jefferson, *The Works of Thomas Jefferson,* ed. Paul Leicester Ford (New York: G. P. Putnam's Sons, 1905), 12:159–60.

11. Thomas Jefferson to Dupont de Nemours, 24 Apr. 1816, in Jefferson, *Writings,* ed. Bergh, 14:487–93. See also Thomas Jefferson to William Ludlow, 6 Sept. 1824, in Jefferson, *Writings,* ed. Bergh, 16:74–76.

12. Philip Alexander Bruce, *History of the Univ. of Virginia, 1819–1919* (New York: Macmillan, 1920), 1:51–55, 1:321–43; Wayne Hamilton Wiley, "Academic Freedom at the Univ. of Virginia: The First Hundred Years—From Jefferson Through Alderman" (Ph.D. diss., Univ. of Virginia, 1973), 92–96, 113–19; Rudolph, *American College,* 124–28; O. Allan Gianniny, Jr., "The Overlooked Approach to Engineering Education: One and a Half Centuries at the Univ. of Virginia, 1836–1986," in *Proceedings of the 150th Anniversary Symposium on Technology and Society,* ed. Howard L. Hartman (Tuscaloosa: College of Engineering, Univ. of Alabama, 1988), 151–55; C. S. Venable, *An Address Delivered Before the Society of Alumni of the Univ. of Virginia* (Richmond, Va.: MacFarlane and Fergusson, 1859), 3–24; *Catalogue of the Univ. of Virginia, Session of 1860–61* (Richmond, Va.: Chas. H. Wynne, 1861), 22.

13. "Original Papers in Relation to a Course of Liberal Education" [Yale Report], *American Journal of Science and Arts* 15 (1829): 297–351; Richard Hofstadter and

C. DeWitt Hardy, *The Development and Scope of Higher Education in the U.S.* (New York: Columbia Univ. Press, 1952), 15–16; Joe L. Kincheloe, "Building God's Kingdom: The Holy Mission of Antebellum Evangelical Colleges," *Southern Studies* 2 (Summer 1991): 103–12; Melvin I. Urofsky, "Reforms and Response: The Yale Report of 1828," *History of Education Quarterly* 5 (Mar. 1965): 53–67; David B. Potts, "American Colleges in the 19th Century: From Localism to Denominationalism," *History of Education Quarterly* 11 (Winter 1971): 368.

14. Potts, "American Colleges," 363–68; Brubacher and Rudy, *Higher Education*, 61, 417; Tewksbury, *Founding of American Colleges*, 66–131; Burton J. Bledstein, *The Culture of Professionalism: The Middle Class and the Development of Higher Education in America* (New York: Norton, 1976), 237–43; Ellwood P. Cubberly, *The History of Education* (Boston: Houghton Mifflin, 1920), 705. Disagreement exists over the mortality rate of antebellum schools. See Robert T. Blackburn and Clifton F. Conrad, "The New Revisionists and the History of Higher Education," *Higher Education* 15 (1986): 215–17.

15. "Univ. of Louisiana," *De Bow's Review* 1 (May 1846): 431n; Philip Lindsley, "Baccalaureate Address at Cumberland College, 1829," in *The Works of Philip Lindsley, D.D.* (Nashville, Tenn.: W. T. Berry and Co., 1859), 160–61. The proliferation of colleges is representative of an antebellum phenomenon described by Robert H. Wiebe as *parallelism*, in which private entrepreneurs and governmental entities engaged in various types of competitive and duplicative enterprises that evolved in isolation from each other. These included the building of canals, railroads, utopian communities, and other ventures. See Robert H. Wiebe, *The Opening of American Society: From the Adoption of the Constitution to the Eve of Disunion* (New York: Knopf, 1984), 287–90, 360–69.

16. Richard Hofstadter, "The Age of the American College," in *The Development of Academic Freedom in the U.S.*, edited by Richard Hofstadter and Walter P. Metzger (New York: Columbia Univ. Press, 1955), 209–23. Most historians initially accepted Hofstadter's interpretation of the negative impact of sectarian colleges on higher education. Revisionists argue that denominational colleges enhanced academic opportunities for many people. For revisionist interpretations, see James Axtell, "The Death of the Liberal Arts College," *History of Education Quarterly* 11 (Winter 1971): 339–52; Blackburn and Conrad, "New Revisionists," 211–30; Jack C. Lane, "The Yale Report of 1828 and Liberal Education: A Neorepublican Manifesto," *History of Education Quarterly* 27 (Fall 1987): 325–38; Potts, "American Colleges," 363–80; and Douglas Sloan, "Harmony, Chaos, and Consensus: The American College Curriculum," *Teachers College Record* 73 (Dec. 1971): 221–51. On Southern denominational colleges, see Albea Godbold, *The Church College of the Old South* (Durham, N.C.: Duke Univ. Press, 1944). Godbold remains one of the most cited sources on the subject of denominational higher education. An updated study is needed.

17. Francis Wayland, *Thoughts on the Present Collegiate System in the U.S.* (Boston: Gould, Kendall and Lincoln, 1842), 32–42, 76–111, 132–49; Francis Wayland, *The Educational Demand of the People of the U.S.* (Boston: Phillips, Sampson and Co., 1855); Francis Wayland, *Report to the Corporation of Brown Univ. and Changes in the System of Collegiate Education* (Providence, R.I.: George H. Whitney, 1850); Henry P. Tappan, *University Education* (New York: George P. Putnam, 1851), 35–67; J. S. B. Thacher to Gov. A. G. Brown, 24 Nov. 1848,

printed in *Governor's Message Delivered at the Biennial Session [of the Mississippi State Legislature], Jan. 1848, and Accompanying Documents* (N.p.: [1848?]), 17–26; Brubacher and Rudy, *Higher Education,* 108–9.

18.   Isaac Croom, *Address Delivered Before the Greensboro Agricultural Society on the 2d of May, 1850* ([Greensboro, Ala.]: n.p., [1850?]), 7; B. L. C. Wailes, *Address Delivered in the College Chapel Before the Agricultural, Horticultural, and Botanical Society of Jefferson College* (Natchez, Miss.: Daily Courier Office, 1841), 5–7. See also: excerpts from Edmund G. Ruffin's "Premium Essay on Agricultural Education," quoted in Ch[arles] H. Williams, "Agricultural Education," *Southern Planter* 13 (July 1853): 217–19; "Agricultural Schools," *Farmer's Register* 1 (Jan. 1843): 16–17; "Constitution of the Texas Agricultural Society," Transactions of the Texas State Agricultural Society 1 (1853): 6; J. D. B. De Bow, "Commerce and Agriculture Subjects of University Instruction," *De Bow's Review* 3 (June 1847): 502–6; A. Yell, "Governor's Message, 8 Nov. 1842," *Journal of the House of Representatives . . . of the State of Arkansas* (Little Rock: State Printer, 1842), appendix, pp. 11–12. On Southerners' interest in science in the antebellum period, see Ronald L. Numbers and Janet S. Numbers, "Science in the Old South: A Reappraisal," *Journal of Southern History* 48 (May 1982): 163–84; and Paul F. Paskoff, "Invention and Culture in the Old South, 1790–1860," unpub. paper delivered at Works-in-Progress Seminar, Department of History, LSU, Baton Rouge, La., 1993.

19.   Carl B. Wilson, "The Baptist Manual Labor School Movement in the U.S.: Its Origin, Development and Significance," *Baylor Bulletin* 40 (Dec. 1937): 9–159; L. F. Anderson, "The Manual Labor School Movement," *Educational Review* 46 (June–Dec. 1913): 369–86; Edgar W. Knight, ed., *A Documentary History of Education in the South Before 1860* (Chapel Hill: Univ. of North Carolina Press, 1953), vol. 4: *Private and Denominational Efforts,* ch. 2. On manual labor schools in Virginia, see Cornelius J. Heatwole, *A History of Education in Virginia* (New York: Macmillan, 1916), 155–64; and John B. May, "The Life of John Lee Buchanan" (Ph.D. diss., Univ. of Virginia, 1937), 12–18.

20.   Augustus B. Longstreet, *Address Delivered Before the Faculty and Students of Emory College, Oxford, Ga.* (Augusta, Ga.: W. T. Thompson, 1840), 9–12; emphasis original.

21.   Isaac I. Stevens to Dear Uncle, 6 July 1836, cited in Hazard Stevens, *The Life of Isaac Ingalls Stevens* (Boston: Houghton Mifflin, 1900), 1:37–38; *Baptist Weekly Journal,* 16 Nov. 1832, cited in Carl B. Wilson, "Baptist Manual Labor," 101–2; *American Annals of Education and Instruction* 3 (Jan. 1833): 92–93; *American Annals of Education and Instruction* 5 (Aug. 1835): 377.

22.   William Gilham, "Report," attached to Francis H. Smith, *Special Report of the Superintendent of VMI, on Scientific Education in Europe* (Richmond, Va.: Ritchie, Dunnavant and Co., 1859), 57–59. See also "University Lectures," *De Bow's Review* 2 (Mar. 1852): 336; and Philip Lindsley, "Inaugural Address . . . January 12, 1825," in *The Works of Philip Lindsley, D.D.,* by Philip Lindsley (Nashville, Tenn.: W. T. Berry and Co., 1859), 28–45.

23.   Charles D. Johnson, *Higher Education of Southern Baptists* (Waco, Tex.: Baylor Univ. Press, 1955), 147–48; Wm. H. Ruffner, J. R. Anderson, and W. T. Sutherlin, "Report of Committee for the Plan of Organization for the Virginia A&M College," in *Virginia A&M College: Its History and Organization* (N.p., n.d.), 31; Carl B. Wilson, "Baptist Manual Labor"; Edgar W. Knight, *Documentary History,* 4:124–32; *Tallahassee*

Floridian, 24 Jan. 1832; C. D. Fishburne to D. H. Hill, Jr., 8 Feb. 1890, in box 94.6, Daniel Harvey Hill, Jr., Papers, NCDAH. In at least one case, advocates of manual labor schools attempted to combine the two "utopian" schemes. The South Carolina Agricultural Society recommended that South Carolina establish manual labor schools and that their students raise silkworms. See *Proceedings of the Agricultural Convention and of the State Agricultural Society of S.C., from 1839 to 1845* . . . (Columbia, S.C.: Summer and Carroll, 1846), 17–19.

24. Merle Curti, *The Social Ideas of American Educators* (New York: Charles Scribner's Sons, 1935), 102–23; Ernest Lee Tuveson, *Redeemer Nation: The Idea of America's Millennial Role* (Chicago: Univ. of Chicago Press, 1968), 76; Thomas Newton Wood, *An Address Delivered Before the Two Literary Societies of the Univ. of Alabama, in the Rotunda, July 4th, 1840* (Tuscaloosa, Ala.: M. D. J. Slade, 1840), 16; Cooper, *Address,* Dec. 1821, 7. See also Jacob Thompson, *Address Delivered on Occasion of the Opening of the Univ. of the State of Mississippi . . . Nov. 6, 1848* (Memphis, Tenn.: Franklin Book and Job Office, 1849), 5.

25. Gavin Wright, *The Political Economy of the Cotton South: Households, Markets, and Wealth in the 19th Century* (New York: Norton, 1978), 7–8, 44–55, 107–8, 116–18, 123; Heatwole, *History of Education in Virginia,* 100–124; Eugene W. Hilgard to L. L. Williams, 31 Jan. 1859, in folder 1, box 1, Eugene W. Hilgard Papers, Mississippi Department of Archives and History, Jackson; Leonidas Polk and Stephen Elliot, *Address of the Commissioners for Raising the Endowment of the Univ. of the South* (New Orleans, La.: B. M. Norman, Publisher, 1859); *De Bow's Review* (Mar. 1852): 336; Roger W. Shugg, *Origins of Class Struggle in Slavery and After, 1840–1875* (1936; reprint, Baton Rouge: LSU Press, 1968), 69–75; Hugh McQueen, *An Address Delivered Before the Alumni and Graduating Class of the Univ. of North Carolina . . . June 26, 1839* (Raleigh, N.C.: Raleigh Register, 1839), 24–25; "On Public Education in Virginia," *Southern Literary Messenger* 13 (Nov. 1847): 686–87; Eugene D. Genovese, Roll, Jordan, *Roll: The World the Slaves Made* (New York: Vintage, 1974), 561–63. On proslavery ideology, see Drew Gilpin Faust, ed., *The Ideology of Slavery: Proslavery Thought in the Antebellum South, 1830–1860* (Baton Rouge: LSU Press, 1981), 1–20; and David Donald, "The Proslavery Argument Reconsidered," *Journal of Southern History* 37 (Feb. 1971): 3–18.

26. A. Clarkson, "The Basis of Northern Hostility to the South," *De Bow's Review* 3 (Jan. 1860): 11–12; William R. Barksdale, *The True Office of the College: An Address, Delivered Before the Alumni Association of the Univ. of Mississippi, July 15, 1857* (Memphis, Tenn.: Bulletin Co., 1857), 12; James W. Massie, *An Address Delivered Before the Society of Alumni of VMI, July 3rd, 1857* (Richmond, Va.: MacFarlane and Fergusson, 1857), 34; emphasis original.

27. James H. Hammond, *An Oration Delivered Before the Two Societies of the South Carolina College, on the 4th of Dec. 1849* (Charleston, S.C.: Walker and James, 1850), 22–23; W. T. Walthall, *First Annual Address, Delivered Before the Mobile Teachers' Institute, Dec. 15th, 1856* (Mobile, Ala.: Daily Register, 1857), 7–15; emphasis original.

28. Samuel A. Cartwright, "The Education, Labor, and Wealth of the South," in *Cotton Is King and Pro-Slavery Arguments . . . ,* ed. E. N. Elliott (Augusta, Ga.: Pritchard, Abbott, and Loomis, 1860), 882; William Harper, "Memoir on Slavery," in *The Pro-Slavery Argument as Maintained by the Most Distinguished Writers of the Southern States . . .* (Philadelphia:

Lippincott, Gramb and Co., 1853), 3–4; [Thomas Roderick Dew], "Abolition of Negro Slavery," *American Quarterly Review* 12 (Sept. 1832): 189–265.

29. George Fitzhugh, "Southern Thought," *De Bow's Review* 23 (Oct. 1857): 338–50; William H. Stiles, *Southern Education for Southern Youth: An Address Before the Alpha Pi Delta Society of the Cherokee Baptist College, Delivered at the Commencement on 14th July, 1858* (Savannah, Ga.: Power Press of George N. Nichols, 1858), 14–24; Harper, "Memoir on Slavery," 22–25 (emphasis original). See also Eugene D. Genovese, *The Slaveholders' Dilemma: Freedom and Progress in Southern Conservative Thought, 1820–1860* (Columbia: Univ. of South Carolina, 1992), 32–37.

30. Fitzhugh, "Southern Thought," 338–50; Stiles, *Southern Education,* 14–24.

31. Massie, *Address Delivered 1857,* 31–53; Genovese, *Slaveholders' Dilemma,* 33–37; Eric Foner, *Free Soil, Free Labor, Free Men* (London: Oxford Univ. Press, 1970), 311–13; Eugene D. Genovese, *The Political Economy of Slavery: Studies in the Economy and Society of the Slave South* (New York: Pantheon, 1965), 243–51.

32. Genovese argues that Southern intellectuals separated spiritual or moral progress from material progress, generally rejecting the former and displaying "deep ambivalence toward" the latter. See Genovese, *Slaveholders' Dilemma,* 3–37. I find that Southern proslavery theorists' were ambivalent about progress *because of the difficulty* they had in separating material from spiritual progress. For definitions of progress in the antebellum period, see Noah Webster, *An American Dictionary of the English Language* . . . , 2 vols. (New York: S. Converse, 1828), and also editions published in 1852, 1855, and 1859. All definitions of progress given by Webster's in 1828 and 1859 are virtually identical. See also J. E. Worcester, *Comprehensive Pronouncing and Explanatory Dictionary of the English Language* . . . (Burlington, Vt.: Chauncey Goodrich, 1831); and Charles Richardson, *A New Dictionary of the English Language,* 2 vols. (Philadelphia: E. H. Butler and Co., 1847). On mainstream Western conceptions of inevitable and beneficial progress, see Bury, *Idea of Progress,* 2; Clarke A. Chambers, "The Belief in Progress in 20th-Century America," *Journal of the History of Ideas* 19 (Apr. 1958): 198; Pirie, *Trial and Error,* 9–10; Charles E. Rosenberg, *No Other Gods: On Science and American Social Thought* (1961; reprint, Baltimore, Md.: Johns Hopkins Univ. Press, 1976), 140; Wagar, *Good Tidings,* 3–10.

33. Hinton Rowan Helper, *The Impending Crisis of the South: How to Meet It* (New York: Burdick Brothers, 1857), 41, 56, *passim.*

34. Kemp P. Battle, *History of the Univ. of North Carolina,* 1:654–56. Hedrick's name appears in the dedication to Helper's *Compendium of the Impending Crisis of the South* (New York: A. B. Burdick, 1860). See the following, all in Benjamin Sherwood Hedrick Papers, SHC-UNC: clipping from an unidentified North Carolina newspaper, 1856, in box 3, folder 31; H. R. Helper to Prof. Hedrick, 15 Oct. 1856, in folder 7, box 1 (emphasis original); B. S. Hedrick to H. R. Helper, 27 Oct. 1856, in folder 7, box 1; H. R. Helper to Prof. B. S. Hedrick, 5 May 1859, in folder 15, box 2.

35. Peter Kolchin, *American Slavery,* 1619–1877 (New York: Hill and Wang, 1993), 187; John Murdoch, *Home Education and the Claims of Oakland College: Delivered Before the Belles Lettres Society and Adelphic Institute of Oakland College on Commencement Day, June 29th, 1854* (New Orleans, La.: Office of the Picayune, 1854), 30, 37, 40; Albert T. Bledsoe, *Address Delivered at the First Annual Commencement of the Univ. of Mississippi,*

July 12, 1849 (Oxford, Miss.: Organizer Office, 1849), 15; emphasis original. George Frederick Holmes, *Inaugural Address, Delivered on Occasion of the Opening of the Univ. of the State of Mississippi, Nov. 6, 1848* (Memphis, Tenn.: Franklin Book and Job Office, 1849), 19; Stiles, *Southern Education,* 8; Massie, *Address Delivered 1857,* 31–44; emphasis original.

36. Barksdale, *True Office of the College,* 4–12; R. D. Hamilton, *An Address Delivered Before the Students of Jefferson College, Washington, Miss., at the Commencement, July 25, 1855* (Natchez, Miss.: Daily Courier Book and Job Office, 1855), 3–11; G. H. Martin, *Address Delivered Before the Philomathean and Hermenian Societies, at Clinton, Miss., July 25, 1859* (Vicksburg, Miss.: Daily and Weekly Whig Steam Book and Job Office, 1859), 17–24; George F. Holmes, *Inaugural Address,* 19–20; J. H. Thornwell, *Letter to His Excellency Governor Manning on Public Instruction in South Carolina* (Columbia, S.C.: R. W. Gibbes and Co., 1853), 6; Walthall, *First Annual Address,* 10; George Junkin, *Christianity: The Patron of Literature and Science. An Address Delivered Feb. 22, 1849, on the Occasion of the Author's Inauguration as President of Washington College, Va.* (Philadelphia: n.p., 1849), 32; W. M. Wightman, *Inaugural Address Delivered at the Opening of the Southern Univ., Greensboro, Ala.* (Marion, Ala.: George C. Rogers, 1859), 3–11.

37. Thornwell, *Letter to His Excellency,* 17–18; John Wood Pratt, *An Address Delivered Before the Society of the Alumni of the Univ. of Alabama, July 8th, 1850* (Tuscaloosa, Ala.: M. D. J. Slade, 1850), 6–7. On conservative fears that the dynamic economy of the antebellum period threatened social distinctions, see Michael P. Johnson, *Toward a Patriarchal Republic: The Secession of Georgia* (Baton Rouge: LSU Press, 1977); and T. Michael Parrish, *Richard Taylor: Soldier Prince of Dixie* (Chapel Hill: Univ. of North Carolina Press, 1992), 16, 38–39, 51–52, 112–23.

38. Curti, *Social Ideas,* 102–23; Kasson, *Civilizing the Machine,* 8; Rosenberg, *No Other Gods,* 140; Bledsoe, *Address,* 8–14; Martin, *Address at Clinton,* 24. See also Walthall, *First Annual Address,* 13–15; Harper, "Memoir on Slavery," 92–93; Thornwell, *Letter to His Excellency,* 19.

39. Josiah C. Nott, "Two Lectures on the Natural History of the Caucasian and Negro Races," in *The Ideology of Slavery: Proslavery Thought in the Antebellum South, 1830–1860,* ed. Drew Gilpin Faust (Baton Rouge: LSU Press, 1981), 235; Hammond, *Oration,* 8–9; Honeywell, *Educational Work of Jefferson,* 251; Hellenbrand, *Unfinished Revolution,* 111–14, 130–36; Boorstin, *Lost World,* 93–98, 224; Albert T. Bledsoe, "Liberty and Slavery; or, Slavery in the Light of Moral Political Philosophy," in *Cotton Is King and Pro-Slavery Arguments . . . ,* ed. E. N. Elliott (Augusta, Ga.: Pritchard, Abbott, and Loomis, 1860), 295–96, 342, 382–417; Stiles, *Southern Education,* 23; James P. Holcombe, *An Address Delivered Before the Society of Alumni of the Univ. of Virginia, at Its Annual Meeting, Held in the Public Hall, June 29th, 1853* (Richmond, Va.: MacFarlane and Fergusson, 1853), 9, 19–23; J. P. Holcombe, *An Address Delivered Before the 7th Annual Meeting of the Virginia State Agricultural Society, Nov. 4th, 1858* (Richmond, Va.: MacFarlane and Fergusson, 1858), 9; Nott, "Two Lectures," 235.

40. Bledsoe, *Address,* 20; Jack P. Maddex, Jr., "Proslavery Millennialism: Social Eschatology in Antebellum Southern Calvinism," *American Quarterly* 31 (Spring 1979): 46–62.

41. Bledsoe, "Liberty and Slavery," 290–311, 338–58; A. B. Longstreet, "Letters on

the Epistle of Paul to Philemon, on the Connection of Apostolical Christianity with Slavery," in "The Letters of Augustus Baldwin Longstreet," ed. J. R. Scafidel (Ph.D. diss., Univ. of South Carolina, 1976), 170–222; Stiles, *Southern Education*, 10; *An Address on Southern Education, Delivered July 18, 1859, Before the Faculty, Trustees, Students, and Patrons of "Madison College," Sharon, Miss.* (Washington, D.C.: n.p., 1859), 5–9; Francis Wayland, *Elements of Moral Science* (New York: Cooke and Co., 1835). Wayland published other editions between 1835 and 1865. In each, he hardened his position against slavery.

42. Ekirch, *Idea of Progress*, 206–7, 214–15, 225–51. Ekirch argues that Southern intellectuals, in contrast to their Northern counterparts, provided a "qualified affirmation" of the idea of progress for the South. He is correct in noting that some Southern intellectuals accepted the materialistic aspects of progress and understood the importance of progress in the public's imagination. He is also correct in his observation that Southerners united slavery with the idea of progress. Ekirch fails to recognize, however, that many of the Southern intellectuals he identifies as progressivists, including Hammond, Harper, Nott, and Thornwell, feared progress as much as they affirmed it. Unlike Northern progressivists, they remained apprehensive about republican cycles, lacked faith in the inevitability of progress, tied progress to the conservative institution of slavery, rejected spiritual progress, and limited the idea of progress to Caucasians. Southern academia also largely rejected materialism and utility, both necessary components of scientific progress.

43. Hammond, *Oration*, 24–28.

44. Alexander M. Clayton, *Address Delivered at the First Annual Commencement of the Univ. of Mississippi . . . July 12, 1849* (Oxford, Miss.: Organizer Office, 1849), 5–16; emphasis original. See also W. W. Avery, *Address Delivered Before the Two Literary Societies of the Univ. of North Carolina, June 4, 1851* (Raleigh, N.C.: William W. Holden, 1851), 10–22.

45. F. W. Keyes, *An Address Delivered Before the Alumni Association of the Univ. of Mississippi on the 5th Day of July, 1859* (Oxford, Miss: n.p., 1859), 8–13, 20–21; A. B. Norton, *Remarks of A. B. Norton in the Texas House of Representatives Upon the University Question . . .* (Austin, Tex.: John Marshall and Co., 1858), 6–8; Ashbel Smith, *Letter from Doctor Ashbel Smith to the Trustees of the Memphis Univ. . . . , 25 Jan. 1849* ([Memphis, Tenn.]: Enquirer, n.d.), 3–7; Reports of the Department of Chemistry, by R. T. Brumby, to the Univ. of Alabama Board of Trustees, MSS, 13 Dec. 1841, 7 Dec. 1843, and 17 Dec. 1845, in folder 1519, box 7, Record Group 1, Trustee Records, University Archives, Univ. of Alabama, Tuscaloosa; Report of the Department of Chemistry, by F. A. P. Barnard, to the Univ. of Alabama Board of Trustees, MS, 4 July 1854, in folder 1519, box 7, Record Group 1, Trustee Records, University Archives, Univ. of Alabama, Tuscaloosa.

46. Walter Monteiro, *Address Delivered Before the Neotrophian Society of the Hampton Academy, on the 28th of July, 1857* (Richmond, Va.: H. K. Ellyson, 1857), 7–19; Hugh Blair Grigsby, *Oration Delivered Before the Students of William and Mary College, July 4, 1859* (N.p., n.d.), 4. Progressivist Southerners joined other Americans in celebrating native inventors who, Kasson notes in *Civilizing the Machine*, "became the objects of a national cult" during the mid-19th century (p. 41). See also Philip St. George Cocke to

B. S. Ewell, 30 June 1859, in box 1, Benjamin Stoddert Ewell Papers, University Archives, College of William and Mary, Williamsburg, Va.; Philip St. George Cocke to Henry A. Wise, Feb. 1859, in Francis H. Smith, *Special Report, 1859,* 4–5; Wm. T. Hamilton, *Address on the Importance of Knowledge, Delivered . . . Dec. 11th, 1841* (Tuscaloosa, Ala.: Office of the Independent Monitor, 1841), 10; and Aaron V. Brown, *Address Delivered Before the Literary Societies of the Univ. of North Carolina, . . . May 31, 1854* (Nashville, Tenn.: J. F. Morgan, 1854), 7.

47. Francis H. Smith, "Superintendent's Report," 25 June 1851, *RBVVMI,* July 1850, p. 7. See also M. F. Maury, *Address Delivered Before the Literary Societies of the Univ. of Virginia . . . 28th June, 1855* (Richmond, Va.: H. K. Ellyson, 1855), 12–15, 18–24.

48. Report of the Prudential Committee, in Board of Trustees, Univ. of Georgia, Minutes, 6 Nov. 1855, typescript copy, in University Archives, Univ. of Georgia, Athens; Report of A. Church, in Board of Trustees, Univ. of Georgia, Minutes, 6 Nov. 1855 and 15 Oct. 1856; Board of Trustees, Univ. of Georgia, Minutes, 2 Nov. 1859; *Catalogue of the Trustees, Officers and Alumni of the Univ. of Georgia, from 1785 to 1894* (Atlanta, Ga.: Foote and Davies Co., 1894).

49. Robin Brabham, "Defining the American University: The Univ. of North Carolina, 1865–1875," *North Carolina Historical Review* 57 (Oct. 1980): 431; Kemp P. Battle, *History of the Univ. of North Carolina,* 1:552–53, 1:660–61; Jno. Kimberly to My Dear Hal, 12 Feb. 1857, in folder 7, box 1, John Kimberly Papers, SHC-UNC; Board of Trustees, Univ. of North Carolina, Minutes, 26 Jan. 1859, in University Archives, Univ. of North Carolina, Chapel Hill.

50. "Address of Dr. Landon C. Garland," in *Minutes of the Convention Which Formed the Alabama Educational Association . . . July 24 25, 1856* (Selma, Ala.: Selma Reporter and Job Printing Office, 1857), 8–13; Willis G. Clark, "The Promise of Education," in *Memorial Record of Alabama* (Madison, Wisc.: Brant and Fuller, 1893), 1:159; James B. Sellers, *History of the Univ. of Alabama* (University, Ala.: Univ. of Alabama Press, 1953), 1:78, 1:153–55; Basil Manly, *Report on Collegiate Education, Made to the Trustees of the Univ. of Alabama, July 1852* (Tuscaloosa, Ala.: M. D. J. Slade, 1852), 8–17.

51. G. F. H. [George F. Holmes], "Sir William Hamilton's Discussions," *Southern Quarterly Review* 8 (Oct. 1853): 299–336; George F. Holmes, *Inaugural Address,* 15–18; Auguste Comte, *The Essential Comte: Selected from Cours de Philosophie Positive,* ed. Stanislav Andreski (New York: Barnes and Noble, 1974), 126–27; Drew Gilpin Faust, *A Sacred Circle: The Dilemma of the Intellectual in the Old South, 1840–1860* (Baltimore, Md.: Johns Hopkins Univ. Press, 1977), 64; Neal C. Gillespie, *The Collapse of Orthodoxy: The Intellectual Ordeal of George Frederick Holmes* (Charlottesville: Univ. of Virginia Press, 1972), 123–50; John N. Waddel, *Historical Discourse Delivered on the Quarter-Centennial Anniversary of the Univ. of Mississippi on Wednesday, June 25th, 1873* (Oxford, Miss.: Board of Trustees, 1873), 10–11, 18–21; John Donald Wade, *Augustus Baldwin Longstreet: A Study of the Development of Culture in the South* (Athens: Univ. of Georgia Press, 1969), 296–313; Allen Cabaniss, *The Univ. of Mississippi: Its First Hundred Years* (Hattiesburg: Univ. and College Press of Mississippi, 1971), 3–20.

52. F. A. P. Barnard, *Improvements Practicable in American Colleges* (Hartford, Conn.: F. C. Brownell, 1856), 3–15; Board of Trustees, Univ. of Mississippi, Minutes, 25 June 1860, in Archives and Special Collections, Williams Library, Univ. of Mississippi, Oxford,

Miss.; William Faulkner, *Absalom, Absalom!* (New York: Random House, 1936; reprint, New York: Vintage Books, 1987), 89, 115, 474. Under Barnard, the number of students at the university declined from 264 to 198. See Waddel, *Historical Discourse,* 13. Barnard's attitude toward practical education and the classics changed dramatically after the Civil War. As postbellum president of Columbia College, he proposed that colleges expand the number of courses they offered in the applied sciences and create elective systems in which students could select classical or scientific studies. Barnard argued that colleges and universities must adjust to the demands of a new age. See William J. Chute, *Damn Yankee! The First Career of Frederick A. P. Barnard, Educator, Scientist, Idealist* (Port Washington, N.Y.: National University Publications, Kennikat Press, 1978), 188–90.

53. A. B. Longstreet to ?, [30 Nov. 1859,] in "The Letters of Augustus Baldwin Longstreet," ed. J. R. Scafidel (Ph.D. diss., Univ. of South Carolina, 1976), 586–89; Joseph LeConte, *The Autobiography of Joseph LeConte,* ed. William Dallam Armes (New York: D. Appleton and Co., 1903), 155–58, 163–64; Hollis, *Univ. of South Carolina,* 1:194–211; Thomas Dyer, *Univ. of Georgia,* 89; James Moore Goode, "The Confederate University: The Forgotten Institution of the American Civil War" (Master's thesis, Univ. of Virginia, 1966), 15n.

Chapter 2. A Separate Education and the Lesson of Civil War

1. Francis H. Smith, *Introductory Address to the Corps of Cadets of VMI, on the Resumption of Academic Duties, Sept. 2, 1856* (Richmond, Va.: MacFarlane and Fergusson, 1856), 21–22; emphasis original.

2. Rachel Bryan Stillman, "Education in the Confederate States of America, 1861–1865" (Ph.D. diss., Univ. of Illinois, 1972), 65–69; "The Great Southern Convention in Charleston," *De Bow's Review* 16 (June 1854): 638–39; "Our School Books," *De Bow's Review* 3 (Apr. 1860): 434–40; Stiles, *Southern Education,* 9.

3. Thomas Jefferson to J. Bannister, Jr., 15 Oct. 1785, in Jefferson, *Works of Thomas Jefferson,* ed. Ford, 5:186–87; John Adams to Thomas Jefferson, 23 Jan. 1825, in Cappon, *Adams-Jefferson Letters,* 2:606–7.

4. W. A. Scott, *The Education We Want: A Discourse, Pronounced on the 23rd of Nov., 1844 . . .* (New Orleans, La.: Besancon, Ferguson and Co., 1845), 13–15; Aaron V. Brown, *Address Before the Literary Societies,* 7–19; Stiles, *Southern Education,* 26–27; Monteiro, *Address Delivered Before the Neotrophian Society,* 10.

5. *Catalogue of the Officers and Students of Mercer Univ., 1860–1861* (Penfield, Ga.: n.p., 1861), [p. 8]; emphasis original. See also *An Address on Southern Education,* 5.

6. "Our School Books" (1860), 435–40; "Great Southern Convention," 638–39; "Future Revolution in Southern School Books," *De Bow's Review* 5 (May–June 1861): 606–14; Anthony Vallas to G. Mason Graham, 19 July 1859, in folder 162, box 12, Anthony Vallas Letters, Walter L. Fleming Collection, Louisiana and Lower Mississippi Valley Collections, LSU Libraries, Baton Rouge. See also John S. Ezell, "A Southern Education for Southrons," *Journal of Southern History* 17 (Aug. 1951): 303–25.

7. Thacher to Gov. A. G. Brown, 24 Nov. 1847, in *Governor's Message, 1848, and Accompanying Documents,* 20. See also Edward Baptist, *Address Delivered Before the*

Trustees, Faculty, and Students of Howard College . . . Nov. 16, 1846 (Tuscaloosa, Ala.:
M. D. J. Slade, 1846), 8; *A Review of the Actions of the Trustees in the Trial of Chancellor
F. A. P. Barnard, and Defence of the Prosecutor* (N.p.: [1860]); *Record of the Testimony and
Proceedings, in the Matter of the Investigation, by the Trustees of the Univ. of Mississippi, on
the 1st and 2nd of March, 1860, of the Charges Made by H. R. Branham Against the
Chancellor of the University* (Jackson, Miss.: Mississippian Office, 1860); Keyes, Address
Delivered 1859, 19.

8. Board of Trustees, Univ. of Georgia, Minutes, 6 Nov. 1855.

9. *Louisiana Democrat* (Alexandria), 13 July 1859.

10. *Catalogue, Officers and Students, Mercer Univ., 1860–61,* 28–32. Only 10 of the
university's 153 students enrolled in the scientific course.

11. *Constitution and Statutes of the Univ. of the South . . .* (Nashville, Tenn.: Bang, Walker
and Co., 1860), article 6; Leonidas Polk, *A Letter to the Rt. Rev. Bishops . . .* (New Orleans, La.:
B. M. Norman, 1856), 1–3; "Account of the Ceremonies, &c., at the Laying of the Corner
Stone of the Univ. of the South, Wednesday, Oct. 10, 1860," in *Univ. of the South Papers,* ser.
A, no. 1 (Sewanee, Tenn.: Univ. of the South Press, 1888).

12. C. W. Sears to the Board of Administrators, Univ. of Louisiana, n.d., in J. S.
Copes, *Report of a Committee of the Board of Administrators, of the Univ. of Louisiana,
Upon the Organization of the Collegiate Department. Read, Dec. 23d, 1856,* Appendix M
(New Orleans, La.: E. C. Wharton, 1857).

13. Copes, *Report of a Committee, Univ. of Louisiana,* 6–12; John P. Dyer, *Tulane:
Biography of the University, 1834–1965* (New York: Harper and Row, 1966), 27.

14. John Hope Franklin, *The Militant South, 1800–1861* (Cambridge, Mass.: Belknap
Press of Harvard Univ. Press, 1956), 129–70; Lester Austin Webb, "The Origin of
Military Schools in the U.S. Founded in the 19th Century" (Ph.D. diss., Univ. of North
Carolina, 1958), 51–53, 73–113, 257–61.

15. Sidney Forman, *West Point: A History of the U.S. Military Academy* (New York:
Columbia Univ. Press, 1950), 25–82; James Kip Finch, *A History of the School of
Engineering, Columbia Univ.* (New York: Columbia Univ. Press, 1954), 4–5; Daniel Hovey
Calhoun, *The American Civil Engineer: Origins and Conflict* (Cambridge, Mass.: Technol-
ogy Press, Massachusetts Institute of Technology, 1960), 37–53; H. G. Good, "New
Data on Early Engineering Education," *Journal of Educational Research* 29 (Sept. 1935–
May 1936): 37; "Report of the Board of Visitors to the Secretary of War, U.S. Military
Academy, 20 June 1839," in *Army and Navy Chronicle* 9 (July 1839): 1–5; McGivern, *First
Hundred Years,* 29–38.

16. *RBVVMI,* July 1850, pp. 3–4; Francis H. Smith, *Special Report,* 1859, 17; Philip St.
George Cocke, quoted in Francis H. Smith, "Superintendent's Report," *RBVVMI,* July
1857, p. 25.

17. Francis H. Smith, "Superintendent's Report," *RBVVMI,* July 1850, pp. 7–8;
Francis H. Smith, "Superintendent's Report," *RBVVMI,* July 1857, pp. 23–24.

18. Francis H. Smith, "Superintendent's Report," *RBVVMI,* July 1856, pp. 5, 51; Francis
H. Smith, "Superintendent's Report," *RBVVMI,* July 1857, p. 25.

19. Francis H. Smith, *Introductory Address to the Corps of Cadets, 1856,* 12–13;
Francis H. Smith to Wm. H. Richardson, 14 Jan. 1854, in *RBVVMI,* 1854, p. 7; Webb,
"Origin of Military Schools," 84–99. The Louisiana institution hired the nephew of

Francis Henney Smith, Francis W. Smith, a graduate of VMI, as professor of chemistry and geology. See F. H. Smith to G. Mason Graham, 12 July 1859, in folder 150, box 11, Francis H. Smith Letters, Walter L. Fleming Collection; and Mrs. Francis W. Smith, "Lieut.-Colonel Francis W. Smith, C.S.A.: Professor of Chemistry and Geology and Commandant of Cadets at the Louisiana State Seminary," *Alumnus* [LSU] 5 (Oct. 1909): 12–14. In 1859, the Florida seminary hired George M. Edgar, a VMI graduate, as professor of mathematics and military tactics. After his resignation the following year, the school replaced him with another VMI graduate, James H. Lane. Lane also quickly resigned, and the seminary filled the post with still another VMI alumnus, J. Lucius Cross. See D. McNeill Turner to D. S. Walker, 25 Aug. 1859, in *Tallahassee Floridian and Journal*, 10 Sept. 1859. See also *Tallahassee Floridian and Journal*, 3 Sept. 1859, 7 July 1860, 22 Sept. 1860, and 1 Dec. 1860.

20. Webb, "Origin of Military Schools," 53–113, 257; Andrew, "Soldiers, Christians, and Patriots," 680. The aforementioned schools that incorporated "polytechnic" in their appellations are the Searcy Polytechnic School, Searcy, Ark., and the Southern Polytechnic Institute, La Grange, Ala. See Acts *Passed at the 12th Session of the General Assembly of the State of Arkansas,* 189; "Polytechnic Education," *De Bow's Review,* new ser., vol. 2 (Oct. 1859): 486; *Official Register of the Faculty, or Academic Staff, and Military Staff with the Rules and Regulations of the Alabama Military and Scientific Institute, Near Tuskegee, Ala.* (Tuskegee, Ala.: Macon Republican, 1845). See also the *Raleigh Register and North Carolina Gazette,* 25 Aug. 1826. According to Webster's 9th *Collegiate Dictionary* (Springfield, Mass.: Merriam-Webster, 1983), the word *polytechnic* is derived from the Greek word *polytechnos,* defined as "skilled in many arts." The word entered the English language in 1805.

21. "Polytechnic Education," 486.

22. George Mason Graham, "The Autobiography of George Mason Graham: Contributed by His Grandson, Dr. G. M. Stafford," *Louisiana Historical Quarterly* 20 (Jan. 1937): 46–47, 54–57; G. Mason Graham to W. T. Sherman, 7 Sept. 1859, in *Gen. W. T. Sherman as College President,* ed. Walter L. Fleming (Cleveland, Oh.: Arthur H. Clark, 1912), 34–37; G. Mason Graham to Gov. [Thomas O.] Moore, 26 May 1860, in Fleming, *Sherman as College President,* 215–18; William T. Sherman, *Memoirs of Gen. William T. Sherman* (New York: D. Appleton and Co., 1875), 1:146–47; *Official Register of the Officers and Cadets of the State Seminary of Learning and Military Academy of Louisiana, Near Alexandria, Parish of Rapides, for 1860–61 and 1862* (Alexandria, La.: Louisiana Democrat Office, 1862).

23. Franklin, *Militant South,* 139–40, 165–66; *North Carolina Journal of Education* 3 (Dec. 1860): 357; D. H. Hill, *A Consideration of the Sermon on the Mount* (Philadelphia: William S. and Alfred Martien, 1858), 8–9; D. H. Hill, *Elements of Algebra* (Philadelphia: J. B. Lippincott, 1857). See Hal Bridges, "D. H. Hill's Anti-Yankee Algebra," *Journal of Southern History* 22 (May 1956): 220–22.

24. Franklin, *Militant South,* 139–40, 165–66; *North Carolina Journal of Education* 3 (Dec. 1860): 357; D. H. Hill, *Sermon on the Mount,* 8–9; D. H. Hill, *Elements of Algebra;* "Southern School-Books," *De Bow's Review* 1 (Sept. 1852): 258–66; emphasis original. Marguerite Gilstrap argues that Hill is the author of this 1852 article. See Gilstrap, "Daniel Harvey Hill, Southern Propagandist," *Arkansas Historical Quarterly* 2 (Mar.–Dec. 1943): 46.

25. Franklin, *Militant South,* 165–66; Henry E. Shepard, "Gen. D. H. Hill—A Character Sketch," *Confederate Veteran* 25 (Sept. 1917): 411–12; J. W. Ratchford to D. H. Hill, Jr., n.d., in box 94.6, Daniel Harvey Hill, Jr., Papers.

26. *Tuscaloosa (Ala.) Independent Monitor,* 10 Oct. 1859.

27. Ibid.; Aug. J. Smith, James L. Kemper, and Wm. H. Richardson, "Report of Committee on Instruction," in *RBVVMI,* July 1856, p. 9. The work referred to may be Thomas R. Dew, *An Essay on Slavery* (Richmond, Va.: J. W. Randolph, 1849). See also "Southern School-books" (1852), 265–66.

28. *De Bow's Review* 3 (Feb. 1860): 239; L. C. Garland and J. J. Ormond, *[Military Department—Univ. of Alabama]* (N.p.: [1861]), 1. The title page is missing from this report located in the Alabama Collection, Gorgas Library, Univ. of Alabama, Tuscaloosa. P. O. Hebert to G. M. Graham, 14 Feb. 1859, in folder 91, box 8, P. O. Hebert Letters, Walter L. Fleming Collection, Louisiana and Lower Mississippi Valley Collections, LSU Libraries, Baton Rouge; Graham, "Autobiography," 54–57.

29. W. T. Sherman to Mrs. Sherman, 29 Oct. 1859, in Fleming, *Sherman as College President,* 43–45; W. T. Sherman to Thomas Ewing, Jr., 23 Dec. 1859, in Fleming, *Sherman as College President,* 89. It is likely that Sherman judged the intentions of the Board of Supervisors accurately. If their plans for the school included aiding secession, they hardly would have appointed an Ohioan with a reputedly abolitionist brother (U.S. Rep. John Sherman) as its superintendent, or hired two foreign professors, Anthony Vallas of Hungary and E. Berte St. Ange of France, making nonsoutherners more than half the five-member faculty. See W. L. Bringhurst, "Recollections of the Old Seminary," *Alumnus* [LSU] 5 (Oct. 1909): 15–16.

30. Simeon Colton, *An Address Delivered at His Inauguration to the Presidency of Mississippi College, July 30, A.D. 1846* (Jackson, Miss.: Southron Office, 1846), 22; Caleb Huse, *The Supplies for the Confederate Army: How They Were Obtained in Europe and How Paid For* (Boston: T. R. Marvin and Son, 1904), 5–6. On student rebellions in the antebellum South, see John A. Reesman, "A School for Honor: South Carolina College and the Guard House Riot of 1856," *South Carolina Historical Magazine* 84 (Oct. 1983): 195–213; W. G. Clark, "Promise of Education," 156; Kemp P. Battle, *History of the Univ. of North Carolina,* 1:100, 1:200–204, 1:619; and Coulter, *College Life,* 72.

31. Garland and Ormond, *[Military Department],* 5; Sellers, *History of Univ. of Alabama,* 1:258–63; W. G. Clark, "Promise of Education," 160; *Regulations for the Univ. of Alabama at Tuscaloosa . . .* (Nashville, Tenn.: Southern Methodist Publishing House, 1861), 26, 39; *Catalogue of the Officers and Students of the Univ. of Alabama for 1860–1861* (Nashville, Tenn.: Southern Methodist Publishing House, 1861).

32. *Floridian and Journal,* 10 Sept. 1859 and 7 July 1860.

33. Thornwell, *Letter to His Excellency,* 5; "South Carolina Military Academies," *Southern Quarterly Review* 10 (July 1854): 191–204.

34. F. A. P. Barnard, *Report on the Organization of Military Schools, and to the Trustees of the Univ. of Mississippi, Nov. 1861* (Jackson, Miss.: Cooper and Kimball, 1861). Published *Report of the Trustees of the Univ. of Mississippi,* 21 Nov. 1861, pp. 5, 11. The title page is missing from this report, located in the Mississippi Department of Archives and History.

35. Board of Trustees, Univ. of Mississippi, Minutes, 25 June 1860 and 1 Oct. 1861; *Report of the Trustees of the Univ. of Mississippi,* 21 Nov. 1861, pp. 8, 10–11.

36. *Report of the Trustees of the Univ. of Mississippi*, 21 Nov. 1861, pp. 7–8.

37. F. A. P. Barnard, *An Oration Delivered Before the Citizens of Tuscaloosa, Ala., July 4th, 1851* (Tuscaloosa: J. W. and J. F. Warren, 1851), 17–22, 30–32.

38. Frederick A. P. Barnard, *Memoirs of Frederick A. P. Barnard*, ed. John Fulton (New York: Macmillan, 1896), 286–89; Jefferson Davis, *Address Before the Phi Sigma and Hermean Societies, of the Univ. of Mississippi, Oxford, July 15, 1852* (Memphis, Tenn.: Appeal Book and Job Office, 1852), 4–16.

39. David F. Boyd, "William Tecumseh Sherman: First Superintendent of the Louisiana State Seminary, Now the Louisiana State Univ.," *Alumnus* [LSU] 5 (Oct. 1909): 9–10; William T. Sherman, *Memoirs*, 1:152–61, 1:164.

40. Kemp P. Battle, *History of the Univ. of North Carolina*, 1:725; Allen Alexander Lloyd and Pauline O. Lloyd, *History of the Town of Hillsborough, 1754–1982* (N.p., n.d.), 148–49, in North Carolina Collection, Univ. of North Carolina Library, Chapel Hill; *Catalogue of the Officers of North Carolina College at Mount Pleasant . . . 2nd Collegiate Year Ending July 1861 . . . Chartered Jan. 1859* (Salisbury, N.C.: North Carolina Watchman Office, 1861), 16.

41. Wayne Flynt, "Southern Higher Education and the Civil War," *Civil War History* 14 (Sept. 1968): 211–25; James Goode, "Confederate University," vi, 3–5, 51, 67–71; William H. Battle, *Address Delivered Before the Two Literary Societies of the Univ. of North Carolina, June 1st, 1865* (Raleigh, N.C.: Wm. B. Smith and Co., 1866), 5; Gianniny, "Overlooked Approach," 158; Bringhurst, "Recollections," 15–17; Henderson, *Campus of the First State University*, 181–85; Brabham, "Defining the American University," 435; Heatwole, *History of Education in Virginia*, 151–57; C. A. Graves, "General Lee at Lexington," in *Gen. Robert E. Lee After Appomattox*, ed. Frank L. Riley (New York: Macmillan, 1922), 38–39n.

42. "Agricultural Requirements of the South," *De Bow's Review* 7 (Jan. and Feb. 1862): 87–103.

43. Edward S. Joynes, *The Education of Teachers in the South: Embracing a Letter from Prof. Edw'd S. Joynes to Geo. P. Tayloe, Esq. . . .* (Lynchburg, Va.: Virginia Power-Press Book and Job Office, 1864), 4–20. Joynes's biblical quotation is from II Corinthians 5:17. See also Francis H. Smith, *Discourse on the Life and Character of Lt. Gen. Thos. J. Jackson (C.S.A.), Late Professor of Natural and Experimental Philosophy in VMI* (Richmond, Va.: Ritchie and Dunnavant, 1863), 3–5. On the importance of religion to Confederate identity, see Drew Gilpin Faust, *The Creation of Confederate Nationalism: Ideology and Identity in the Civil War South* (Baton Rouge: LSU Press, 1988), 22–40, 60–62; and Mitchell Snay, *Gospel of Disunion: Religion and Separatism in the Antebellum South* (New York: Cambridge Univ. Press, 1993), 1–2, 211–18.

44. Joynes, *Education of Teachers*, 4–20. For a view similar to that expressed by Joynes with regard to the education of Southern women, see "Education of Southern Women," De Bow's Review 6 (Oct.–Nov. 1861): 381–90; Christie Anne Farnham, *The Education of the Southern Belle: Higher Education and Student Socialization in the Antebellum South* (New York: New York Univ. Press, 1994), 3, 20, 182–83. Farnham argues that Southern parents provided their daughters with collegiate education for conservative reasons. Such education, she notes, identified them as upper-class ladies "worthy of protection, admiration, and chivalrous attention."

45. "The Dead Languages," *De Bow's Review*, new ser., vol. 5 (Mar. 1861): 316–20.

46. "Dead Languages," 317–19; Edward S. Joynes, *Education After the War: A Letter Addressed to a Member of the Southern Educational Convention, Columbia, S.C., 28th April, 1863* (Richmond, Va.: MacFarlane and Fergusson, 1863), 6–15; emphasis original.

47. *Proceedings of the Convention of Teachers of the Confederate States Assembled at Columbia, S.C., April 28th, 1863* (Marion, Ga.: Burke, Boykin and Co., 1863), 7–8; C. H. Wiley et al., *Address to the People of North Carolina* (N.p.: [ca. 1861–65]), 2–15.

48. James Goode, "Confederate University," 71–78, 83–86, 147, 170–74; Flynt, "Southern Higher Education," 216–17; L. C. Garland to Jno. G. Shorter, 17 Feb. 1863, in folder 3, box 636, Landon C. Garland Letters, William Stanley Hoole Special Collections Library, Univ. of Alabama, Tuscaloosa; L. C. Garland to T. H. Watts, 17 Mar. 1864, in folder 3, box 636, Garland Letters; L. C. Garland to Thomas H. Watts, 25 Jan. 1864, in folder 3, box 636, Garland Letters; emphasis original.

49. L. C. Garland to Gov. Shorter, 1 May 1863, in folder 3, box 636, Garland Letters; Mark Twain [Samuel L. Clemens], "The Private History of a Campaign that Failed," in *The American Claimant and Other Stories and Sketches,* by Mark Twain, 255–82 (New York: P. F. Collier and Son, 1899); Flynt, "Southern Higher Education," 217.

50. Kemp P. Battle, *History of the Univ. of North Carolina,* 1:733–37; Thomas Dyer, *Univ. of Georgia,* 106; H. A. London, "The University During the War," *Univ. of North Carolina Record* (June 1911): 78–82; Wagstaff, *Impressions,* 13; Flynt, "Southern Higher Education," 216–17; Bringhurst, "Recollections," 16; Fleming, *Louisiana State Univ., 1860–1896* (Baton Rouge: LSU Press, 1936), 109–12; Anthony Vallas, *History of the Louisiana State Seminary, 1864* (Baton Rouge: n.p., 1935), 7.

51. Paul Brandon Barringer, James Mercer Garnett, and Rosewell Page, eds., *Univ. of Virginia: Its History, Influence, Equipment and Characteristics . . .* (New York: Lewis Publishing Co., 1904), 1:131, 1:136, 1:172–73; Bringhurst, "Recollections," 15–18; "Forty Years Ago," *Alumni Bulletin of the Univ. of Virginia* 4 (Oct. 1904): 288; Lawrence A. Cremin, *American Education: The National Experience, 1783–1876* (New York: Harper and Row, 1980), 511–12; Flynt, "Southern Higher Education," 216–23; James Goode, "Confederate University," 71–78, 83–86, 147, 170–74; Wagstaff, *Impressions,* 13.

52. Board of Trustees, Univ. of Georgia, Minutes, 1 Aug. 1860, 1 July 1862, 1 July 1863, and 30 June 1864; Andrew A. Lipscomb, "Report," in Board of Trustees, Univ. of Georgia, Minutes, 4 July 1861.

53. Board of Visitors, Univ. of Virginia, Minutes, 27 May 1861 and 16 July 1861, Manuscripts Dept., Alderman Library, Univ. of Virginia, Charlottesville; *Catalogue, Univ. of Virginia, 1860–61,* 4; Gianniny, "Overlooked Approach," 155, 158; Bruce, *History of Univ. of Virginia,* 3:311–12.

54. L. C. Garland to Th. H. Watts, 29 Mar. 1864, in folder 3, box 636, Garland Letters; Francis H. Smith, *Discourse on Thos. J. Jackson,* 3–5; Francis H. Smith, *Introductory Lecture Read Before the Corps of Cadets, on the Resumption of the Academic Duties of VMI, at the Alms House, Richmond, Va., Dec. 28, 1864* (Richmond, Va.: MacFarlane and Fergusson, 1865), 1–2, 6–7.

55. "The Times and the War," *De Bow's Review* 6 (July 1861): 3; Burwell [Boykin Lewis] to Rose [Garland], 16 Jan. 1863, in box 1, Burwell Boykin Lewis Papers, Special Collections Library, Duke Univ., Durham, N.C. G. W. Smith hailed from Kentucky and John C. Pemberton from Pennsylvania. Expressions of approval for scientific generals

also appeared in the North. William T. Sherman lauded U. S. Grant's military ability as "scientific." Sherman admirers praised the modern means he used to conduct military operations. See Charles Royster, *The Destructive War: William Tecumseh Sherman, Stonewall Jackson, and the Americans* (New York: Knopf, 1991), 337, 366.

56. William LeRoy Broun, "Confederate Ordnance During the War," *Journal of the U.S. Artillery* 9 (Jan.–Feb. 1898): 1–13; P. H. Mell, "Dr. William LeRoy Broun," *Confederate Veteran* 10 (May 1902): 225; draft of William LeRoy Broun to M. L. Butler, n.d. [Sept. or Oct. 1888?], in folder 78, box 6, William LeRoy Broun Collection, University Archives, Draghon Library, Auburn Univ., Auburn, Ala. This draft is a response to M. L. Butler to William LeRoy Broun, 27 Sept. 1888, in folder 77, box 6, William LeRoy Broun Collection, Auburn. Josiah Gorgas, "Notes on the Ordnance Department of the Confederate Government," *SHSP* 12 (Jan.–Feb. 1884): 90.

57. Vandiver, *Ploughshares into Swords*; Board of Trustees, Univ. of Georgia, Minutes, 15 Oct. 1856; W. G. Clark, "Promise of Education," 159–60; Francis P. Venable, "Sketch of John William Mallet," typescript, in folder 134, box 3, Francis Preston Venable Papers, SHC-UNC; Mark Mayo Boatner III, *The Civil War Dictionary* (New York: David McKay, 1959), 88; Geo. W. Rains, *History of the Confederate Powder Works: An Address by Invitation Before the Confederate Survivors Association . . . April 26th, 1882* (Augusta, Ga.: Chronicle and Constitutionalist, 1882), 3–30; Joseph LeConte, *Autobiography*, 184–85; Capt. J. W. Mallet to Prof. Kimberly, 11 June 1862, in folder 37, box 3, Kimberly Papers; May, "Life of Buchanan," 53, 63.

58. Typescript copy of Josiah Gorgas, "Editorial Recounting Operations of the Ordnance Bureau," *Daily Richmond (Va.) Enquirer,* 24 Nov. 1864, in folder 5, box 678, Gorgas Family Papers, William Stanley Hoole Special Collections Library, Univ. of Alabama, Tuscaloosa; William LeRoy Broun, "Confederate Ordnance," 1–13; Gorgas, "Notes on the Ordnance Department," 67–94; J. W. Mallet, "Work of the Ordnance Bureau," *SHSP* 37 (Jan.–Dec. 1909): 1–20; Walter L. Fleming, "Industrial Development in Alabama During the Civil War," *South Atlantic Quarterly* 3 (July 1904): 260–72; Emory M. Thomas, *Revolutionary Experience,* 87–99, 135–36.

Chapter 3. Progress and the Academic Origins of the New South

1. Charles Forster Smith, "Southern Colleges and Schools," *Atlantic Monthly* 54 (Oct. 1884): 543. Stillman, "Education in the Confederate States," 417–18; Flynt, "Southern Higher Education," 218–25; Stetar, "Development of Southern Higher Education," 35, 113.

2. James Goode, "Confederate University," 52; *Catalogue of the Trustees, Faculty, and Students of the Univ. of North Carolina, 1860–61* (Chapel Hill, N.C.: John B. Neathery Book, Job and Card, 1861), 8–9; Mrs. Francis W. Smith, "Lieut.-Colonel Francis W. Smith, C.S.A.: Professor," 12–14; Flynt, "Southern Higher Education," 218–25; *Report of the Trustees of the Univ. of Mississippi, 21 Nov. 1861,* 5–7; Arkansas Industrial Univ., "Official Report of Col. Geo. M. Edgar, President, Fayetteville, June 7, 1885," MS, in box 2, Board of Trustee Records, 1868–1934, University Archives, Univ. of Arkansas, Fayetteville; Eugene Hilgard, "A Confederate Scientist at War," ed. Walter E. Pittman, *Civil War Times Illustrated* 25 (Mar. 1986): 20–25; John K. Bettersworth, "'The Cow in

the Front Yard': How a Land-Grant College Grew in Mississippi," *Agricultural History* 53 (Jan. 1979): 62; Joseph LeConte, *Autobiography*, 243.

3. Donald S. Frazier, "Losses and Numbers," in *Encyclopedia of the Confederacy*, ed. Richard N. Current (New York: Simon and Schuster, 1993), 1:337–40; Emory M. Thomas, *The Confederate Nation, 1861–1865* (New York: Harper and Row, 1978), 207–11; Charles R. Wilson, *Baptized in Blood*, 143–60; Derrell Roberts, "The Univ. of Georgia and Georgia's G.I. Bill," *Georgia Historical Quarterly* 49 (Dec. 1965): 418–23; Fleming, *Louisiana State Univ.*, 142–48; Cabaniss, *Univ. of Miss.: First Hundred Years*, 64.

4. The 14 schools are Alabama A&M, Univ. of Alabama, Arkansas Industrial Univ., Clemson A&M, Univ. of Georgia, LSU, Mississippi A&M, Univ. of Mississippi, North Carolina A&M, Univ. of North Carolina, Univ. of South Carolina, Univ. of Tennessee, Texas A&M, and Virginia A&M. The survey covers the years 1878–96 and includes only those acting presidents or chancellors whose positions were made permanent. Only the Univs. of Texas and Virginia, which were governed by faculty chairs during this period, are not included among state universities and A&M colleges. However, at least one faculty chair at the Univ. of Virginia, mathematics professor Charles S. Venable (1870–73, 1886–88), served as a Confederate officer. The State of Georgia divided its Morrill grant among a number of branch campuses of the Univ. of Georgia. The leaders of these institutions are excluded. Florida did not establish any stable state institutions of collegiate grade until after 1900. See William G. Dodd, *History of West Florida Seminary* (Tallahassee, Fla.: n.p., 1952), 44–99. Of those schools surveyed, only the Univ. of North Carolina (two administrations) and the Univ. of Tennessee (two administrations) had no Confederate veterans serve as president. However, Kemp P. Battle, North Carolina's president from 1876 to 1891, had worked as the chief administrative officer of a railroad which primarily hauled coal from Chatham County, N.C., to Confederate ordnance factories. See Kemp P. Battle, *Memories of Tar Heel*, 172–98. Survey compiled from: Hesseltine, *Confederate Leaders*, 77–92; Thomas Dyer, *Univ. of Georgia*, 118–33; *Auburn's First 100 Years, 1856–1956* (N.p.: Auburn Univ., [1956]); Cabaniss, *Univ. of Miss.: First Hundred Years*, 81–120; Fleming, *Louisiana State Univ.*, 130–475; Hollis, *Univ. of South Carolina*, 2:94–196; Sellers, *History of Univ. of Alabama*, 1:325–40; Duncan Lyle Kinnear, *The First Hundred Years: A History of Virginia Polytechnic Institute and State Univ.* (Blacksburg, Va.: VPI Educational Foundation, 1972), 95–134; Robert A. Leflar, *The First 100 Years: Centennial History of the Univ. of Arkansas* (Fayetteville: Univ. of Arkansas Foundation, 1972), 37–67; Alice Elizabeth Reagan, *North Carolina State Univ.: A Narrative History* (Ann Arbor, Mich.: Edwards Brothers, 1987), 2; Robert S. Lambert, "The Builder of a College: Henry Aubrey Strode, 1890–1893," in *Tradition: A History of the Presidency of Clemson Univ.*, ed. Donald M. McKale (Macon, Ga.: Mercer Univ. Press, 1988), 21; John L. Idol, Jr., "The Controversial Humanities Professor, Edwin Boon Craighead, 1893–1897," in *Tradition: A History of the Presidency of Clemson Univ.*, ed. Donald M. McKale (Macon, Ga.: Mercer Univ. Press, 1988), 34; Henry C. Dethloff, *A Centennial History of Texas A&M Univ., 1876–1976* (College Station: Texas A&M Univ. Press, 1975), 1:39–70. On the prevalence of veterans in positions of leadership at Southern schools, see also Andrew, "Soldiers, Christians, and Patriots," 702–3; and Hesseltine, *Confederate Leaders*, 77–92. On the

Univ. of Virginia, see Virginius Dabney, *Mr. Jefferson's University: A History* (Charlottesville: Univ. Press of Virginia, 1981), 30. On the Univ. of Texas, see Elizabeth Silverthorne, *Ashbel Smith of Texas: Pioneer, Patriot, Statesman, 1805–1886* (College Station: Texas A&M Univ. Press, 1982), 217–22.

5. Andrew, "Soldiers, Christians, and Patriots," 703; Fleming, *Louisiana State Univ.,* 142–48; Cabaniss, *Univ. of Miss.: First Hundred Years,* 64; Virginius Dabney, *Mr. Jefferson's University,* 29–30; Thomas Dyer, *Univ. of Georgia,* 118–33; *Auburn's First 100 Years,* 6–14; Leflar, *First 100 Years,* 37–67; Dethloff, *Centennial History of Texas A&M,* 39–70; Hollis, *Univ. of South Carolina,* 2:21; Sellers, *History of Univ. of Alabama,* 1:325–40; Brabham, "Defining the American University," 437; Kemp P. Battle, *Sketches of the History of the Univ. of North Carolina,* 54; Boatner, *Civil War Dictionary,* 88; Charles R. Wilson, *Baptized in Blood,* 143–60.

6. Unsigned fragment of letter to Samuel H. Lockett, 3 Oct. 1879, in folder 27 box 2, Samuel Henry Lockett Papers, SHC-UNC; William Preston Johnston to R. E. Lee, 26 Oct. 1866, in Robert Edward Lee Papers, Washington and Lee Univ., Lexington, Va.; William LeRoy Broun, application for bankruptcy, 10 Mar. 1869, U.S. District Court for the Northern Georgia District, in box 2, folder 22, William LeRoy Broun Collection, Auburn; R. E. Lee to Wm. M. Green, 23 Sept. 1868, in Robert Edward Lee Papers; "Richard Morton Venable," *LSU Quarterly* 6 (Apr. 1911): 86; Harrison Hale, *Univ. of Arkansas, 1871–1948* (Fayetteville: Univ. of Arkansas Alumni Association, 1948), 80; Edmund Berkeley and Dorothy Smith Berkeley, *A Yankee Botanist in the Carolinas: The Rev. Moses Ashley Curtis, D.D. (1808–1872)* (Berlin: J. Cramer, 1986), 208–9. A number of former Confederate generals or politicians were employed by insurance agencies. (1) *Stephen D. Lee.* See "S. D. Lee, Superintendent of Agencies, Alabama Gold Life Insurance Company," letterhead, n.d., in John Francis Hamtramck Claiborne Papers, Selected Items, University Archives, Mississippi State Univ., Starkville, on microfilm provided by SHC-UNC. (2) *James Longstreet.* See Gen. James Longstreet, president, Great Southern and Western Life and Accident Insurance Co., New Orleans, La., to Stephen D. Lee, 2 May 1866, in Stephen D. Lee Papers. Microfilm version available at University Archives, Mississippi State Univ., Starkville. Original MS collection in Stephen Dill Lee Papers, SHC-UNC. (3) *D. H. Maury.* See Gen. D. H. Maury, Special Agent of the Equitable Life Assurance Society, New York City, to Stephen D. Lee, n.d., in Stephen D. Lee Papers. (4) *A. P. Stewart.* See Hesseltine, *Confederate Leaders,* 80. (5) *John B. Gordon.* See Jno. B. Gordon, president, Southern Life Insurance Co., to William LeRoy Broun, 2 Dec. 1868, in folder 21, box 2, William LeRoy Broun Collection, Auburn. (6) *Braxton Bragg.* See Bragg to Josiah Gorgas, 22 June 1870, in folder 13, box 674, Josiah Gorgas, Incoming Correspondence (Various), 1839–1878, Gorgas Family Papers. On the profitability of life insurance companies in the postbellum U.S., see Bledstein, *Culture of Professionalism,* 46.

7. J. Randolph Tucker, *Life and Character of Col. William Allan, Late Principal of McDonogh School: An Address Delivered Nov. 21, 1889* (McDonogh, Md.: Published by Boys of the School, 1889), 9; Jefferson Davis to Edmund Kirby Smith, 1 Sept. 1875, in folder 56, box 4, Edmund Kirby Smith Papers, SHC-UNC; Sellers, *History of Univ. of Alabama,* 1:327; R. E. Colston to William LeRoy Broun, 4 July 1872, in folder 35, box 3, William LeRoy Broun Collection, Auburn; Alexander M. Clayton to Matthew Fontaine

Maury, 22 Aug. 1869, in vol. 31, Matthew Fontaine Maury Papers, Library of Congress, Washington, D.C.; James H. Lane to Robert E. Lee, 20 Nov. 1865, in Robert Edward Lee Papers; William Preston Johnston to Robert E. Lee, 26 Oct. 1866, in Robert Edward Lee Papers.

8. J. W. Clapp, *Address Delivered at the Univ. of Mississippi, on Behalf of the Board of Trustees on Commencement Day, June 29, 1866* (Memphis, Tenn.: Public Ledger Office, n.d.), 12.

9. William Preston Johnston, *Problems of Southern Civilization: An Address Delivered Before the Polytechnic Institute of Alabama, . . . June 10, 1891* (N.p.: [1891]), 7; Wm. LeRoy Broun to Wm. Preston Johnston, 14 Feb. 1891, in folder 21, box 30, William Preston Johnston Collection, Manuscripts and Rare Books, Howard-Tilton Memorial Library, Tulane Univ., New Orleans, La.; William LeRoy Broun, "Confederate Ordnance," 11; Atticus G. Haygood, *The New South: Gratitude, Amendment, Hope. A Thanksgiving Sermon for Nov. 25, 1880* (Oxford, Ga.: n.p., 1880), 8. See also D. H. Hill, *The Old South: An Address . . . June 6, 1887, Before the Society of the Army and Navy of the Confederate States in the State of Maryland* (Baltimore, Md.: Andrew J. Conlon, 1887), 4.

10. D. H. Hill, *Old South,* 18–19; D. H. Hill, *The Confederate Soldier in the Ranks: An Address . . . Before the Virginia Division of the Association of the Army of Northern Virginia, . . . Oct. 22, 1885 . . .* (Richmond, Va.: Wm. Ellis Jones, Book and Job, 1885), 6; D. H. H. [Daniel Harvey Hill], "Education," pt. 1, *Land We Love* 1 (May 1866): 9; D. H. H. [Daniel Harvey Hill], "Education," pt. 3, *Land We Love* 1 (Aug. 1866): 235–39; *Official Register of LSU and A&M College, 1877–1878* (New Orleans, La.: A. W. Hyatt, 1878), 46; emphasis original. A. J. Peeler, Address Before the State A&M College of Texas, Thursday, June 26, 1877 (Austin, Tex.: Statesman Steam Book and Job Office, 1877), 22; Sid S. Johnson, Texans Who Wore the Gray [Tyler, Tex.: n.p., 1907], 71–72. See also Stephen D. Lee, "The Seed Corn of the Southern Confederacy," clipping from an unidentified newspaper, in Blewett Lee Scrapbook, vol. 1, Stephen D. Lee Museum, Columbus, Miss.

11. D. H. H. [Daniel Harvey Hill], "Education," pt. 2, *Land We Love* 1 (June 1866): 90–91. See also Francis H. Smith, *Gymnastic and Technical Education in VMI . . . An Introductory Lecture on the Resumption of Academic Exercises in the Institution, Sept. 5th, 1871* (New York: D. Van Nostrand, 1871), 20–21; Wm. M. Burwell to Matthew F. Maury, 5 Jan. 1869, in vol. 28, Matthew Fontaine Maury Papers; W. M. Burwell, *Address Delivered Before the Faculty and Students of LSU, on Wed., 25th June, 1871 . . .* (N.p.: Price Current, [1871?]), 7–8.

12. Samuel H. Lockett, "Technical Education," MS, n.d. [ca. 1873], in folder 52, box 3, ser. A, Samuel Henry Lockett Papers, SHC-UNC. Emphasis original.

13. Stephen D. Lee, "Details of Important Work by Two Telegraph Operators, Christmas Eve, 1862, Which Prevented the Almost Complete Surprise of Confederate Army at Vicksburg," clipping from an unidentified newspaper, in Blewett Lee Scrapbook, vol. 1; Stephen D. Lee, "Address at Industrial Institute and College" [ca. 1900], clipping from an unidentified newspaper, in Blewett Lee Scrapbook, vol. 1.

14. D. F. Boyd, "Sherman," 10; Spencer Ford, "Address," Battalion [Texas A&M] (Jan. 1898): 22–23. See also D. H. H. [Daniel Harvey Hill], "Education," pt. 3, pp. 238–39.

15. D. H. H. [Daniel Harvey Hill], "Education," pt. 1, pp. 3–4, 9.

16. Typescript copy of Isaac Taylor Tichenor, *6th Annual Report to the Board of*

Directors of the A&M College of Alabama, 25 June 1877, on microfilm, Isaac Taylor Tichenor Papers, Special Collections, Draghon Library, Auburn Univ., Auburn, Ala. See also manuscript fragment entitled "Southern Agriculture," in folder 4, box 2, William C. Stubbs Papers, SHC-UNC. Although the manuscript's author is not identified, the writer refers to his Kentucky birth, and large passages bear wording identical to Tichenor, *6th Report,* cited above. Tichenor befriended and worked with William C. Stubbs (in whose collection the manuscript is found) at Alabama A&M. Thus evidence strongly suggests that the manuscript originated with Tichenor. See typescript copy of Isaac Taylor Tichenor, *5th Annual Report to the Board of Directors of the A&M College of Alabama, 8 Jan. 1877,* on microfilm, in Tichenor Papers.

17. Francis H. Smith, *Introductory Address to the Corps of Cadets of VMI, on the Resumption of the Academic Exercises, Sept. 10, 1866* (N.p.: Published by Order of the Board, [1866]), 10; D. H. H. [Daniel Harvey Hill], "Education," pt. 1, pp. 3–4, 9–11; D. H. H. [Daniel Harvey Hill], "Education," pt. 3, pp. 235–39.

18. Edward S. Joynes to M. F. Maury, 10 Nov. 1869, in vol. 32, Matthew Fontaine Maury Papers; M. F. Maury, "Inaugural Address of the President of the Univ. of Alabama," clipping from an unidentified newspaper, in scrapbook [1871], vol. 1, Eugene Allen Smith Collection, William Stanley Hoole Special Collections Library, Univ. of Alabama, Tuscaloosa; J. W. Mallet, *Chemistry Applied to the Arts: A Lecture Delivered Before the Univ. of Virginia, May 30, 1868* (Lynchburg, Va.: Schaffter and Bryant, 1868), 13–14.

19. William Preston Johnston, "Lecture First: The Uses of History," MS [ca. 1870s], in folder 1, box 48, Johnston Collection; R. E. Lee to Cyrus H. McCormick, 28 Nov. 1865, in copy of Letter Book I, Robert Edward Lee Papers; see also R. E. Lee to J. B. Baldwin, 22 Nov. 1865, in Robert Edward Lee Papers; Ralph W. Donnelly, "Scientists of the Confederate Nitre and Mining Bureau," *Civil War History* 2 (Dec. 1956): 88–89; George Templeton Strong, *The Diary of George Templeton Strong,* ed. Allan Nevins and Milton Halsey Thomas (New York: Macmillan, 1952), 2:200, 2:326–27. McCulloh also spelled his name "McCulloch," which is the traditional spelling of the family name. He used "McCulloh" while a professor at Columbia College (1854–63) and both spellings while at Washington College. He consistently used the third "c" in his name by the late 1870s. See Milton Halsey Thomas, "Professor McCulloh of Princeton, Columbia, and Points South," *Princeton Univ. Literary Chronicle* 9 (Nov. 1947): 18n; *Catalogue of the Washington College, Va., for the Collegiate Year Ending June, 1869* (Baltimore, MD.: John Murphy and Company, 1869), 6; R. S. McCulloch to R. E. Lee, 18 Feb. 1869, in Robert Edward Lee Papers, University Archives, Washington & Lee Univ., Lexington, Va.; R. E. Lee to R. S. McCulloh, 28 Sept. 1869, in Robert E. Lee Letters, Mississippi Department of Archives and History, Jackson; and correspondence between McCulloch and D. F. Boyd in folder 116, box 10, Richard S. McCullock [sic] Letters and Related Items, Walter L. Fleming Collection.

20. Donnelly, "Scientists," 88–89; Milton Halsey Thomas, "Professor McCulloh," 23–27.

21. Josiah Gorgas, Journals, MS, 17 Jan. 1871, in folder 3, box 676, Gorgas Family Papers; James L. Morrison, Jr., *"The Best School in the World": West Point, the Pre–Civil War Years, 1833–1866* (Kent, Oh.: Kent State Univ., 1986), 97; Forman, *West Point,* 139.

Gorgas's journals are available in print; see Josiah Gorgas, *The Journals of Josiah Gorgas, 1857–1878,* ed. Sarah Woolfolk Wiggins (Tuscaloosa: Univ. of Alabama Press, 1995).

22. Frank L. Riley, "What General Lee Read After the War," in *General Robert E. Lee After Appomattox,* ed. Frank L. Riley (New York: Macmillan, 1922), 158; William Preston Johnston, *An Address Before the Louisiana State Public School Teachers Association . . . Dec. 28th, 1893* (New Orleans, La.: L. Graham and Son, 1894), 16; D. F. Boyd, "Some Ideas on Education: The True Solution of the Question of 'Color' in Our Schools, Colleges, and Universities, etc.," MS, 1875, in folder 7, box 2, Walter L. Fleming Collection. Wm. LeRoy Broun, *Science-Education: An Address . . . Delivered at the Annual Commencement of the A&M College of Alabama* (Auburn, Ala.: n.p., 1880), 7–8; William Preston Johnston, *High Schools in Louisiana and Tulane Univ.* (New Orleans, La.: n.p., 1893), 5–6.

23. J. L. M. Curry, *Address Before the Alabama Polytechnic Institute, Auburn, Ala., June 14th, 1899* (Montgomery, Ala.: Brown Printing Co., 1899), 21–22; D. H. Hill, *University Address by Gen. D. H. Hill of Georgia, Delivered . . . June 20, 1888, Before the Regents, Faculty, and Students of the Univ. of Texas* (Austin, Tex.: State Printing Office, 1888), 6; Francis H. Smith, *Gymnastic and Technical Education,* 20–21; Kemp P. Battle, "The Head and the Hand: The Practical Side of College Life—Problems of the Day. Anniversary Oration Before the Students of South Carolina College, Delivered June 23, 1886," typescript, in folder 345, box 28, Charles W. Dabney Papers; Tichenor, *6th Report;* Benjamin H. Hill, [Sr.], "Speech Delivered Before the Alumni Society of the Univ. of Georgia . . . July 31, 1871," in Benjamin H. Hill, [Sr.], *Senator Benjamin H. Hill of Georgia: His Life, Speeches, and Writings,* comp. Benjamin H. Hill, Jr. (Atlanta, Ga.: T. H. P. Bloodworth, 1893), 347; Hilary Herbert, *An Address Delivered Before the Society of Alumni of the Univ. of Virginia, On Commencement Day, June 29, 1887* (Lynchburg, Va.: J. P Bell and Co., 1887), 8–9; B. M. Palmer, *The Address . . . Delivered on the First Day of the New Year and Century in the First Presbyterian Church, New Orleans, La.* [N.p.: 1900?], 6–16. Title page is missing on the copy in Rare Book Room, Gorgas Library, Univ. of Alabama, Tuscaloosa.

24. R. L. Dabney, *The New South: A Discourse Delivered at the Annual Commencement of Hampden-Sidney College, June 15, 1882, Before the Philanthropic and Union Literary Societies* (Raleigh, N.C.: Edwards, Broughton and Co., 1883), 12. The diplomat referred to is Aleksandr Mikhaylovich Gorchakov, Russia's Imperial Chancellor (1868–82) and Minister of Foreign Affairs (1856–82); R. L. Dabney to D. H. Hill, in folder 2, box 1, Daniel Harvey Hill Papers, SHC-UNC; D. H. H. [Daniel Harvey Hill], "Education," pt. 1, p. 11; Johnston, *Problems of Southern Civilization,* 5.

25. William Preston Johnston, *Decoration Day [Address] at the Graves of Lee and Jackson, June 2nd, 1875* (Lexington, Va.: n.p., 1875); Tichenor, 6th Report. See also D. H. Hill, *Confederate Soldier,* 4, 18–19; D. H. Hill, *Old South,* 4; William LeRoy Broun, "Address Delivered on Memorial Day Before the Students of the Alabama Polytechnic Institute in May, 1891," in William LeRoy Broun, *Dr. William LeRoy Broun,* comp. Thomas L. Broun (New York: Neale Publishing Co., 1912), 232–36; Clapp, *Address Delivered,* 4; Benjamin H. Hill, "Address Delivered Before the Southern Historical Society, at Atlanta, Ga., Feb. 18, 1874," in B. H. Hill, *Sen. Benjamin H. Hill of Georgia,* 406. On the defensiveness and sensitivity of white Southerners concerning their defeat, see Waldo W. Braden, "'Repining Over an Irrevocable Past': The Ceremonial Orator in a Defeated

Society, 1865–1900," in *Rhetoric of the People: "Is There Any Better or Equal Hope in the World?,"* ed. Harold Barret (Amsterdam, Netherlands: Rodopi NV, 1974), 273–301; and Gaines M. Foster, *Ghosts of the Confederacy: Defeat, the Lost Cause, and the Emergence of the New South* (New York: Oxford Univ. Press, 1987), 20–35, 115–19. On the importance of honor to Southerners and other Americans, see Cash, *Mind of the South;* Bertram Wyatt-Brown, *Honor and Violence in the Old South* (New York: Oxford Univ. Press, 1986); and Gerald Linderman, *Embattled Courage: The Experience of Combat in the American Civil War* (New York: Free Press, 1987). Confederate veterans transmitted their sensitivity to defeat to subsequent generations of Southerners. Not even W. J. Cash proved immune. See Cash, *Mind of the South,* 69.

26. D. H. Hill, *Confederate Soldier,* 18–19; Gorgas, Journals, 31 Aug. 1865. See also "Address of Prof. Wm. Preston Johnston of Washington and Lee Univ., Before the Educational Association of Virginia, at Staunton, Va., July 10, 1872," clipping from an unidentified newspaper, in folder 24, box 15, Johnston Collection; A. C. Avery, *Memorial Address on Life and Character of Lieutenant General D. H. Hill, May 10th, 1893* (Raleigh, N.C.: Edwards and Broughton, 1893), 12; Francis H. Smith, *Introductory Address, 1866,* 12; and Herman Hattaway, *General Stephen D. Lee* (Jackson: Univ. Press of Mississippi, 1976), 207.

27. Gorgas, Journals, 31 Aug. 1865.

28. William LeRoy Broun, "Memorial Address," typescript dated Apr. 1896, in folder 8, box 1, Leroy Stafford Boyd Collection, University Archives, Draghon Library, Auburn Univ.; D. F. Boyd, "Sherman," 4.

29. J. L. M. Curry, "Education at the South," *Texas Journal of Education* 2 (Mar. 1882): 80–82; Haygood, *New South,* 8–9; B. B. Lewis, *Baccalaureate Address Delivered at 50th Annual Commencement of the Univ. of Alabama, July 7, 1881* (N.p., n.d.), 2–4, in Alabama Collection; Dabney Lipscomb, "General Stephen D. Lee: His Life, Character, and Services," *Publications of the Mississippi Historical Society* 10 (1909): 30–31; Johnston, *Problems of Southern Civilization,* 7–9; William Preston Johnston, *The Work of the University in America: An Address Before the South Carolina College on Commencement Day, June 25th, 1884* (Columbia, S.C.: Presbyterian Publishing House, 1884), 4–5, 19; Phillip S. Paludan, *"A People's Contest": The Union and the Civil War, 1861–1865* (New York: Harper and Row, 1988), 372–74; Abraham Lincoln, "Second Inaugural Address," 4 Mar. 1865, in *The Collected Works of Abraham Lincoln,* ed. by Roy P. Basler (New Brunswick, N.J.: Rutgers Univ. Press, 1953), 8:332–33. On the symbiosis of Providence and progress, see Spadafora, *Idea of Progress in Britain,* 4, 104, 369. On the concept that the Civil War allowed the U.S. to continue its progressivist destiny, see Royster, *Destructive War,* 383–85.

30. Lewis, *Baccalaureate Address, 1881,* 4; Tichenor, *5th Report;* B. B. Lewis, *Memorial Address . . . At the Laying of the Memorial Stone of the New University Hall, May 5, 1884; and Baccalaureate Address, Delivered on Commencement Day, June 18, 1884* (N.p., n.d.), 4, in Alabama Collection; Curry, "Education at the South," 80–82; William Preston Johnston, "Higher Education in the South," *Regents' Bulletin* 9 (Aug. 1892): 12–25, in folder 21, box 49, Johnston Collection; Joseph W. Taylor, *The Young Men of the New South: Their Education, Duties and Rewards. An Address Delivered before the Phi Sigma and Hermean Societies, at Commencement of the Univ. of Mississippi, on June 23, 1869 . . .*

(Memphis, Tenn.: Hite and Corwine, 1869); Clapp, *Address Delivered*, 5. See also Haygood, *New South*, 12.

31. See Edward L. Ayers, *The Promise of the New South: Life After Reconstruction* (New York: Oxford Univ. Press, 1992); Paul M. Gaston, *The New South Creed: A Study in Southern Mythmaking* (New York: Alfred A. Knopf, 1970); Dewey Grantham, *Southern Progressivism: The Reconciliation of Progress and Tradition* (Knoxville: Univ. of Tennessee Press, 1983); Howard N. Rabinowitz, *The First New South* (Arlington Heights, Ill.: Harlan Davidson, 1992); Jonathan M. Wiener, *Social Origins of the New South: Alabama, 1860–1885* (Baton Rouge: LSU Press, 1978); Woodward, *Origins of the New South*.

32. Gaston, *New South Creed*, 105–6.

33. D. F. Boyd, *Address of Superintendent, Louisiana State Seminary, to the Graduating Class, Delivered June 30, 1869* (New Orleans, La.: Jas. A. Gresham, 1869), 10; Henry D. Clayton, "Commencement Address," typescript, n.d. [ca. 1886–89], in folder 9, box 318, Henry DeLamar Clayton Collection, William Stanley Hoole Special Collections Library, Univ. of Alabama, Tuscaloosa; Horace Harding to the Board of Trustees of the Univ. of Alabama, 17 Oct. 1876, in folder 1520, box 7, Record Group 1, Trustee Records, University Archives, Univ. of Alabama, Tuscaloosa; Walter B. Hill to Mary Clay Hill, [3?] July 1869, in Walter B. Hill, *College Life in the Reconstruction South: Walter B. Hill's Student Correspondence, Univ. of Georgia, 1869–1871*, ed. G. Ray Mathis, Univ. of Georgia Libraries Miscellanea Publications No. 10 (Athens: Univ. of Georgia Libraries, 1974), 97; "Address of Stephen D. Lee," *Jackson (Miss.) Clarion-Ledger*, 20 June 1889; Wm. Preston Johnston, *The University: Its Dangers and the Remedies. An Address . . . at the Commencement of the Univ. of Texas, June 14, 1884* (Austin, Tex.: Warner and Co., 1884), 22; Lewis, *Baccalaureate Address, 1881*, 3–4; Samuel H. Lockett, "Immigration to Louisiana. Her Fitness for White Immigrants, How to Get Them," MS [ca. 1867–73], in folder 49, box 3, Samuel Henry Lockett Papers, SHC-UNC; *Official Register of the Louisiana State Seminary . . . 1869* (New Orleans: n.p., 1869), 16–17; Mallet, *Chemistry Applied to the Arts*, 4–7; M. F. Maury, "Circular," in vol. 26, Matthew Fontaine Maury Papers; Ashbel Smith, "Address on the Laying of the Corner Stone of the Univ. of Texas," in *Catalogue of the Univ. of Texas for 1883–1884* (Austin, Tex.: E. W. Swindells, 1884), 55; *Montgomery Advertiser*, 22 Apr. 1886; Tichenor, *5th Report* and *6th Report;* Francis H. Smith, *Introductory Address, 1866*, 10; William LeRoy Broun, "Industrial Education," in *Report of the Board of Supervisors of LSU . . . 1877–78* (New Orleans, La.: Office of the Democrat, 1878), appendix, p. 17.

34. John T. Morgan, *Address . . . Before the Erosophic and Philomathic Societies of the Univ. of Alabama, July 6th, 1875* ([Tuscaloosa, Ala.?]: n.p., 1875). The biblical reference is to Proverbs 3:2. Boatner, *Civil War Dictionary*, 566–67; Haygood, *New South*, 9, 12. See Exodus 13:21 and 14:19, 24. Joseph W. Taylor, *Young Men of the New South*, 23. Compare with Exodus 3:8 and Revelation 22:20. See also Robert A. Hardaway, "Condition of the South," typescript made from a clipping from an unidentified newspaper in Robert A. Hardaway, "Book," 104–7, compiled between 1870 and 1900, on microfilm #3006, SHC-UNC. On the South's religious tradition, see Anne C. Loveland, *Southern Evangelicals and the Social Order, 1800–1860* (Baton Rouge: LSU Press, 1980), 264–65; Faust, *Creation of Confederate Nationalism*, 22–33; and Charles Reagan Wilson, "The Religion of the Lost Cause: Ritual and Organization of the Southern Civil Religion," *Journal of Southern History* 46 (May 1980): 219–38. On the

integral relationship between millennialism and the idea of progress, see Tuveson, *Redeemer Nation;* and Ekirch, *Idea of Progress.*

35. Edmund Kirby Smith, untitled MS draft of commencement address for an unnamed school for girls, n.d., in folder 67, box 5, Edmund Kirby Smith Papers; A. G. Clopton, "From the Eulogy on the Life and Character of Ashbel Smith," in *Catalogue of the Univ. of Texas for 1886–87* (Austin, Tex.: State Printing Office, 1887), 105; [William] LeRoy Broun, "Technical Education: Baccalaureate Address of President LeRoy Broun, of the A&M College," *Montgomery Weekly Advertiser,* 7 July 1885, clipping in folder 21, box 3, McBryde Family Papers, SHC-UNC; William LeRoy Broun, "Industrial Education," 17; William Preston Johnston, "Address Before the Camera Club," MS, in folder 20, box 49, Johnston Collection. See also Mallet, *Chemistry Applied to the Arts,* 4–7; [Francis Henry Smith], untitled MS draft of a speech on technical education, n.d., in box 1, Harrison, Smith, and Kent Family Papers, Manuscripts Department, Alderman Library, Univ. of Virginia, Charlottesville; Benjamin H. Hill, [Sr.], "Speech Delivered Before the Alumni, July 31, 1871," 335; Maury, "Inaugural Address."

36. Burwell, *Address at LSU, 1871,* 7; Benjamin H. Hill, "Speech Delivered 1871," 340; Eugene W. Hilgard, *Address on Progressive Agriculture and Industrial Education, Delivered Before the Mississippi A&M Fair Association, at Jackson, Nov. 14th, 1872* (Jackson, Miss.: Clarion Book and Job Office, 1873), 5; William T. Sutherlin, *Address Delivered Before the Mechanics' Association of Danville, Va., Mar. 11, 1867* (Richmond, Va.: Enquirer Steam Presses, 1867), 26–27; Morgan, *Address to Erosophic and Philomathic, 1875,* 4–6; Tichenor, *5th Report;* Harding to Board of Trustees, Univ. of Alabama, 17 Oct. 1876; Lewis, *Baccalaureate Address, 1881,* 3; John Goode, quoted in Kemp P. Battle, *History of the Univ. of North Carolina,* 2:385.

37. John Lee Buchanan, "Address Delivered before the Calliopean and Hermesian Societies, June 16th, 1874," in May, "Life of Buchanan," appendix, pp. 98, 106; emphasis original. Kinnear, First Hundred Years, 99–110; Wm. LeRoy Broun, *Improvements Required in Southern Colleges: Read Before the Teachers' Association of Georgia, in Macon, Dec. 19th, 1867* (Macon, Ga.: J. W. Burke and Co., 1868), 3n. See also Andrew A. Lipscomb, "Report," in Board of Trustees, Univ. of Georgia, Minutes, 25 July 1871; and William H. McGuffey, professor of moral philosophy at the Univ. of Virginia, quoted in Herbert, *Address Before Univ. of Virginia,* 8.

38. Joseph W. Taylor, *Young Men of the New South,* 10; D. F. Boyd, *Address of Superintendent, 1869;* Burwell, *Address at LSU, 1871,* 7; Hilgard, *Address on Progressive Agriculture,* 11–12, 26–31; emphasis original. Concerning the human effort necessary to bring about the millennium, see Cremin, *American Education: National Experience,* 17–18, 36–37, 57.

39. William LeRoy Broun, *Science-Education,* 14–15; Burwell, *Address at LSU, 1871,* 7. Benjamin H. Hill, [Sr.], "Speech Delivered Before the Alumni, July 31, 1871," 335; *Jackson (Miss.) Clarion,* 23 June 1886. See also David F. Boyd, "Appeal to the People of Louisiana," in *Official Register of LSU . . . 1871–1872* (New Orleans, La.: A. W. Hyatt, 1872), 74–75.

40. Harding to the Board of Trustees, 17 Oct. 1876; William LeRoy Broun, "Industrial Education," 27. Compare with D. F. Boyd, "Sherman," 10. On the friendship between Boyd and Broun, see their correspondence in box 7, folder 57, William LeRoy

Broun Letters, Walter L. Fleming Collection, LSU; and in the William LeRoy Broun Collection, Auburn.

41. Bartholomew Egan, *Address Delivered at the Commencement Exercises of the Louisiana State Seminary and Military Academy* (Alexandria, La.: n.p., 1866), 5–7; Peeler, *Address at Texas A&M, 1877,* 2; Josiah Granville Leach, *History of the Bringhurst Family, with Notes on the Clarkson, De Peyster and Boude Families* (Bossier City, La.: Everett Companies, 1989), 66, 83–84; Andrew B. Booth, ed., *Records of Louisiana Confederate Soldiers and Louisiana Commands* (Spartanburg, S.C.: Reprint Co., 1984), 1:118; Bringhurst quoted in typescript copy of "Davis Memorial Day," *College Journal* [Texas A&M] 1 (Dec. 1889): 11–13, in W. L. Bringhurst Vertical File, University Archives, Texas A&M Univ., College Station. See also Clapp, *Address Delivered,* 4; and N. H. R. Dawson to B. S. Ewell, 11 May 1887, in box 2, Ewell Papers. On Northern attitudes toward reconciliation, see Nina Silber, *The Romance of Reunion: Northerners and the South, 1865–1900* (Chapel Hill: Univ. of North Carolina Press, 1993).

42. Burwell, *Address at LSU, 1871,* 13–14; R. M. Venable to David Boyd, 30 Sept. 1873, in folder 164, box 12, Richard M. Venable Letters and Related Items, 1865–1882, Walter L. Fleming Collection.

43. Benjamin S. Ewell to Charles S. Sumner, 16 Mar. 1867, in box 1, Ewell Papers; copy of printed letter from Henry Ward Beecher to [potential William and Mary subscriber], 9 Apr. 1867, in box 1, Ewell Papers; U. S. Grant to Benj. S. Ewell, 30 Apr. 1867, in box 1, Ewell Papers; U. S. Grant to the Public, 22 Dec. 1868, box 1, Ewell Papers; A. E. Burnside to Benj. S. Ewell, n.d., box 1, in Ewell Papers; W. T. Sherman to [potential William and Mary subscriber] 19 Apr. 1869, in box 1, Ewell Papers; Geo. B. McClellan to Benj. S. Ewell, 6 Dec. 1869, in box 1, Ewell Papers; Circular [announcing Ewell's support for Grant's presidency], 18 May 1872, in box 1, Ewell Papers.

44. D. F. Boyd, in *Official Register of LSU and A&M College, 1877–78,* 80–82; D. F. Boyd, *Address of Superintendent, 1869,* 3; Leroy S. Boyd, "Recollections of the Early History of Nu Chapter of Kappa Alpha Fraternity at the Alabama Polytechnic Institute, Arlington, Va., Nov. 22, 1933," in Leroy Stafford Boyd Collection, Auburn Univ.; Isaac Taylor Tichenor, *4th Annual Report to the Board of Directors of the A&M College of Alabama, 12 July 1875,* on microfilm, in Tichenor Papers.

45. Richard Sears McCulloch to David F. Boyd, 17 Oct. 1877, in folder 116, box 10, Richard S. McCullock [sic] Letters and Related Items, Walter L. Fleming Collection; *Proceedings of the 3rd Annual Convention of the Association of American Agricultural Colleges and Experiment Stations . . . 1889* (Washington, D.C.: GPO, 1890), 11; Board of Trustees, Univ. of Mississippi, Minutes, 19 June 1869; *Columbus (Miss.) Patron of Husbandry,* 26 June 1880; Eugene A. Smith to W. G. Clark, 11 June 1887, in folder 86, box 4, Record Group 1, Trustee Records, University Archives, Univ. of Alabama, Tuscaloosa; Charles Phillips to John Kimberly, 8 July 1875, in folder 55, box 4, Kimberly Papers; *Montgomery Daily Advertiser,* 20 Sept. 1883; William C. Stubbs to D. F. Boyd, 25 May 1885, in folder 4, box 1, David F. Boyd Papers, University Archives, Draghon Library, Auburn Univ.; John Eaton to William LeRoy Broun, 28 Apr. 1880, in folder 53, box 4, William LeRoy Broun Collection, Auburn; J. M. Gregory to Wm. LeRoy Broun, 13 July 1868, in folder 19, box 2, William LeRoy Broun Collection, Auburn; Johnston, *University: Dangers and Remedies,* 8–9; Samuel H. Lockett, "Report of Visit to Various Schools, Colleges, Universities and Public Works in the Northern States and Canada," in *Annual Report to the Board of Supervisors [of LSU] for*

1871–1872 (New Orleans: n.p., 1872), 73–85; letters from various academics to David F. Boyd, included in *Annual Report of LSU, for the Year 1874, to the Governor of Louisiana* (New Orleans, La.: Republican Office, 1875), 34–65; Kemp P. Battle, *History of the Univ. of North Carolina,* 2:122; C. S. Venable to William LeRoy Broun, 9 Apr. 1878, in folder 46, box 3, William LeRoy Broun Collection, Auburn; Alexander Hogg, "Lacks and Needs of the South Educationally: The Development of Her Natural Resources, the Remedy," *Addresses and Journal of Proceedings of the National Educational Association . . . 1876* (Salem, Oh.: Office of the National Teacher, 1876), 73–76; Mayo, *Training of Teachers in the South.*

46. James C. Clark, *The Murder of James A. Garfield: The President's Last Days and the Trial and Execution of His Assassin* (Jefferson, N.C.: McFarland, 1993).

47. Board of Supervisors for LSU and Agricultural and Mechanical College, Minutes, 2 July 1881, in LSU Official Papers; William Preston Johnston to Dear Wife, 3 July 1881, in folder 12, box 20, Johnston Collection; typescript copy of letter from Ashbel Smith to Oran M. Roberts, 19 July 1881, in Oran Milo Roberts Papers, Box 2F476, Center for American History, Univ. of Texas, Austin.

48. James C. Clark, *Murder of Garfield;* Minutes of the Faculty, Arkansas Industrial Univ., MS, 23 Sept. 1881, on microfilm, University Archives, Univ. of Arkansas; Johnston, *University: Dangers and Remedies,* 15. See also *[Louisiana] Journal of Education* 3 (Nov. 1881): 211.

49. A. D. Mayo, *The Third Estate in the South: An Address Delivered Before the American Social Science Association, at Saratoga, N.Y., Sept. 2d, 1890* (Boston: George H. Ellis, 1890), 16; Alva Woods, *Valedictory Address, Delivered Dec. 6, 1837, at the Close of the 7th Collegiate Year of the Univ. of the State of Alabama* (Tuscaloosa, Ala.: Marmaduke J. Slade, 1837), 3–7; Ashbel Smith, *Address Delivered in the Chapel at West Point Before the Officers and Cadets of the U.S. Military Academy . . . June 16, 1848* (New York: W. L. Burroughs, 1848), 7–16; John A. Campbell, *Address Delivered Before the Alumni Society of the Univ. of Georgia* (Athens, Ga.: J. S. Peterson, 1853); W. W. Avery, *Address Delivered 1851,* 13; Alexander M. Clayton, *Commencement Address . . . Read Before the Law Students of the Univ. of Mississippi on the 26th Day of June, 1860* (Oxford, Miss.: n.p., 1860), 6. On the "Cult of the Anglo-Saxon" in American thought, see Paul F. Boller, Jr., *American Thought in Transition: The Impact of Evolutionary Naturalism, 1865–1900* (Lanham, N.Y.: Univ. Press of America, 1981), 212–26; Richard Hofstadter, *Social Darwinism in American Thought, 1860–1915* (Philadelphia: Univ. of Pennsylvania Press, 1945), 146–54; and Peter Novick, *That Noble Dream: The "Objectivity Question" and the American Historical Profession* (New York: Cambridge Univ. Press, 1988), 80–84.

50. Lewis, *Baccalaureate Address, 1881,* 2; D. H. Hill, *University Address, 1888,* 4–6; Johnston, *Problems of Southern Civilization,* 6–7. See also William Preston Johnston, "Origin of the English People," MS, n.d., in folder 9, box 49, Johnston Collection; Edmund Kirby Smith, untitled MS draft of commencement address for an unnamed school for girls, n.d.; D. H. H. [Daniel Harvey Hill], "Education," pt. 2, p. 85; William LeRoy Broun, *Science-Education,* 9; Kemp P. Battle, *History of the Univ. of North Carolina,* 2:535–36; Curry, *Address Before the Institute, 1899,* 3–5.

51. Boller, *American Thought;* Hofstadter, *Social Darwinism,* 147–53; Nisbet, *History of the Idea,* 286–95.

52. Kemp P. Battle, *Memories of Tar Heel,* 266–67; 293; William LeRoy Broun, *Improvements Required,* 27; B. B. Lewis, *Baccalaureate Address: A Plea for Popular*

Institutions (N.p., n.d.), 4–7, pamphlet in Burwell Boykin Lewis Vertical File, William Stanley Hoole Special Collections Library, Univ. of Alabama, Tuscaloosa. *The Montgomery Daily Advertiser* published the address on 19 Sept. 1883. H. H. Dinwiddie, *Industrial Education in Our Common Schools . . . A Paper Read Before the Texas State Teachers Convention . . . at Waco, Texas, July 1, 1885* (Fort Worth, Tex.: Loving Printing Co., 1886), 5; Buchanan, "Address," in May, "Life of Buchanan," appendix, pp. 97–107; William Preston Johnston, untitled typescript labeled "Speech at a Meeting of Scientists," in Untitled Addresses, Johnston Collection; "In Memory of Professor [John W.] Mallet," Alumni Bulletin [Univ. of Virginia] 6 (Jan. 1913): 21; Johnston, *Problems of Southern Civilization,* 9; Johnston, *Louisiana State Public School Teachers Association,* 11, 15; *Catalogue of the Trustees, Faculty, and Students of the Univ. of North Carolina, 1890–1891* (Raleigh: n.p., 1891), 51; Herbert, *Address Before Univ. of Virginia,* 6–10.

53. Gorgas, Journals, 13 Jan. 1867; Matthew Fontaine Maury, *Physical Survey of Virginia, Her Resources, Climate and Productions: Preliminary Report No. 2 . . . July 1, 1877* (Richmond, Va.: N. V. Randolph, 1878), 35–36; S. D. Lee, "The South After the War," in *Confederate Military History,* ed. Clement Anselm Evans (Atlanta, Ga.: Confederate Publishing Co., 1899), 12:349. See Dan T. Carter, *When the War Was Over: The Failure of Self-Reconstruction in the South, 1865–1867* (Baton Rouge: LSU Press, 1985), 166.

54. Hardaway, "Condition of the South," 104–7; D. H. H. [Daniel Harvey Hill], "Education," pt. 2, p. 84. See also Joseph W. Taylor, *Young Men of the New South,* 18–19; Charles Gayarre, "Mr. Cable's Freedman's Case in Equity," *New Orleans Times-Democrat,* 11 Jan. 1885; Mallet, *Chemistry Applied to the Arts,* 6; and Tichenor, *6th Report.*

55. Southern Historical Society, official circular, in folder 99, box 3, James H. Lane Papers, University Archives, Auburn Univ.; Nisbet, *History of the Idea,* 47–48, 103; Tuveson, *Redeemer Nation;* John Lee Buchanan, "Our Relations to the Past and the Future," n.d., in May, "Life of Buchanan," appendix, pp. 170–74; William Preston Johnston, "History: Its Place in a Liberal Education. Address of Wm. Preston Johnston, of Washington and Lee Univ., Before the Educational Association of Virginia, at Staunton, Va., July 10, 1872," in bound volume entitled *Addresses and Essays, First President of Tulane* (n.p., n.d.), 6, 10, in Rare Books, Howard-Tilton Memorial Library, Tulane Univ., New Orleans, La.

56. Hal Bridges, *Lee's Maverick General: Daniel Harvey Hill* (New York: McGraw-Hill, 1961), 1, 273–77; Charles R. Wilson, *Baptized in Blood,* 37; Harold Eugene Mahan, "The Final Battle: The Southern Historical Society and Confederate Hopes for History," *Southern Historian* 5 (Spring 1984): 32. See also *A Correspondence Between Generals Early and Mahone* (N.p.: n.p., [ca. 1871]), in folder 97, box 3, James H. Lane Papers; J. B. Hood to S. D. Lee, 29 Nov. 1866, in Stephen Dill Lee Papers, on microfilm, Mississippi State Univ., courtesy of SHC-UNC; Stephen D. Lee to J. H. F. Claiborne, 15 May 1878, in Claiborne Papers.

57. Johnston, "History: Its Place in a Liberal Education," 7, 10–11, 13; Johnston, "Lecture First: Uses of History"; Tucker, *Col. William Allan,* 14–15; Jefferson Davis to S. D. Lee, n.d., in Stephen Dill Lee Papers; D. H. Hill, *Old South,* 14–20; Riley, "What General Lee Read," 160–61; J. B. Henneman, "Historical Studies in the South Since the War," *Sewanee Review* 1 (May 1893): 320–39; Wendell H. Stephenson, "Herbert B. Adams and Southern Historical Scholarship at the Johns Hopkins Univ.," *Maryland Historical Magazine* 42 (Mar. 1947): 2–19; Novick, 33, 38; Bledstein, *Culture of Professionalism,* 326.

58. Robert E. Lee Memorial Association, circular [ca. 1870], in Stephen Dill Lee Papers; *Alabama Historical Reporter* [announcement], vol. 1, Jan. 1880, p. 4, in folder 108, box 316, Henry DeLamar Clayton Collection; Louisiana Historical Association identification card issued to William Preston Johnston, in folder 7, box 31, Johnston Collection; C. M. Wilcox to Samuel H. Lockett, 19 Nov. 1868, in folder 16, box 1, Samuel Henry Lockett Papers, SHC-UNC; D. H. Hill to S. D. Lee, 29 June 1866, in Stephen Dill Lee Papers.

59. William LeRoy Broun, "The Red Artillery: Confederate Ordnance During the War," *SHSP* 26 (1898): 365–76; this article was published first as William LeRoy Broun, "Confederate Ordnance During the War," *Journal of the U.S. Artillery* 9 (Jan.-Feb. 1898): 1–13. D. H. Hill, "Address Before the Mecklenburg (N.C.) Historical Society," *SHSP* 1 (1876): 389–98; William Preston Johnston, "Zagony's Charge with Fremont's Body-Guard—A Picturesque Fol-de-rol," *SHSP* 3 (1877): 195–96; S. D. Lee, "The Second Battle of Manassas—A Reply to General Longstreet," *SHSP* 6 (1878): 59–70; Mallet, "Work of the Ordnance Bureau," 1–20.

60. Southern Historical Society, official circular; William Preston Johnson, untitled MS [ca. 1870s], in folder 12, box 50, Johnston Collection; emphasis original. See also Benjamin H. Hill, "Address Delivered Feb. 18, 1874," 405; and R. L. Gibson to William Preston Johnston, 7 Apr. 1891, in folder 3, box 31, Johnston Collection.

61. Southern Historical Society, official circular.

62. See Foster, *Ghosts;* Gaston, *New South Creed;* and Charles R. Wilson, *Baptized in Blood*.

63. William Preston Johnson, untitled MS [ca. 1870s]; William LeRoy Broun, "Address on Memorial Day, 1891," 237; Lewis, *Baccalaureate Address, 1881,* 3–4; Samuel H. Lockett, "Address at Memorial Celebration" [Montgomery, Ala.], MS, 1 May 1875, in folder 23, box 2, Samuel Henry Lockett Papers, SHC-UNC.

64. E. Merton Coulter, "The New South: Benjamin H. Hill's Speech Before the Alumni Society of the Univ. of Georgia, 1871," *Georgia Historical Quarterly* 57 (Summer 1973): 183.

65. Johnston, *Problems of Southern Civilization,* 3–19.

66. David French Boyd, *Reminiscences of the War in Virginia,* ed. T. Michael Parrish (Baton Rouge: U.S. Civil War Center, 1994); D. F. Boyd, *Address . . . on the Anniversary of the Delta Rifles, 4th Louisiana Regiment, Confederate States Army, at Port Allen, West Baton Rouge, La., May 20th, 1887* (Baton Rouge, La.: Capitolian-Advocate Book and Job Print, 1887), 4–7, 11; emphasis original. D. H. Hill, *Old South,* 6.

67. Wiener, *Social Origins,* 215–19; Gaston, *New South Creed;* Charles R. Wilson, *Baptized in Blood,* 81–86.

68. On the immense popularity of commencements and other ceremonial speaking occasions in the 19th century, see E. Merton Coulter, "A Famous Univ. of Georgia Commencement, 1871," *Georgia Historical Quarterly* 57 (Fall 1973): 347–61; and Waldo W. Braden and Harold Mixon, "Epideictic Speaking in the Post–Civil War South and the Southern Experience," *Southern Communication Journal* 54 (Fall 1988): 48.

Chapter 4. Obstacles to Progress

1. [Isaac Taylor Tichenor], "Southern Agriculture," in Stubbs Papers.
2. D. H. H. [Daniel Harvey Hill], "Education," pt. 1, pp. 8–9, and pt. 3, p. 239;

Tichenor, *6th Report;* D. F. Boyd, quoted in Germaine M. Reed, *David French Boyd: Founder of LSU* (Baton Rouge: LSU Press, 1977), 93; emphasis original. Hardaway Hunt Dinwiddie, "Valedictory Address, Class of 1867, VMI, July 4, 1867," photocopy from *Alumni Review* [VMI] (1985) in Hardaway Hunt Dinwiddie Vertical File, University Archives, Texas A&M Univ., College Station; "Hardaway Hunt Dinwiddie," photocopy from *Texas Farm and Ranch* [1 Jan. 1888], in Dinwiddie Vertical File; *5th Annual Report of the A&M College of Texas, Session 1880–1881* (Brenham, Tex.: Sentinel Print, 1881), 4; H. H. Dinwiddie, "Report of the Chairman of the Faculty" in *Report of the Agricultural and Mechanical College of Texas* [1885] (Austin: E. W. Swindells, State Printer, 1885), 5. See also James Allen Cabaniss, *A History of the Univ. of Mississippi* (University, Miss.: Univ. of Mississippi, 1949), 79–89; and Paul H. Buck, *The Road to Reunion, 1865–1900* (Boston: Little, Brown, 1947), 35–38.

3. William LeRoy Broun, "Baccalaureate Address Delivered at the A&M College, Auburn, Ala., June, 1888," in William LeRoy Broun, *Dr. William LeRoy Broun,* 245.

4. Benjamin H. Hill, [Sr.], "Speech Delivered Before the Alumni, July 31, 1871"; Coulter, "New South," 183.

5. Brooks, *Univ. of Georgia Under 16,* 46; Thomas Dyer, *Univ. of Georgia,* 107–11; Board of Trustees, Univ. of Georgia, Minutes, 28 June and 4 July 1866.

6. Andrew A. Lipscomb to William LeRoy Broun, in folder 17, box 2, William LeRoy Broun Collection, Auburn; William LeRoy Broun, *Improvements Required.*

7. S. Maupin to Wm. LeRoy Broun, 21 July 1868, and Geo. W. Rains to William LeRoy Broun, 27 July 1868, both in folder 19, box 2, William LeRoy Broun Collection, Auburn; W. M. Shirley to William LeRoy Broun, 28 Nov. 1870, in folder 27, box 2, William LeRoy Broun Collection, Auburn; J. M. Gregory to W. LeRoy Broun, 13 July 1868, in folder 19, box 2, William LeRoy Broun Collection, Auburn.

8. Draft of proposal for reorganization of Univ. of Georgia, MS, 13 Nov. 1868, in folder 21, box 2, William LeRoy Broun Collection, Auburn; Charles Forster Smith, "Southern Colleges," 553; Board of Trustees for the Univ. of Georgia, *Present Organization and Proposed Plan of Expansion of the Univ. of Georgia* (Athens, Ga.: Southern Banner, 1872); Board of Trustees, Univ. of Georgia, Minutes, 28 July and 2 Aug. 1869.

9. Board of Trustees, Univ. of Georgia, Minutes, 28 July 1874, 28 July 1869, and 25 July 1871.

10. Edward S. Joynes to W. L. Broun, 24 Aug. 1868, in folder 19, box 2, William LeRoy Broun Collection, Auburn; Milton W. Humphreys to Colonel Broun, 28 Jan. 1902, in William LeRoy Broun, *Dr. William LeRoy Broun,* 55–56; Milton W. Humphreys, "William LeRoy Broun," in William LeRoy Broun, *Dr. William LeRoy Broun,* 48; Edward S. Joynes to C. C. Thach, in William LeRoy Broun, *Dr. William LeRoy Broun,* 57–58; Robert E. Lee, Jr., "Why General Lee Accepted the Presidency of Washington College," in *General Robert E. Lee After Appomattox,* ed. Frank L. Riley (New York: Macmillan, 1922), 16–21; Thomas L. Connelly, *The Marble Man: Robert E. Lee and His Image in American Society* (Baton Rouge: LSU Press, 1977), 28.

11. R. E. Lee to J. B. Baldwin, 22 Nov. 1865, copy of Letter Book I, Robert Edward Lee Papers; R. E. Lee to Cyrus H. McCormick, 28 Nov. 1865, in Robert Edward Lee Papers; R. E. Lee to C. H. Latrobe, 18 Jan. 1867, copy of Letter Book II, Robert Edward Lee Papers; Board of Trustees, Washington College, Minutes, MS, 24 Oct. 1865, University Archives,

Washington and Lee Univ., Lexington, Va.; R. E. Lee to M. G. Harman, 22 Nov. 1865, copy of Letter Book I, Robert Edward Lee Papers; *Catalogue of the Washington College, Va., for the Collegiate Year Ending June 1866* (N.p.: Johnson and Schaffter, 1866), 5–12; *Catalogue, Washington College, 1869*, 6–7, 16; Edward S. Joynes, "Lee, the College President," in *Robert E. Lee: Centennial Celebration of His Birth, Held Under the Auspices of the Univ. of South Carolina on the 19th Day of Jan., 1907* (Columbia, S.C.: State Company, 1907), 29n.

12. Extract of Faculty Minutes, provided by E. C. Gordon, MS, June 1868, in folder 172, Trustee Papers, University Archives, Washington and Lee Univ.; R. S. McCulloch to R. E. Lee, 18 Feb. 1869, in Robert Edward Lee Papers; William LeRoy Broun, *Improvements Required*, 15; *Lexington (Va.) Southern Collegian*, 29 Oct. 1870; Kemp P. Battle, "Head and Hand." See also Burwell, *Address at LSU*, 1871, 9–13; and Joynes, "Lee, College President." On Lee's popularity after his death, see Connelly, *Marble Man*, 27–162.

13. S. Maupin to Wm. LeRoy Broun, 21 July 1868, in folder 19, box 2, William LeRoy Broun Collection, Auburn; *Catalogue of the Univ. of Virginia . . . 1867–68*, 24–28; Mallet, *Chemistry Applied to the Arts*, 13–14.

14. Francis H. Smith, *Introductory Address, 1866*, 10–11; Francis H. Smith, *Gymnastics and Technical Education*, 21.

15. James T. Murfee, *A New Scheme of Organization, Instruction, and Government for the Univ. of Alabama, with Report on Construction of Building* (Tuscaloosa, Ala.: John F. Warren, 1867); N. T. Lupton to W. LeRoy Broun, 11 Jan. 1872, in folder 33, box 3, William LeRoy Broun Collection, Auburn; Sellers, *History of Univ. of Alabama*, 1:291–317, 1:444–45; Robert J. Norrell, *A Promising Field: Engineering at Alabama, 1837–1987* (Tuscaloosa: Univ. of Alabama Press, 1990), 35–40.

16. Donnelly, "Scientists," 89–90.

17. *Historical Catalogue of the Officers and Alumni of the Univ. of Alabama, 1821 to 1870* (Selma, Ala.: Armstrong and Martin, 1870), 35; "Univ. of Alabama," circular [1871 or 1872], in scrapbook, vol. 2 (1872–79), Eugene Allen Smith Collection; M. F. Maury, "Inaugural Address"; Donnelly, "Scientists," 89–90.

18. D. F. Boyd to William LeRoy Broun, 23 Oct. 1873, in folder 40, box 3, William LeRoy Broun Collection, Auburn; D. F. Boyd to William LeRoy Broun, 11 Dec. 1877, in folder 51, box 4, William LeRoy Broun Collection, Auburn; *Report of the Board of Supervisors for LSU, 1877–78*, appendix, p. 17; Germaine M. Reed, *David French Boyd*, 93; *Official Register of the Louisiana State Seminary . . . 1866* (New Orleans: Crescent Job Print, 1866), 10; *Official Register of the Louisiana State Seminary . . . 1867* (New Orleans: Crescent Office Print, 1867), 15–16; *Report of the Board of Supervisors for the Louisiana State Seminary . . . 1870* (New Orleans: n.p., 1870), 23; D. F. Boyd to Wm. H. Fishback, 30 July 1887, in Letters, University Archives, Univ. of Arkansas; "Richard Morton Venable," 86; Fleming, *Louisiana State Univ.*, 148; *New Orleans Republican*, 10 and 11 Aug. 1867.

19. *Historical Catalogue of the Univ. of Mississippi, 1849–1909* (Nashville, Tenn.: Marshall and Bruce Co., 1910), 18–21; Hilgard, "Confederate Scientist," 21–23; Hilgard, *Address on Progressive Agriculture;* Eugene W. Hilgard, *Report on Organization of the Department of Agriculture and the Mechanic Arts, Aug. 29, 1871* (N.p., n.d.).

20. Board of Trustees, Univ. of Mississippi, Minutes, 15–17 Aug. 1870; *Historical Catalogue, Univ. of Mississippi, 1849–1909*, 74–76, 98; *Catalogue of the Officers and Trustees of the Univ. of Mississippi at Oxford, Miss., 22nd Session* (Oxford, Miss.: n.p., 1874), 19, 28–30,

38–40, 44–47; "In Memory of Professor Mallet," 3–47; Board of Trustees of the State [Miss.] Univ., *Where Shall I Send My Son? An Address to the People of Mississippi* (N.p.: [1876]), 8, 14–19; *Jackson (Miss.) Clarion-Ledger,* 4, 7, and 11 July 1889; E. Mayes to William LeRoy Broun, 22 July 1889, in folder 81, box 6, William LeRoy Broun Collection, Auburn.

21. Joseph M. Hill, *Biography of Daniel Harvey Hill: Lieutenant General, Confederate States of America: Educator, Author, Editor* ([Little Rock, Ark.?]: Official Publications of the Arkansas History Commission, n.d.), 32; Dan T. Carter, *When the War Was Over,* 118; "Hillsborough Military Academy," circular [1867], in folder 18, box 2, John Lancaster Bailey Papers, SHC-UNC.

22. E. Kirby Smith to William Preston Johnston, 31 Aug. 1869, located with "Western Military Academy," circular, in folder 15, box 14, Johnston Collection. Smith's school should not be confused with the Western Military Institute which operated in Georgetown, Ky., and closed permanently shortly after the start of the Civil War. See Mabel Altsetter and Gladys Watson, "Western Military Institute, 1847–1861," *Filson Club History Quarterly* 10 (Apr. 1936): 100–115; S. H. Lockett to D. F. Boyd, 28 July 1873, in folder 105, box 9, Samuel H. Lockett Letters and Related Items, Walter L. Fleming Collection; Lockett, "Technical Education."

23. A. A. Lloyd and P. O. Lloyd, *Town of Hillsborough,* 150–51; Joseph Howard Parks, *General Edmund Kirby Smith, C.S.A.* (Baton Rouge: LSU Press, 1954), 497; Joseph M. Hill, *Biography of D. H. Hill,* 32; Samuel H. Lockett to D. F. Boyd, 2 Dec. 1873, in folder 105, box 9, Samuel H. Lockett Letters, LSU; *2nd Annual Report to the Board of Directors of the A&M College of Alabama, 30 July 1873,* on microfilm in Tichenor Papers; Board of Trustees, Univ. of Georgia, Minutes, 27 July 1877; Eugene W. Hilgard to D. F. Boyd, in *Annual Report of LSU for 1874,* 531.

24. *Catalogue, Washington College, 1869,* 56–61; Tucker, *Col. William Allan,* 7; William M. Burwell, "General Lee as Teacher," *De Bow's Review* 6 (July 1869): 540–47.

25. Circular, "To Our Friends in the United States," endorsed by W. F. [sic] Hardee, Alex. P. Stewart, R. S. Ewell, C. M. Wilcox, W. N. Pendleton, F. S. Marmaduke, [P.] G. T. Beauregard, R. Taylor, S. B. Buckner, F. [sic] B. Hood, Braxton Bragg, and J. A. Early, in folder 6, box 55, Johnston Collection; Joseph W. Taylor, *Young Men of the New South,* 19; Joseph W. Taylor, *Address Before the Literary Societies of Washington and Lee Univ., on Commencement Day, June 22, 1871* (Baltimore, Md.: J. Murphy, 1871); *Catalogue of Washington and Lee Univ. . . . 1877* (Lynchburg, Va.: Bell, Browne & Co., 1877), 10, 16–24; Connelly, *Marble Man,* 30–32.

26. S. D. Lee, *The A&M College of Mississippi: Its Origin, Object, Management and Results, Discussed in a Series of Papers* (Jackson, Miss.: Clarion-Ledger, 1889), 14; *Charleston (S.C.) News and Courier,* 26 Aug. and 26 June 1885; Charles W. Dabney, "President Battle and the University," typescript, 1928, in folder 274, box 21, Charles William Dabney Papers.

27. Kemp P. Battle, *History of the Univ. of North Carolina,* 2:9–11; Brabham, "Defining the American University," 427–55; Henderson, *Campus of the First State University,* 194–95; Kemp P. Battle, *Memories of Tar Heel,* 172–98, 247; Kemp P. Battle, *History of the Univ. of North Carolina,* 1:764–67; James L. Leloudis, *Schooling the New South: Pedagogy, Self, and Society in North Carolina, 1880–1920* (Chapel Hill: Univ. of North Carolina Press, 1996), 55.

28. *By-Laws of the Univ. of South Carolina, as Revised and Adopted by the Board of Trustees, at the Annual Meeting in 1866 . . .* (Columbia, S.C.: W. W. Deane, 1867);

Prospectus of the Univ. of South Carolina, 1866 (Columbia, S.C.: Southern Presbyterian Review, 1866); Joseph LeConte, *Autobiography,* 235–39.

29. Joseph LeConte, *Autobiography,* 235–39; *Reorganization of the Univ. of South Carolina in 1873, and Catalogue for 1872–73* (N.p., n.d.); *Catalogue of the Univ. of South Carolina, 1872–73* (N.p., n.d.); B. B. Babbitt, *Report of the Chairman of the Faculty of the Univ. of South Carolina in Response to a Resolution of the House of Representatives and of the Senate, Passed Feb. 18, 1875* (Columbia, S.C.: Republican Printing Co., 1875); Hollis, *Univ. of South Carolina,* 2:3–79; Fisk Parsons Brewer, "South Carolina University—1876," ed. William P. Vaughn, *South Carolina Historical Magazine* 76 (Oct. 1875): 225–31.

30. *Historical Catalogue, Univ. of Mississippi, 1849–1909,* 74; James Allen Cabaniss, *A History of the Univ. of Mississippi* (University, Miss.: Univ. of Mississippi, 1949), 79–89; Josephine M. Posey, *Against Great Odds: The History of Alcorn State Univ.* (Jackson: Univ. Press of Mississippi, 1994), 3–4.

31. Board of Supervisors for LSU, Minutes, 5 Apr. 1886; Germaine M. Reed, *David French Boyd,* 55–190.

32. D. F. Boyd, "Ideas on Education."

33. Atticus G. Haygood, *Our Brother in Black: His Freedom and His Future* (New York: Phillips and Hunt, 1881), 144–58; Hugh C. Bailey, *Liberalism in the New South: Southern Social Reformers and the Progressive Movement* (Coral Gables, Fla.: Univ. of Miami Press, 1969), 34; Horace Mann Bond, *Negro Education in Alabama: A Study in Cotton and Steel* (Washington, D.C.: Associated Publishers, 1939), 105–15, 198–203, 214–25; W. Stuart Towns, "Atticus G. Haygood: Neglected Advocate of Reconciliation and a New South," *Southern Studies* 26 (Spring 1987): 39; typescript fragment of draft of J. M. McBryde to A. P. B. [A. P. Butler], n.d., in folder 23, box 3, McBryde Family Papers; Benjamin H. Hill, [Sr.], "Speech Delivered Before the Alumni, July 31, 1871," 343; Kemp P. Battle, "Head and Hand"; Bauman, "Confronting the New South," 96–98; Booker T. Washington, *Up from Slavery: An Autobiography* (1900; reprinted by Corner House Publishers, Williamstown, Mass., 1978). For correspondence between Washington and Curry, see Louis R. Harlan, ed., *The Booker T. Washington Papers* (Urbana: Univ. of Illinois Press, 1974), vols. 2 and 3; Booker T. Washington to William LeRoy Broun, 15 Oct. 1890, in Harlan, *Booker T. Washington Papers,* 3:87–90.

34. "Branch Normal College of the Arkansas Industrial Univ., Pine Bluff, Arkansas," in *8th Catalogue of the Arkansas Industrial Univ. . . . for the Year Ending June 10th, 1880* (Little Rock: Arkansas Democrat, 1880), 91–114; "Georgia State Industrial College for Colored Youths," in *Univ. of Georgia: General Catalogue, 1900–1901* (Atlanta, Ga.: Foote and Davies Co., 1901), 155–250; *Reports: Southern Univ., 1899–1900* (New Orleans, La.: n.p., [1900?]), 25–32; Bond, *Negro Education,* 262–69; A. H. Colquitt to D. H. Hill, 17 Dec. 1878, in box 93.2, Daniel Harvey Hill Papers, NCDAH; Brubacher and Rudy, *Higher Education,* 79; Caesar F. Toles, "Regionalism in Southern Higher Education" (Ph.D. diss., Univ. of Michigan, 1953), 75–78; Bauman, "Confronting the New South," 96; *Biennial Report: Southern Univ. and A&M College, Sessions 1910–1911, 1911–1912* (New Orleans, La.: n.p., [1912?]), 25; Oran M. Roberts, *General Message on the Judiciary, Education, the Department of Insurance, Statistics and History, Railroads, Etc., to the 17th Legislature of the State of Texas . . . Jan. 11, 1881* (Galveston, Tex.: News Book and Job, 1881), 10; *Report of the Prairie View Normal School Located in Waller County [Tex.]* (Austin, Tex.: Smith, Hicks and Jones, 1889); Wagstaff, *Impressions,* 35.

35. A. J. Peeler, for the Board of Directors of the State Normal School of Texas, for

Colored Students, to Gov. O. M. Roberts, 7 Jan. 1881, in *Message Accompanying the Report of the Board of the A&M College of the State of Texas* (Galveston, Tex.: News Book and Job, 1881), 47–48; Kemp P. Battle, "Head and Hand."

36. Peeler, *Address at Texas A&M*, 1877, 15; Kemp P. Battle, "Head and Hand"; "Negro Education," *Jackson (Miss.) Clarion-Ledger*, 4 July 1889.

37. Samuel H. Lockett, untitled address delivered at Calhoun College and Jacksonville Female Academy, [29 June 1874], in folder 130, box 8, Samuel Henry Lockett Papers, SHC-UNC. See also H. R. Thomas to the Editor, *Charleston (S.C.) News and Courier*, 22 July 1887, clipping in folder 21, box 3, McBryde Family Papers.

38. Fleming, *Louisiana State Univ.*, 146–59, 221, 256–58; Germaine M. Reed, *David French Boyd*, 67–71; Germaine M. Reed, "David Boyd, LSU, and Louisiana Reconstruction," *Louisiana Studies* 14 (Fall 1975): 259–76; *Official Register of LSU*, 1871–72, 5–6, 10; "Roll of Officers and Cadets of LSU, Session 1874–1875," typescript, in folder 7, LSU Official Papers; *Baton Rouge (La.) Daily Reveille*, 17 Sept. 1953.

39. Hale, *Univ. of Arkansas*, 9–40; Thomas S. Staples, *Reconstruction in Arkansas, 1862–1874* (New York: Longmans, Green and Co., 1923), 328–35; Guerdon D. Nichols, "Breaking the Color Barrier at the Univ. of Arkansas," *Arkansas Historical Quarterly* 27 (Spring 1968): 3; Harrison Hale, "Glimpses of Univ. of Arkansas History," *Arkansas Historical Quarterly* 6 (Winter 1947): 436; "Catalogue of the Arkansas Industrial Univ. for 18[74–75]," in *3rd Report of the Arkansas Industrial Univ.* (Fayetteville, Ark.: Democrat Book and Job, 1875), 8–11; A. W. Bishop, "Farewell Address," in *3rd Report of the Arkansas Industrial Univ.*, 108–10; *6th Catalogue of the Arkansas Industrial Univ.* (Little Rock, Ark.: A. H. Sevier, 1878), 15–17.

40. Montgomery, Folmsbee, and Green, *To Foster Knowledge*, 65–86; Jack P. Maddex, Jr., *The Virginia Conservatives, 1867–1879: A Study in Reconstruction Politics* (Chapel Hill: Univ. of North Carolina Press, 1970), 3–100; T. P. Abernethy, *Historical Sketch of the Univ. of Virginia* (Richmond, Va.: Dietz Press, 1948), 25; Thomas Dyer, *Univ. of Georgia*, 109–22; Hollis, *Univ. of South Carolina*, 2:44, 2:131–32, 2:138–39, 2:141. The Univ. of Alabama suffered little from partisan conflict after Maury's election to the presidency in 1871 until the end of Reconstruction in Alabama in 1875. See Sellers, *History of Univ. of Alabama*, 310–20.

41. Waddel, *Historical Discourse*, 11; Dumas Malone, *The Public Life of Thomas Cooper, 1783–1839* (Columbia: Univ. of South Carolina Press, 1961), 259–70, 337–67; Kelley, "Additional Chapters," 18–23; S. A. Goodwin, *Commencement Sermon Delivered Before the Students of the Univ. of Columbus, Sunday, June 26th, 1876 . . . Subject: Excellency of the Knowledge of Christ* (Columbus, Miss.: Excelsior Book and Job, 1876), 2–5; *Catalogue of the Trustees, Faculty and Students, Wofford College, Spartanburg, S.C., 1861* (Spartanburg, S.C.: Express Office, 1861), 15; *Catalogue, Officers and Students, Mercer Univ., 1860–61*, 29; *Catalogue of the Officers and Students of the Furman Univ. for 1860–61* (Charleston, S.C.: Evans and Cosswell, 1861), 25.

42. Norrell, *Promising Field*, 46; Lewis, *Baccalaureate Address, 1881*, 5; Glenn R. Conrad, ed., *Dictionary of Louisiana Biography* (New Orleans: Louisiana Historical Association, 1988), 2:759–60; George Soule, *Address by Col. Geo. Soule, President of Soule Commercial College and Literary Institute, New Orleans, La., at the 32nd Anniversary and Commencement, June 30th, 1888* (N.p.: [1888?]), 3–4.

43. Barringer, Garnett, and Page, *Univ. of Virginia*, 2:4–5; Francis H[enry] Smith, *Thoughts on the Discord and Harmony Between Science and the Bible: Delivered Before the American Institute of Christian Philosophy, 27th July 1888* (New York: Wilbur B. Ketchum, [1888?]). See also Samuel H. Lockett, "The Correlation of Medicine with the Exact Sciences and Mechanic Arts," [1881?], MS with typescript copy in folder 28, box 2, ser. A, Samuel Henry Lockett Papers, SHC-UNC. On the efforts by Victorians to reconcile Christianity and evolutionary science, see James R. Moore, *The Post-Darwinian Controversies: A Study of the Protestant Struggle to Come to Terms with Darwin in Great Britain and America, 1870–1900* (London: Cambridge Univ. Press, 1979).

44. Robert L. Stuart to Col. [D. F.] Boyd, 4 Oct. 1883, in folder 1, box 1, David F. Boyd Papers, Auburn; Thos. D. Boyd to D. F. Boyd, 23 Oct. 1883, folder 1, box 1, David F. Boyd Papers, Auburn; *Catalogue of the State A&M College of Alabama, 1883–1884* (N.p., n.d.); James H. Lane to D. F. Boyd, 29 May 1885, in folder 4, box 1, David F. Boyd Papers, Auburn; D. F. Boyd to H. D. Clayton, 9 Feb. 1884, in folder 2, box 1, David F. Boyd Papers, Auburn; D. F. Boyd to J. T. Murfee, 5 Apr. 1884, folder 2, box 1, David F. Boyd Papers, Auburn; D. F. Boyd to [the] Young Gentlemen of the Corps of Cadets, General Orders No. 1, 26 Sept. 1883, MS, in folder 1, box 1, David F. Boyd Papers, Auburn; David F. Boyd, "Commencement Address, 1884," MS, in folder 2, box 1, David F. Boyd Papers, Auburn; J. S. Newman to William Leroy Broun, 4 Jan. 1884, in folder 62, box 5, William LeRoy Broun Collection, Auburn; Leroy S. Boyd, "Recollections"; Ashbel Smith to W. Leroy Broun, 16 Nov. 1882, in folder 55, box 4, William LeRoy Broun Collection, Auburn; *Catalogue, Univ. of Texas, 1883–84*, 1–3, 28; Silverthorne, *Ashbel Smith of Texas*, 210–22; photocopy of W. LeRoy Broun to H. D. Clayton, 7 May 1883, in folder 56, box 4, William LeRoy Broun Collection, Auburn; original cited as located in Henry DeLamar Clayton Collection; photocopy of William LeRoy Broun to H. D. Clayton, 31 May 1883, in folder 56, box 4, William LeRoy Broun Collection, Auburn; original cited as located in Henry DeLamar Clayton Collection.

45. *Louisiana Capitolian* (Baton Rouge), 6 Nov. 1880; Dinah Daniel Richard, "The Southern Oratory of William Preston Johnston" (Ph.D. diss., Louisiana State Univ., 1982), 38–40; William Preston Johnston, *Report . . . to the Board of Administrators on the Plan of Organization of Tulane Univ., June 4th, 1883* (New Orleans, La.: A. W. Hyatt, 1883). See also William Preston Johnston, typescript, [speech at a meeting of scientists, probably the New Orleans Academy of Sciences], n.d., in folder 21, box 49, Johnston Collection.

46. George M. Edgar, "A Contribution to the History of the Battle of New Market, May 15th, 1864," typescript, n.d., in folder 16, box 2, George M. Edgar Papers, UNC-SHC; George M. Edgar, "Studies of the Wilderness," typescript, n.d., in folder 18, Edgar Papers; George M. Edgar, "History of the Battle of Winchester, 19th Sept. 1864," MS, in folder 18, box 2, Edgar Papers; George M. Edgar, "Outline of Advantages the South Would Have Had in Entering the Family of Nations, If Successful," in vol. 4, MS notebook, folder 24, box 2, Edgar Papers; George M. Edgar, *Biennial Report of the Board of Trustees of Arkansas Industrial Univ. to His Excellency, Simon P. Hughes, Governor of Arkansas* (Little Rock, Ark.: A. M. Woodruff, 1886); "Arkansas Industrial Univ. Official Report of Col. Geo. M. Edgar, President, Fayetteville, June 7th, 1885," MS, in box 2, subser. 2, ser. 2, Board of Trustees' Records, University Archives, Univ. of Arkansas.

47. William Mercer Green, *Address Delivered Before the Board of Trustees of the Univ. of*

the South, Sewanee, Tenn., Monday of Commencement Week, July 28, 1878 (Sewanee, Tenn.: Mountain News, [1878?], 7–8.

48. Tichenor, 5th Report; Lockett, "Correlation of Medicine with Science"; William LeRoy Broun, Improvements Required, 27.

49. Report of the A&M College of Texas [1885], 11–12.

50. Draft of the Constitution and Statutes of the Univ. of the South (New Orleans, La.: Bulletin Book and Job Office, 1860); Arthur Benjamin Chitty, Jr., Reconstruction at Sewanee: The Founding of the Univ. of the South and Its First Administration, 1857–1872 (Sewanee, Tenn.: University Press, 1954), 105–79; "In Memory of Professor Mallet," 18; Vandiver, Ploughshares into Swords, 288–89; George R. Fairbanks, History of the Univ. of the South, at Sewanee, Tennessee, from Its Founding by the Southern Bishops, Clergy, and Laity of the Episcopal Church in 1857 to the Year 1905 (Jacksonville, Fla.: H. and W. B. Drew Co.), 160–61; Gorgas, Journals, 16 June 1865, 3 May and 1 July 1866, and 3 Mar. and 7 June 1868.

51. Fairbanks, Univ. of the South, 176–334; Chitty, Reconstruction at Sewanee, 105–6, 125, 142, 179; J. Gorgas to William LeRoy Broun, 25 Oct. 1877, in folder 51, box 4, William LeRoy Broun Collection, Auburn; J. Gorgas to S. H. Lockett, 31 Jan. 1878, in folder 26, box 2, Samuel Henry Lockett Papers, SHC-UNC; Charles R. Wilson, Baptized in Blood, 143–60; Vandiver, Ploughshares into Swords, 304; N. H. R. Dawson to J. Gorgas, 5 July 1878, in folder 12, box 674, Gorgas Family Papers; Board of Trustees, Univ. of Alabama, Minutes, 4 July 1878, on microfilm, University Archives, Univ. of Alabama. Gorgas also received an offer to serve as professor of engineering at LSU; see D. F. Boyd to J. Gorgas, 15 July [1878], in folder 13, box 674, Gorgas Family Papers; and Gorgas, Journals, 16 July 1878.

52. First Report of the Arkansas Industrial Univ. with a Normal Department Therein (Little Rock: Little Rock Printing & Publishing Co., 1873), 21–22; 7th Catalogue of the Arkansas Industrial Univ. [1879] (Little Rock: Blocher & Mitchell, 1879), 21; Catalogue of the Officers and Students of the Univ. of Mississippi, at Oxford, Miss., 31; Catalogue of the Univ. of South Carolina, 1867, N.p., 1867, 4, 7; 6th Catalogue, Arkansas Industrial Univ. [1878], 37; Board of Trustees, Univ. of Georgia, Minutes, 5 Aug. 1874; Kemp P. Battle, History of the Univ. of North Carolina, 1:475.

53. Burwell, Address at LSU, 1871, 11; Roy [Broun] to Dear Father [William LeRoy Broun], 8 Apr. 1884, in folder 66, box 5, William LeRoy Broun Collection, Auburn; Montgomery, Folmsbee, and Green, To Foster Knowledge, 92–93; Board of Trustees, Univ. of Georgia, Minutes, 27 July 1877.

54. Dethloff, Centennial History of Texas A&M, 1:39–50, 1:70–76.

55. Fred A. Bailey, "Oliver Perry Temple and the Struggle for Tennessee's Agricultural College," Tennessee Historical Quarterly 36 (Spring 1977): 44–61; Montgomery, Folmsbee, and Green, To Foster Knowledge, 70, 77, 92–100, 106–70; Columbia (S.C.) State, 12 Jan. 1912, in folder 21, box 3, McBryde Family Papers; draft of [Samuel H. Lockett] to Thos. W. Humes, n.d., in folder 26, box 2, Samuel Henry Lockett Papers, SHC-UNC. Internal evidence suggests that Lockett wrote this draft between Nov. 1877 and Sept. 1878. Clipping from an unidentified newspaper, June 1882, in folder 21, box 3, McBryde Family Papers; Hollis, Univ. of South Carolina, 2:103–15.

56. Board of Trustees, Univ. of Georgia, Minutes, 28 July 1875 and 27 July 1877; Thomas Dyer, Univ. of Georgia, 103–4, 122–33.

57. D. H. Hill, "Report to the Board of Trustees for the Arkansas Industrial Univ.," MS, 1880, box 93.5, Daniel H. Hill Papers, NCDAH; Board of Trustees, Mississippi A&M College, Minutes, MS, 15 Mar. 1888, on microfilm, University Archives, Mississippi State Univ., Starkville; John J. Wilmore, "Some Phases of Engineering Education in the South," *Proceedings of the Society for the Promotion of Engineering Education* 6 (1898): 62–64; Jennings L. Wagoner, "Higher Education and Transitions in Southern Culture: An Exploratory Apologia," *Journal of Thought* 18 (Fall 1983): 109–10; Andrew A. Lipscomb to William LeRoy Broun, 8 Jan. 1868, in folder 17, box 2, William LeRoy Broun Collection, Auburn; Andrew A. Lipscomb to William LeRoy Broun, 2 Apr. 1872, in folder 34, box 3, William LeRoy Broun Collection, Auburn; F. H. Smith to M. F. Maury, 12 Mar. 1869, in vol. 30, Matthew Fontaine Maury Papers; Tichenor, *6th Report;* D. F. Boyd, *Address of Superintendent, 1869,* 4; Wagstaff, *Impressions,* 31.

58. Board of Supervisors of LSU, Minutes, 2 Apr. 1883; Kemp P. Battle, *History of the Univ. of North Carolina,* 1:781; Kemp P. Battle, *Memories of Tar Heel,* 244; Norrell, *Promising Field,* 24; Thomas Dyer, *Univ. of Georgia,* 122, 129–30; clipping from *Alabama Christian Advocate,* 1 Apr. 1885, in scrapbook, vol. 5 (1886–87), Eugene Allen Smith Collection; H. D. Clayton to William LeRoy Broun, 8 Oct. 1888, in folder 79, box 6, William LeRoy Broun Collection, Auburn; J. L. M. Curry, "Annual Report of the Hon. J. L. M. Curry, General Agent of the Peabody Fund," *Texas Journal of Education* 2 (Oct. 1881): 241.

59. Board of Trustees, Univ. of Arkansas, Minutes of Meetings, MS, 2 June 1887, on microfilm, University Archives, Univ. of Arkansas; Trustees of the State [Miss.] Univ., *Where Shall I Send My Son?* 4; Joseph W. Taylor, *Young Men of the New South,* 10–13; D. F. Boyd, *Louisiana State Univ. Scheme to Raise an Endowment Fund* (New Orleans: n.p., 1872), 4; *Louisiana Democrat* (Alexandria), 29 July 1868; *Report of the Subcommittee on Public and Charitable Institutions, Appointed Jan. 20, 1876* (New Orleans: n.p., [1876?]), 16; Peeler, *Address at Texas A&M, 1877,* 17; J. T. Murfee to Matthew F. Maury, 1 May 1871, in vol. 37, Matthew Fontaine Maury Papers; Egan, *Address at Louisiana State Seminary,* 7; Samuel H. Lockett, untitled commencement address, [29 June 1874], in folder 130, box 8, Samuel Henry Lockett Papers, SHC-UNC; *Knoxville (Tenn.) Daily Tribune,* 23 June 1886.

60. C[harles]. P[hillips]. to [J. Kimberly], 15 July 1875, in folder 55, box 4, Kimberly Papers; Edgar, "Arkansas Industrial Univ., June 7th, 1885"; J. W. Nicholson, *Higher Education at Public Expense Justified: Address of Col. J. W. Nicholson—President of LSU and A&M College on the Occasion of the 7th Annual Convention of the Louisiana Educational Association, Shreveport, La., July 25, 1890* (Baton Rouge, La.: Truth, Job, and Book Office, 1890), pamphlet located in folder 2, James W. Nicholson Papers; *Jackson (Miss.) Clarion-Ledger,* 11 July 1889; Kemp P. Battle, *History of the Univ. of North Carolina,* 2:217; James H. Lane to D. F. Boyd, 5 Nov. 1885, in folder 4, box 1, David F. Boyd Papers, Auburn; R. S. McCulloch to William Preston Johnston, 1 June 1883, in folder 1, box 22, Johnston Collection; *Catalogue, Univ. of Texas, 1886–87,* 73–74; *Official Register of LSU . . . 1870,* 24; *Official Register of LSU . . . 1871–72,* 77–80; *Official Register of LSU . . . 1873,* 75–90; *9th Catalogue of the Arkansas Industrial Univ. . . . 1881,* 66; *11th Catalogue of the Arkansas Industrial Univ. . . . 1883,* 67; Joel Colley Watson, "Isaac Taylor Tichenor and the Administration of the Alabama Agricultural College, 1872–1882" (Master's thesis, Auburn Univ., 1968), 66.

61. Joel C. Watson, "Tichenor and the Administration," 62; *Baton Rouge (La.) Tri-Weekly Advocate,* 30 Aug. 1871; "Biographic Sketch," in *Guide to the Eugene Allen Smith Collection,* typescript, Hoole Library, Univ. of Alabama; *Proceedings of the Alabama Industrial and Scientific Society* 1 (1891): 1–8; Andrew A. Lipscomb, "Report," in Board of Trustees, Univ. of Georgia, Minutes, 28 July 1874.

62. Gaston, *New South Creed,* 105–6; Ayers, *Promise of the New South,* 45; Wiener, *Social Origins,* 156–60, 183–85. While president of the Univ. of Alabama (1880–85), Burwell Boykin Lewis did have some success in gaining political support from Alabama's business community; see Norrell, *Promising Field,* 46.

63. F. H. Smith to M. F. Maury, 17 Mar. 1869, in vol. 30, Matthew Fontaine Maury Papers; emphasis original. *Report of the A&M College of Texas [1887–88]* (Austin: Smith, Hicks, & Jones, State Printers, 1889), xviii–xix; *State Grange [Miss.] and A. & M. College: Compiled from the Official Proceedings by Secretary of State Grange* (N.p.: [1886]), 6–7; *Proceedings of the 14th Annual Session of the Texas State Grange, Held at College Station, Brazos County, Texas . . . 1888* (Dallas, Tex.: Texas Farmer, 1888), 4–5; *Proceedings of the Farmers' State Alliance of Texas: 9th Regular Session, Held in Dallas, Texas . . . 1888* (Dallas, Tex.: Circular Letter Office, 1888), 33–35; S. D. Lee, *A&M College of Mississippi,* 18; N. T. Lupton and Eugene A. Smith, *Addresses Delivered Before the State Agricultural Society in Convention at Selma, Alabama, Feb. 2d, 1888* (Montgomery, Ala.: n.p., 1888); James H. Lane to D. F. Boyd, 5 Nov. 1885, in folder 4, box 1, David F. Boyd Papers, Auburn; *National Agricultural Congress,* circular, 1874, in Letters to A. W. Bishop, box 3, Board of Trustees Records, University Archives, Univ. of Arkansas; "Programme of the Alabama State Agricultural Society, to Be Held at Troy, Ala., Aug. 3d, 4th and 5th, 1887" (N.p., n.d.), in folder 75, box 6, William LeRoy Broun Collection, Auburn; William LeRoy Broun, "Speech Before the Inter-State Farmers' Association," in William LeRoy Broun, *Dr. William LeRoy Broun,* 170–88.

64. *Proceedings of 6th Session of Texas State Grange, 1880,* 36; *Louisiana Capitolian* (Baton Rouge), 29 July 1880; Tichenor, *5th Report;* J. B. Angell to D. F. Boyd, 18 Nov. 1874, in *Annual Report of LSU, 1874,* 50; *Report of the Board of the A&M College of the State of Texas,* 37–38; Sutherlin, *Address Delivered 1867,* 26; D. H. Hill, "Brethren of the Orange County Grange," MS, n.d., in box 93.5, Daniel Harvey Hill Papers, NCDAH.

65. *Proceedings of the Texas State Grange . . . 1887,* appendix, p. 6; *Proceedings of the Texas State Grange . . . 1885,* 7–8, 33–34; *Proceedings of the Texas State Grange . . . 1886,* 39–42; Lawrence Goodwyn, *The Populist Moment: A Short History of the Agrarian Revolt in America* (Oxford, England: Oxford Univ. Press, 1978), 20–25; Wright, *Political Economy,* 164–76; *State Grange and A&M College,* 3. See also *Proceedings of the 3rd Session of the State Grange of the Patrons of Husbandry of South Carolina* (Columbia, S.C.: Wm. Sloane, 1875), 5, in folder 1, box 1, Patrons of Husbandry, South Carolina Papers, 1873–76, Special Collections Library, Duke Univ. Library, Durham, N.C.

66. Portion of Morrill text quoted in William S. Aldrich, "Engineering Education and the State Univ.," *Proceedings of the Society for the Promotion of Engineering Education* 2 (1894): 272–73; Brubacher and Rudy, *Higher Education,* 234; Earle D. Ross, *Democracy's College: The Land-Grant Movement in the Formative State* (Ames: Iowa State College Press, 1942), 60–61.

67. "Report by the Committee of Agriculture and Horticulture for the State College," in Board of Trustees, Univ. of Georgia, Minutes, 4 Aug. 1875; Ruffner, J. R.

Anderson, and Sutherlin, "Report of Committee for the Plan of Organization," 18–22; *Columbus (Miss.) Patron of Husbandry,* 24 July 1880; *Charleston (S.C.) News and Courier,* 15 Aug. 1887, clipping in folder 21, box 3, McBryde Family Papers; Hilgard, *Address on Progressive Agriculture,* 28–31; William LeRoy Broun, "Industrial Education," appendix, pp. 17–23; emphasis original. See also Alex'r Hogg, *Industrial Education (Origin and Progress): State A&M College of Texas* (Galveston, Tex.: Galveston News, 1879), 33.

68.   Alan I. Marcus, *Agricultural Science and the Quest for Legitimacy: Farmers, Agricultural Colleges, and Experiment Stations, 1870–1890* (Ames: Iowa State Univ. Press, 1985), 3–86; Egan, *Address at Louisiana State Seminary,* 7; R. S. McCulloch to [D. F. Boyd], 27 Feb. 1884, in folder 116, box 10, McCullock [sic] Letters; D. F. Boyd, "Industrial Education in Louisiana 1875," in folder 7, box 2, LSU Official Papers; Report of Jerome McNeill to the President and Board of Trustees of Arkansas Industrial Univ., 24 Nov. 1891, in box 6, Biology and Geology Reports 1883–1897, Annual Reports, University Archives, Univ. of Arkansas; copy of William LeRoy Broun to H. D. Clayton, 7 Jan. 1885, in folder 71, box 5, William LeRoy Broun Collection, Auburn; original cited as located in Henry DeLamar Clayton Collection; W. G. Clark, "Promise of Education," 169, 173; H. D. Clayton to W. G. Clark, 11 June 1887, in folder 86, box 4, Record Group 1, Trustee Records, University Archives, Univ. of Alabama, Tuscaloosa; William LeRoy Broun, "Presidential Address," in *Proceedings of the 6th Annual Convention of the Association of American Agricultural Colleges and Experiment Stations, Held at New Orleans, La., Nov. 15–19, 1892* (Washington, D.C.: GPO, 1893), 62; copy of William LeRoy Broun to H. D. Clayton, 3 June 1885, in folder 71, box 5, William LeRoy Broun Collection, Auburn; original cited as located in Henry DeLamar Clayton Collection; William LeRoy Broun, *Science Education,* 14–15.

69.   John M. McBryde to the Farmers of Tennessee, 22 July 1879, clipping from unidentified newspaper in folder 21, box 3, McBryde Family Papers; J. M. McBryde, *Agricultural Education: An Address Delivered Before the State Legislature, Dec. 12th, 1882* (Columbia, S.C.: Charles A. Calvo, Jr., 1883), 6; H. R. Thomas to the Editor, *Charleston (S.C.) News and Courier,* 22 July 1887, folder 21, box 3, McBryde Family Papers.

70.   *State Grange and A&M College,* 1–7; "B. R. Tillman in Newberry: His Talk to the Farmers," *Newberry (S.C.) Observer,* 26 Aug. 1886, newspaper clipping in folder 21, box 3, McBryde Family Papers; B. R. Tillman to the Editor, *Charleston (S.C.) News and Courier,* 11 Jan. 1886, in folder 21, box 3, McBryde Family Papers; *Charleston (S.C.) News and Courier,* 15 Aug. 1887.

71.   Wm. J. Robertson to Moses White, 13 May 1879, in folder 1, box 1, McBryde Family Papers; Jno. R. Page to Moses White, 13 May 1879, in McBryde Family Papers; McBryde, *Agricultural Education;* John M. McBryde to the Farmers of Tennessee, 22 July 1879, clipping from unidentified newspaper in folder 21, box 3, McBryde Family Papers.

72.   "The College of the State: First Annual Report of the New Board of Supervisors," *Charleston (S.C.) Weekly News and Courier,* 26 Aug. 1885; *Columbia (S.C.) Daily Register,* 16 May 1891, in folder 3, box 1, McBryde Family Papers; see Hollis, *Univ. of South Carolina,* 2:128–96; Robert M. Calhoun, "James Woodrow," in *American National Biography* (New York: Oxford Univ. Press, 1999), 23:804–5; Buz M. Walker, "These Fifty Years, 1880–1930," typescript, in Buz M. Walker President's File (1925–30), University Archives, Mississippi State Univ.; Reagan, *North Carolina State Univ.,* 15–20; E. Mayes to William LeRoy Broun, 22 July 1889; Edward Mayes, "Report of the Chairman of the

Faculty for 1889," in Board of Trustees, Univ. of Mississippi, Minutes, 6 Aug. 1889; *Catalogue, Univ. of North Carolina, 1890–91,* 52–61.

73. Board of Trustees, Arkansas Industrial Univ., Minutes, 18 Apr. 1887, 2 and 7 June 1887; Edgar, *Biennial Report to Governor, 1886;* Hale, *Univ. of Arkansas,* 55, 63–64; E. H. Murfee, "Biennial Report of the President," in *Biennial Report of the Board of Trustees of the Arkansas Industrial Univ. to His Excellency, Simon P. Hughes, Governor of Arkansas* (Little Rock, Ark.: Press Printing Co., 1889), 11–16; *13th Catalogue of the Arkansas Industrial Univ. . . . 1885* (Little Rock: Mitchell & Bettis, 1885), 16; *15th Annual Catalogue of the Arkansas Industrial Univ. . . . 1887* (Little Rock: Mitchell & Bettis, 1887), 17.

74. For the extensive correspondence among Southern academics, see the following collections: David F. Boyd Papers, University Archives, Auburn Univ.; David F. Boyd Papers, Louisiana and Lower Mississippi Valley Collections, LSU Library; William LeRoy Broun Collection, Auburn; Daniel Harvey Hill Papers, NCDAH; Johnston Collection; Stephen D. Lee, President's Letter Book, University Archives, Mississippi State Univ.; Ashbel Smith Papers, Center for American History; Francis Henney Smith Papers, Archives, VMI.

75. *Catalogue, State A&M College of Alabama, 1883–84; Catalogue, Univ. of Alabama, 1882–83* (Tuscaloosa, Ala.: N.p., 1883);*15th Catalogue, Arkansas Industrial Univ., 1887; Annual Announcement of the Univ. of Georgia* (Athens, Ga.: Banner Job Print., 1891); *Catalogue of the Louisiana State University and Agricultural and Mechanical College, Baton Rouge, Louisiana for 1886–1887* (Baton Rouge: Capitolian-Advocate Book and Job Print, 1887); *First Annual Catalogue of the Officers and Students of the A&M College of Mississippi, 1880–1881* (Jackson, Miss.: Clarion Steam Publishing House, 1881); Edward Mayes, "Report of the Chairman of the Faculty for 1889," in Board of Trustees, Univ. of Mississippi, Minutes, 6 Aug. 1889; Reagan, *North Carolina State Univ.,* 15–20; *Catalogue, Univ. of North Carolina, 1890–91; 5th Annual Report, A&M College of Texas, 1880–81; Catalogue, Univ. of Texas, 1883–84;* Hollis, *Univ. of South Carolina,* 2:128–58; Montgomery, Folmsbee, and Green, *To Foster Knowledge,* 106–70; *Virginia A&M College; Catalogue of the Univ. of Virginia, 1890–1891* (Richmond: N.p., 1891); Wilmore, "Phases of Engineering Education," 63–64.

Chapter 5. Legacy of Progress

1. M. F. Maury to F. H. Smith, 30 Mar. 1867, in folder G-M 1867, Francis Henney Smith Papers. See also Robert E. Lee, [Jr.], *Recollections and Letters of General Robert E. Lee by His Son Captain Robert E. Lee* (New York: Doubleday, Page and Co., 1909), 210.

2. "Southern Education," *Virginia Gazette,* 11 Aug. 1869, reprinted in *Collegian,* 4 Sept. 1869, located in folder 16, box 14, Johnston Collection; Charles R. Wilson, *Baptized in Blood,* 143–60; *Historical Catalogue, Univ. of Mississippi, 1849–1909,* 10; Barringer, Garnett, and Page, *Univ. of Virginia,* vol. 1, 175; Nathaniel E. Harris, *Autobiography: The Story of an Old Man's Life with Reminiscences of 75 Years* (Macon, Ga.: J. W. Burke Co., 1925), 153; Derrell Roberts, "Georgia's G.I. Bill," 418–23.

3. Ruffner, J. R. Anderson, and Sutherlin, "Report of Committee for the Plan of Organization," 5–6, 33; J. N. Craig to the Trustees of the Mississippi A&M College, 19 Mar. 1880, in folder 2, box 1, Edgar Papers; Stephen D. Lee, "Report of the President," in *Report of the Trustees, President and Other Officers of the A&M College of Mississippi, from the Organization of College to Dec. 1st, 1883* (Jackson, Miss.: Clarion Steam Printing Establishment,

1883), 4; William Warren Rogers, "The Founding of Alabama's Land Grant College at Auburn," *Alabama Review* 40 (Jan. 1987): 14–37; Gianniny, "Overlooked Approach," 160–61; "Our University: Some Suggestions from a Friend of the Institution," *Knoxville (Tenn.) Daily Tribune,* 23 June 1886; "Univ. of Alabama," circular [1871 or 1872], in Eugene Allen Smith Collection; *Report of the Board of Supervisors of LSU . . . 1870,* 23; *Report of the Joint Committee on Charitable and Public Institutions to the General Assembly of Louisiana, Jan. 1869* (New Orleans: n.p., 1869), 3–4; *Report of the Board of Supervisors of the Louisiana State Seminary . . . 1867* (New Orleans: N.p., 1867), 12.

4. Abernethy, *Historical Sketch,* 9; Andrew, "Soldiers, Christians, and Patriots," 694–95, 707; *Catalogue of the Officers and Students of the Univ. of Georgia . . . 1874* (Macon, Ga.: J. W. Burke and Co., 1874), 47; *Official Register of LSU, 1871–72,* 27; Sellers, *History of Univ. of Alabama,* 1:486; John K. Bettersworth, *People's College: A History of Mississippi State Univ.* (University: Univ. of Alabama Press, 1953), 66; Oran M. Roberts, *Message,* 41; R. [sic] R. Tillman to the Editor, *Charleston (S.C.) News and Courier,* 27 May 1886, clipping in folder 21, box 3, McBryde Family Papers; *Biennial Report of the Superintendent of Public Instruction to the Governor of the State of Arkansas for the Two Years Ending Sept. 30, 1872* (Little Rock, Ark.: Price and McClure, 1872), 60; Reagan, *North Carolina State Univ.,* 26; William W. Belknap to N. T. Lupton, 24 Nov. 1871, in folder 1209, box 57, Record Group 1, Trustee Records, University Archives, Univ. of Alabama, Tuscaloosa; N. T. Lupton to Chief of Ordnance (Washington, D.C.), 27 May 1872, in folder 1209, box 57, Record Group 1, Trustee Records, University Archives, Univ. of Alabama, Tuscaloosa; M. L. Poland to President of the Univ. of Alabama, 10 June 1872, in box 57, Record Group 1, Trustee Records, University Archives, Univ. of Alabama, Tuscaloosa; Ordnance Office (Washington, D.C.) to Daniel Harvey Hill, 18 Sept. 1878, in box 93.2, Daniel H. Hill Papers, NCDAH; Stephen D. Lee, "President's Report to the Honorable Trustees," in *Biennial Report of the Trustee, President and Other Officers of the A&M College of Mississippi for the Years 1884–85* (Jackson, Miss.: Clarion Steam Publishing Establishment, 1885), 9.

5. Ordnance Office to D. H. Hill, 18 Sept. 1878; *1st Annual Catalogue, A&M College of Mississippi, 1880–81,* 25–27; *5th Annual Report, A&M College of Texas, 1880–81,* 14; Tillman to Editor, *Charleston (S.C.) News and Courier,* 27 May 1886; Kinnear, *First Hundred Years,* 116; Reagan, *North Carolina State Univ.,* 24; D. F. Boyd, *General History of the Seminary Fund and the A&M College Fund, and of the Organization and Work of the Institution Founded Thereon by the State of Louisiana* (Baton Rouge: Bauer Printing Co., 1899), 12.

6. Andrew, "Soldiers, Christians, and Patriots," 683–95. Andrew sees Southern colleges and universities that embraced military instruction as conservative institutions. He does not examine their curricula or explore the ideology of Southern academics beyond the martial and religious elements.

7. Kemp P. Battle, *History of the Univ. of North Carolina,* 2:86; May, "Life of Buchanan," 114–25; James H. Lane to D. F. Boyd, 2 Mar. 1885, in folder 4, box 1, David F. Boyd Papers, Auburn; J. G. James, "President's Report," in *4th Annual Report of the President of the A&M College of Texas with Accompanying Documents* [Nov. 22, 1879–July 1, 1880] (College Station, Tex.: n.p., 1880), 10; Report of the Joint Committee, "The Agricultural and Mechanical College," *Senate [Tex.] Journal,* 4 Mar. 1893, pp. 311–14, in folder 12, box 2, Miscellaneous Publications, Louis Lowry McInnis Papers, University

Archives, Texas A&M Univ., College Station; *Dialectic Reflector* [monthly newspaper of Mississippi A&M], Dec. 1884; two letters from Roy Broun to [William LeRoy Broun], both dated 26 Oct. 1884, in folder 70, box 5, William LeRoy Broun Collection, Auburn.

8. Tillman to Editor, *Charleston (S.C.) News and Courier,* 27 May 1886; *Aiken (S.C.) Recorder,* 8 Sept. 1885, in folder 26, box 4, McBryde Family Papers.

9. H. H. Dinwiddie, "Report of the Chairman of the Faculty," in *Report of the Agricultural and Mechanical College of Texas [1885]* (Austin: E. W. Swindells, State Printer, 1885), 9; Peeler, *Address at Texas A&M,* 1877, 4; Oran M. Roberts, *Message,* 40–42; Report of the Professor of Chemistry, Wm. B. Phillips to Richard C. Jones, 12 June 1891, in folder 1519, box 7, Record Group 1, Trustee Records, University Archives, Univ. of Alabama, Tuscaloosa; Roy Broun to [William LeRoy Broun], 26 Oct. 1884, in folder 70, box 5, William LeRoy Broun Collection, Auburn; Faculty Minutes, Arkansas Industrial Univ., 28 Oct. 1886; J. H. McCleary, *Univ. [of Texas] Address, June 17, 1890* (N.p., n.d.), 16, in bound volume entitled "Univ. of Texas Commencement Addresses," Center for American History; Thomas Dyer, *Univ. of Georgia,* 164–65; Curti, *Social Ideas,* 408; Ric A. Kabat, "Before the Seminoles: Football at Florida State College, 1902–1904," *Florida Historical Quarterly* 70 (July 1991): 21.

10. William Preston Johnston, "The Definition of History," in *Annual Report of the American Historical Association for the Year 1893* (Washington, D.C.: GPO, 1894): 45–53; Johnston, "History: Its Place in a Liberal Education," 1–15; *Catalogue, Univ. of North Carolina, 1890–91,* 51; *Annual Announcement of the Univ. of Georgia with a Catalogue of the Officers and Students, 1881* (Athens: Ga.: Yancey & Cranford, Printers, 1881), 23; *Catalogue of the Univ. of Texas for 1889–90* (Austin, Texas: State Printing Office, 1890), 50–51; *Univ. of Virginia: Its History,* 1:182; Board of Trustees, Mississippi A&M College, Minutes, 14 June 1892; Barringer, Garnett, and Page, *Univ. of Virginia,* 1:186; David Brooks Cofer, *First Five Administrators of Texas A&M College, 1876–1890* (College Station: Association of Former Students of Texas A&M College, 1952), 25–29; Report of J. R. Cole to Jno. G. James, in *5th Annual Report, A&M College of Texas, 1880–81,* 34.

11. R. E. Lee to E. Kirby Smith, 8 Oct. 1866, in folder 53, box 4, Edmund Kirby Smith Papers; Johnston, "History: Its Place in a Liberal Education," 1–15. Johnston's address also appears in a clipping from an unidentified newspaper in folder 24, box 15, Johnston Collection. The last quotation is from the text reported in the newspaper, which differs slightly from the formally published version of the address.

12. Riley, "What General Lee Read," 160–61; R. E. Lee to R. S. McCulloh, 28 Sept. 1869, Robert E. Lee Letters, Miss. Dept. of Archives and History; R. E. Lee to C. F. Lee, Jr., 6 June 1870, in folder 27, box 1, Robert Edward Lee Papers. See also Allen W. Moger, "General Lee's Unwritten 'History of the Army of Northern Virginia,'" *Virginia Magazine of History and Biography* 71 (1963): 341–63.

13. S. D. Lee to E. Kirby Smith, 17 Oct. 1892, in folder 59, box 4, Edmund Kirby Smith Papers; Hattaway, *Stephen D. Lee,* 211; Dabney Lipscomb, "Gen. Stephen D. Lee," 26, 30–31; Fred Arthur Bailey, "The Textbooks of the 'Lost Cause': Censorship and the Creation of Southern State Histories," *Georgia Historical Quarterly* 75 (Fall 1991): 507–8. See also Richard D. Starnes, "Forever Faithful: The Southern Historical Society and Confederate Historical Memory," *Southern Cultures* 2 (Winter 1996): 177–94.

14. Hattaway, *Stephen D. Lee,* 211–12; S. D. Lee to E. Kirby Smith, 17 Oct. 1892;

Dabney Lipscomb, "Gen. Stephen D. Lee," 13–33; Resolution by the Faculty of Mississippi A&M College, 1 May 1899, in Stephen D. Lee Papers.

15. *Confederate Veteran* 5 (Jan. 1897); *Confederate Veteran* 12 (Feb. 1904): 53.

16. Samuel H. Lockett, untitled address to the Southern Historical Society, New Orleans, n.d., in folder 49, box 3, Samuel Henry Lockett Papers, SHC-UNC; Dabney Lipscomb, "Gen. Stephen D. Lee," 17; W. Conard Gass, "Kemp Plummer Battle and the Development of Historical Instruction at the Univ. of North Carolina," *North Carolina Historical Review* 45 (Jan. 1968): 7–18; "Officers for 1898–1899," *Transactions of the Alabama Historical Society* 2 (1897–98): 7; *Report of the Alabama History Commission to the Governor of Alabama, Dec. 1, 1900* (Montgomery, Ala.: Brown Printing Co., 1901), 14–19; Wm. R. Garrett, "The Work of the South in the Building of the United States," *Transactions of the Alabama Historical Society* 3 (1898–99): 27–45.

17. Clarence C. Buell to D. H. Hill, 18 June 1885, in Correspondence 1870–79, box 93.2, Daniel Harvey Hill Papers, NCDAH; photocopy of Clarence C. Buell to D. H. Hill, 29 June 1885, in box 1, Daniel Harvey Hill Papers, Archives Division, Virginia State Library and Archives, Richmond; *Century Magazine*, 1884–87, *passim. Century Magazine* compiled expanded versions of its popular articles by Civil War veterans to create a 32-part, subscription-only series, *Battles and Leaders of the Civil War* (1884–87). *Century* also published these articles in four volumes by the same title in 1887.

18. Jabez Lamar Monroe Curry, *Civil History of the Government of the Confederate States, with Some Personal Reminiscences* (Richmond, Va.: B. F. Johnson, 1901); Dabney Lipscomb, "Gen. Stephen D. Lee," 17; Hesseltine, *Confederate Leaders*, 85; Boatner, *Civil War Dictionary*, 489; *Historical Catalogue, Univ. of Mississippi, 1849–1909*, 74–75.

19. Curry, *Address Before the Institute, 1899*, 3; Johnston, "History: Its Place in a Liberal Education," 15; Thomas Jefferson, *An Essay Towards Facilitating Instruction in the Anglo-Saxon and Modern Dialects of the English Language, for the Use of the Univ. of Virginia* (New York: John F. Trow, 1851); *Official Register of LSU, 1871–72*, 24–25; *Historical Catalogue, Univ. of Mississippi, 1849–1909*, 44–48; *Catalogue of the State A&M College of Texas, Session of 1876–77* (Bryan, Tex.: Pilot Book and Job Office, 1877), 12; Sellers, *History of Univ. of Alabama*, 1:384; *Catalogue, Univ. of Mississippi [1874]*, 17, 27, 29; *Catalogue of the A&M College of Mississippi, 1880–81* (Jackson, Miss.: Clarion Steam Publishing House, 1881), 22–23; Kemp P. Battle, *History of the Univ. of North Carolina*, 2:338–39; *Biennial Report of the Trustees, President, and Other Officers of the Agricultural College of Mississippi for the Years 1890 and 1891* (Jackson, Miss.: R. H. Henry, 1891), 30–31; *Catalogue of the Univ. of Texas, Austin, Tex., for 1891–92*, 21–58; Barringer, Garnett, and Page, *Univ. of Virginia*, 1:182.

20. "Examination in Anglo-Saxon, December 1886," taken by students, MSS, in folder 115, box 5, Dept. of Anglo-Saxon, Univ. of Alabama Examinations, Record Group 1, Trustee Records, University Archives, Univ. of Alabama, Tuscaloosa; *Univ. of Alabama, 53rd Annual Commencement, June 18, 1884* (N.p.: M. I. Burton, [1884]), in scrapbook, vol. 4, 1884–1886, Eugene Allen Smith Collection; *Univ. of Alabama, 54th Commencement, June 17, 1885*, in scrapbook, vol. 4, 1884–1886, Eugene Allen Smith Collection; *Univ. of Alabama Prize Exhibition Orations by Members of the Senior Class, Tuesday, July 3, 1877* (N.p.: J. F. Warren, [1877]), in scrapbook, vol. 2, 1872–1879, Eugene Allen Smith Collection; *Program. Commencement Exercises. A. & M. College of*

Mississippi, 1891 (Starkville, Miss.: O'Brien's Book and Job Office, [1891]), located in Commencement Programs, University Archives, Mississippi State Univ.; Kemp P. Battle, *History of the Univ. of North Carolina,* 2:154, 2:497; Walter B. Hill to Mary Clay Hill, [17 Sept. 1870] and 13 Nov. 1870, in Walter B. Hill, *Student Correspondence,* 190–91, 201.

21. Sutherlin, *Address Delivered 1867,* 22; Lyon Gardiner Tyler, ed., *Encyclopedia of Virginia Biography* (New York: Lewis Historical Publishing Co., 1915), 3:277; Ruffner, J. R. Anderson, and Sutherlin, "Report of Committee for the Plan of Organization"; William Leroy Broun, "Technical Education," *Montgomery Weekly Advertiser,* 7 July 1885. See also Lewis Flint Anderson, *History of Manual and Industrial School Education* (New York: D. Appleton and Co., 1926), 158–62, 178–80; and Charles Alpheus Bennett, *History of Manual and Industrial Education, 1870–1917* (Peoria, Ill.: Manual Arts Press, 1937), 13–52.

22. On the effort by 19th-century American academics to create or accelerate industrialization through technical schools, see Monte A. Calvert, *The Mechanical Engineer in America, 1830–1910* (Baltimore, Md.: Johns Hopkins Univ. Press, 1967).

23. On the Russian system in relation to industrialization and education in Russia and the U.S. (but not specifically the South), see John R. Pannabecker, "Industrial Education and the Russian System: A Study in Economic, Social, and Technical Change," *Journal of Industrial Teacher Education* 24 (Fall 1986): 19–31. See also Peter Kolchin, *Unfree Labor: American Slavery and Russian Serfdom* (Cambridge, Mass.: Belknap Press of Harvard Univ. Press, 1987).

24. William LeRoy Broun, *Science Education,* 8; Boyd to Broun, 11 Dec. 1877; *Official Register of LSU, 1877–78,* 44–45; *Report of the Board of Supervisors of LSU, 1877–78,* appendix, pp. 69–83; *Report of the Board of Supervisors of LSU . . . 1882,* 24; *LSU and A&M College, Baton Rouge, La., Year Ending July 4, 1881* (New Orleans: James A. Gresham, [1881], 14–17; William Preston Johnston, "Manual Training at the Tulane Univ. of Louisiana," in *Industrial Education in the South,* by A. D. Mayo (Washington, D.C.: GPO, 1888), appendix, pp. 60–61.

25. Hardaway, "Book," typescript, R. A. Hardaway to Age Hearld, n.d., 365–68; Hogg, *Industrial Education,* 43–50; R. H. Whitlock, "Department of Mechanics," in *Annual Reports of the Officers and Faculty of the Agricultural and Mechanical College of Texas* (College Station, Tex.: N.p, [1884], no page nos.; Oliver Knight, *Fort Worth: Outpost on the Trinity* (Norman: Univ. of Oklahoma Press, 1953), 161–63; Alexander Hogg, *An Address Prepared for [the] National Educational Association . . . Delivered Also Before the Centennial Bureau of Education, Philadelphia, Sept. 1st, 1876* (Salem, Oh.: W. D. Henkle, 1876), 20–24.

26. Peeler, *Address at Texas A&M, 1877,* 22–23; Hogg, *Industrial Education,* 49–50; Board of Trustees, Mississippi A&M College, Minutes, 5 and 6 Oct. 1880; Oran M. Roberts, Message, 40; McBryde, *Agricultural Education,* 14–15, 20–21; S. D. Lee, "Report of the President" (1883), 10; [Francis Henry Smith,] untitled MS [an address on theology], n.d., in box 1, Harrison, Smith, and Kent Family Papers; Johnston, "Manual Training," 61–63.

27. Kemp P. Battle, "Head and Hand"; Isaac Taylor Tichenor, "Report, 8 January 1877," in Tichenor Papers; Edgar, *Report,* 37; emphasis original. For Gilham, see ch. 1 above.

28. Bettersworth, "Cow in Front Yard," 63–64; John Hugh Reynolds and David Yancey Thomas, *History of the Univ. of Arkansas* (Fayetteville: Univ. of Arkansas, 1910),

462–79, 536–74; Leroy S. Boyd, "Recollections"; Thomas Walter Reed, *'Uncle Tom'*
Reed's Memoir of the Univ. of Georgia, ed. Ray Mathis, Univ. of Georgia Libraries
Miscellanea Publications No. 11 (Athens: Univ. of Georgia Libraries, 1974), 99–100;
Kemp P. Battle, *History of the Univ. of North Carolina,* 2:122; Allen Johnson, ed.,
Dictionary of American Biography (New York: Charles Scribner's Sons, 1935), 1:407–8;
Barringer, Garnett, and Page, *Univ. of Virginia,* 2:12–13; S. W. Geiser, "George Washing-
ton Curtis and Frank Arthur Gulley: Two Early Agricultural Teachers in Texas," *Field and*
Laboratory 14 (Jan. 1946): 1–13; "Faculty Notes," *Longhorn* [Texas A&M] (1903): 20;
John Alfred Heitmann, *The Modernization of the Louisiana Sugar Industry, 1830–1910*
(Baton Rouge: LSU Press, 1987), 230–43; W. A. Martin to L. L. McInnis, 6 Apr. 1891, in
folder 16, box 1, Louis Lowry McInnis Papers.

   29. Eugene W. Hilgard to Col. D. F. Boyd, 11 Feb. 1874, in *Annual Report of LSU for*
1874, 53; Stetar, "In Search of Direction," 358; Charles Forster Smith, "Southern
Colleges," 544–45.

   30. See several letters printed in *Annual Report of LSU for 1874:* Hilgard to Boyd, 11
Feb. 1874, pp. 51–55; E. Kirby Smith to D. F. Boyd, 21 Dec. 1874, p. 65; W. LeRoy
Broun to D. F. Boyd, 20 Nov. 1874, pp. 49–50; W. LeRoy Broun to John R. Page, 21 Dec.
1874, pp. 64–65.

   31. Norrell, *Promising Field,* 78–97; *Univ. of Georgia, General Catalogue, 1900–1901,*
39–40, 126; Reagan, *North Carolina State Univ.,* 22–23; Kemp P. Battle, *History of the*
Univ. of North Carolina, 2:452; Gianniny, "Overlooked Approach," 159–61, 163–64;
Annual Announcement, Univ. of Georgia, with Catalogue of Officers and Students, 1881, 9; O. M.
Roberts, *Faculty Address, June 17, 1890: The Relation of Public Education to the Government of*
Texas (N.p., n.d.), 9, located in bound volume entitled "Univ. of Texas Commencement
Addresses," Center for American History.

   32. *Report of the Board of Supervisors of LSU for the Years 1890–1891 and 1891–1892* (New
Orleans: N.p., 1892), 4–5, 39–40; Aldrich, "Engineering Education," 277–78; Wilmore,
"Phases of Engineering Education," 62; Brubacher and Rudy, *Higher Education,* 79.

   33. Kemp P. Battle, *Memories of Tar Heel,* 250–54; Stephen D. Lee, quoted in Hattaway,
Stephen D. Lee, 173; F. R. Sims, "General Lee at Columbus," *Jackson (Miss.) Clarion-Ledger,* 20
June 1889; *Constitutional Convention, 1890: Report of the Committee Appointed by the State*
Farmers' Alliance in Session at Starkville, to Memorialize the Constitutional Convention Concerning
Certain Matters (N.p.: [1890]), in folder 3, box 1, Charles K. Regan Papers, Mississippi
Department of Archives and History, Jackson; Committee on Education [Constitutional
Convention], Minutes, 15 Aug. 1890, in Regan Papers.

   34. Johnston, *High Schools in Louisiana,* 9; Mallet, *Chemistry Applied to the Arts,* 5–6, 31–
32; Peeler, *Address at Texas A&M, 1877,* 19–27; S. B. Maxey, *University Address . . . Delivered on*
Commencement Day, June 19, 1889, Before the Regents, Faculty, and Students of the Univ. of Texas
(Austin, Tex.: State Printing Office, 1889), 14–16; [Francis Henry Smith], untitled MS draft
of a speech on technical education, n.d.; William LeRoy Broun, "Presidential Address," in
Proceedings of American Agricultural Colleges, 1892, 58–66; Curry, *Address Before the Institute,*
1899, 11, 17–24; Boatner, *Civil War Dictionary,* 830; A. W. Terrell, *Address of Judge A. W. Terrell*
(N.p.: [1884]), 19–22, located in bound volume entitled "Univ. of Texas Commencement
Addresses," Center for American History.

   35. Soule, *Address by Col. Geo. Soule,* 3–4; Andrew A. Lipscomb, "Report," in Board of

Trustees, Univ. of Georgia, Minutes, 25 July 1871; Maxey, *University Address, 1889,* 14–15; [Francis Henry Smith], untitled MS draft of a speech on technical education, n.d. See also James W. Nicholson, *Oration Before the Louisiana State Medical Society* (New Orleans, La.: L. Graham and Son, 1895), pp. 5–12, pamphlet in folder 2, Nicholson Papers.

36. Curry, *Address Before the Institute, 1899,* 24; D. H. Hill, *University Address,* 12–14; Terrell, *Address of Judge Terrell,* 19–20; Johnston, *Problems of Southern Civilization,* 14.

37. Henry Adams recognized the power of the medieval conception of the Virgin Mary to inspire people to transcend their limitations, as demonstrated by the building of the cathedral at Chartres. This inspiration Adams believed was lacking in the industrial 19th century. Samuel Clemens likewise developed a dim view of 19th-century progress and found solace in the medieval heroine Joan of Arc. Henry Adams, *The Education of Henry Adams: An Autobiography* (1918; reprint, New York: Heritage Press, 1942), 353–63; Henry Adams, *Mont-Saint-Michel and Chartres* (1905; reprint, Boston: Houghton Mifflin, 1933); Mark Twain [Samuel Clemens], *Personal Recollections of Joan of Arc . . .* (New York: Harper and Brothers, 1896); Johnston, *Problems of Southern Civilization,* 13–15, 19.

38. Gorgas, "Editorial"; William LeRoy Broun, "Confederate Ordnance," 1–13; Gorgas, "Notes on the Ordnance Department," 67–94; Mallet, "Work of the Ordnance Bureau," 1–20; Emory M. Thomas, *Confederacy as Revolutionary Experience,* 87–99, 135–36; Soule, *Address by Col. Geo. Soule,* 11; Nicholson, *Oration,* 5–8; Ward, "Editor's Note," in Haygood, *New South,* x–xi; Judson C. Ward, ed. "Introduction," to *The New South: Thanksgiving Sermon, 1880* by Atticus G. Haygood (Atlanta, Ga.: The Emory Univ. Library, 1950), x–xi; Peter C. Thomas, "Matthew Fontaine Maury and the Problem of Virginia's Identity," *Virginia Magazine of History and Biography* 90 (Apr. 1982): 236; Curry, *Address Before the Institute, 1899,* 24; Johnston, *Problems of Southern Civilization,* 13–15, 19; William A. Link, *The Paradox of Southern Progressivism, 1880–1930* (Chapel Hill: Univ. of North Carolina Press, 1992), 4–58. On Southern Progressives in the 20th century, see Grantham, *Southern Progressivism.*

39. Samuel H. Lockett, "Woman Enslaved and Woman Free," MS, n.d., in folder 52, box 3, Samuel Henry Lockett Papers, SHC-UNC.

40. Gorgas, *Journals of Josiah Gorgas,* 57; William LeRoy Broun, *Dr. William LeRoy Broun,* 220, 226; Joynes, *Education of Teachers,* 4–20; Curry, *Address Before the Institute, 1899,* 15; emphasis original. Clipping from an unidentified newspaper, in Blewett Lee Scrapbook, vol. 2; Dabney Lipscomb, "Gen. Stephen D. Lee," 28. See also Johnston, *Address to Louisiana Public School Teachers Association,* 12; and Edmund Kirby Smith, untitled MS draft of commencement address for an unnamed school for girls, n.d.

41. Tichenor, *4th Report;* Tichenor, *6th Report;* D. H. Hill to W. P. Johnston, 6 May 1882, in folder 3, box 21, Johnston Collection; M. A. Cohn, "Report of the Secretary of the Board of Trustees Arkansas Industrial Univ., Dec. 31, 1872," in *Biennial Report of the Superintendent of Public Instruction to the Governor of the State of Arkansas for the Two Years Ending Sept. 30, 1872* (Little Rock, Ark.: Price and McClure, 1872), 50–51; Terrell, *Address of Judge Terrell,* 8.

42. *Historical Catalogue, Univ. of Mississippi, 1849–1909,* 74–75; *Jackson (Miss.) Clarion,* 9 June 1886; S. D. Lee to Geo. M. Edgar, 23 Jan. 1885, in S. D. Lee, President's Letter Book, vol. 3; R. W. Jones, "Industrial Institute and College for the Education of White Girls of Mississippi," in *Industrial Education in the South,* by A. D. Mayo (Washington, D.C.: GPO, 1888), appendix, pp. 55–56.

43. Peeler, *Address at Texas A&M, 1877,* 33–34; *Jackson (Miss.) Clarion-Ledger,* 30 Aug. 1888; Curry, *Address Before the Institute, 1899,* 16; Edmund Kirby Smith, untitled MS draft of commencement address for an unnamed school for girls, n.d.

44. R. W. Jones, "Industrial Institute," 55; Stephen D. Lee, quoted in a clipping from an unidentified newspaper, Blewett Lee Scrapbook, vol. 3. Although sympathetic to the expansion of women's rights in general, Lee supported female suffrage in part because, prior to Mississippi's disfranchisement of African Americans in 1890, he believed that female suffrage would "secure white supremacy and to a great extent solve the negro problem."

45. Nicholson, *Oration,* 12; Soule, *Address by Col. Geo. Soule,* 3–4; J. M. McBryde, untitled commencement address, typescript, n.d., in folder 23, box 3, McBryde Family Papers. The novelist is not identified.

46. Kemp P. Battle, *History of the Univ. of North Carolina,* 2:380.

47. Ibid., 2:235, 2:266, 2:331, 2:386, 2:395, 2:465, 2:501; S. D. Lee to Henry W. Grady, 2 Feb. 1887, in S. D. Lee, President's Letter Book, vol. 4; *New Orleans (La.) Picayune,* 30 June 1873; *Commencement Exercises: A&M College of Mississippi,* 1891, 1892, and 1895; A&M College, Auburn, Ala., *3rd Class Declamation, 1890: Thursday, May 1, 8 P.M.* (N.p., n.d.), in folder 88, box 6, William LeRoy Broun Collection, Auburn; *Univ. of Alabama Prize Exhibition Orations, July 3, 1877,* in scrapbook, vol. 2, 1872–1879, Eugene Allen Smith Collection; *Program of Exercises for Commencement Day of the Arkansas Industrial Univ., Fayetteville, Ark., June 17, 1875* (N.p., n.d.), in University Archives, Univ. of Arkansas; *Univ. of Alabama, 54th Commencement, June 17, 1885,* in scrapbook, vol. 4, 1884–1886, Eugene Allen Smith Collection.

48. *Commencement Exercises: A. & M. College of Mississippi, 1895;* Kemp P. Battle, *History of the Univ. of North Carolina,* 2:463; *Commencement Exercises: A. & M. College of Mississippi, 1890;* Thomas Walter Reed, "History of the Univ. of Georgia," typescript in 19 vols., n.d., pp. 5:1257–58, University Archives, Univ. of Georgia; Board of Trustees, Univ. of Georgia, Minutes, 12 July 1887; "The Skeptics of Yesterday Are the Saints of Tomorrow," *College Reflector* [Mississippi A&M] 4 (Oct. 1890): 10; Richard N. Graham, "The Economic Man," *Ozark* [Arkansas Industrial Univ.] 4 (May 1897): 351.

49. Pat Walker, "The Responsibility That Will Devolve on Us," *College Reflector* 5 (Mar. 1892): 16–17; J. D. G. [Guyton], "Was It Defeat?" *College Reflector* 14 (Dec. 1900): 14–16; Kemp P. Battle, *History of the Univ. of North Carolina,* 2:254.

50. *Report of the Board of Supervisors of LSU, 1882,* 21–23; William LeRoy Broun to D. F. Boyd, 27 Nov. 1873, in folder 57, box 7, William LeRoy Broun Letters (1873–87), Walter L. Fleming Collection; *Biennial Report of the Trustees, President and Other Officers of the Mississippi A&M College for the years 1892 and 1893* (Jackson, Miss.: Clarion-Ledger Publishing Company, 1893), 7; *Biennial Report of the Arkansas Industrial Univ. . . . 1895,* 8.

51. *2nd Decennial Catalogue of the Mississippi A&M College, 1890–1900* (Meridian, Miss.: Meridian News, n.d.), 12; *17th Annual Catalogue of the A&M College of Texas, Session 1892–93,* 65; R. A. Hardaway to H. D. Clayton, 12 June 1888, in folder 1520, Record Group 1, Trustee Records, University Archives, Univ. of Alabama, Tuscaloosa; Dan R. Frost and Kou K. Nelson, T*he LSU College of Engineering: Origins and Establishment, 1860–1908* (Baton Rouge: LSU College of Engineering, distributed by LSU Press, 1995), 154; James E. Brittain and Robert C. McMath, Jr., "Engineers and the New South

Creed: The Formation and Early Development of Georgia Tech," *Technology and Culture* 18 (Apr. 1977): 199.

52. Curry, *Address Before the Institute, 1899,* 17–18; Ayers, *Promise of the New South;* Rabinowitz, *First New South;* James C. Cobb, "Beyond Planters and Industrialists: A New Perspective on the New South," *Journal of Southern History* 54 (Feb. 1988): 54–55.

53. Calvert, *Mechanical Engineer;* David F. Noble, *America by Design: Science, Technology, and the Rise of Corporate Capitalism* (New York: Knopf, 1977); Norrell, *Promising Field,* 54–55; Pannabecker, "Industrial Education," 19–37.

54. Thomas Boyd to Boykin Pegues, 29 Nov. 1898, in folder 1, box 1, Boykin W. Pegues Papers; Barringer, Garnett, and Page, *Univ. of Virginia,* 2:11–12, 2:16–17; *Longhorn* (1903): 20–27; Thomas Walter Reed, *'Uncle Tom' Reed's Memoir,* 63n–64n, 68–69; Robert C. McMath, Jr., et al., *Engineering the New South: Georgia Tech, 1885–1985* (Athens: Univ. of Georgia Press, 1985), 97; Heitmann, *Louisiana Sugar Industry,* 236; Foster, *Ghosts,* 180.

55. Edwin A. Alderman, *Sectionalism and Nationality . . . Before the New England Society in the City of New York, Dec. 22, 1906* (N.p., n.d.), 8–13, in [Edwin A.] Alderman, *Addresses* (N.p., n.d.), bound collection of addresses located in the Howard-Tilton Memorial Library. For similar sentiments, see Edwin A. Alderman, *The Growing South: An Address Delivered Before the Civic Forum in Carnegie Hall, New York City, March 22, 1908* (New York: Civic Forum, 1908).

56. Ayers, *Promise of the New South,* 417–23; Curti, *Social Ideas,* 281; Virginius Dabney, *Liberalism in the New South* (Chapel Hill: Univ. of North Carolina Press, 1932), 177–89; Horace H. Cunningham, "The Southern Mind Since the Civil War," in *Writing Southern History: Essays in Historiography in Honor of Fletcher M. Green,* ed. Arthur S. Link and Rembert W. Patrick (Baton Rouge: LSU Press, 1965), 399; Charles William Dabney, *Universal Education in the South* (Chapel Hill: Univ. of North Carolina Press, 1936), 1:182–89, 1:206–5, 1:378–80, and vol. 2; Leloudis, *Schooling the New South,* ch. 2. To his credit, Leloudis acknowledges the influence of Battle's curricular reforms at the Univ. of North Carolina on Alderman and other educational reformers in North Carolina.

57. Charles W. Dabney, "Progress of Renationalization"; Grantham, *Southern Progressivism,* 246–74; Neufeldt and Allison, "Rise of the New South," 252–55; Spencer J. Maxcy, "Progressivism and Rural Education in the Deep South, 1900–1950," in *Education and the Rise of the New South,* ed. Ronald K. Goodenow and Arthur O. White (Boston: G. K. Hall, 1981), 50–52; Woodward, *Origins of the New South,* 396–97, 400–401, 436–38; Charles W. Dabney, "The Watauga Club," typescript, n.d., in folder 274, box 21, Charles W. Dabney Papers; Hugh C. Bailey, *Liberalism in the New South,* 81; Lawrence A. Cremin, *American Education: The Metropolitan Experience, 1876–1980* (New York: Harper and Row, 1988), 216–19; Wagstaff, *Impressions,* 57–59; James Knox Powers, "Co-education in Alabama," [probably 1897], typescript, in James Knox Powers Vertical File, William Stanley Hoole Special Collections Library, Univ. of Alabama, Tuscaloosa; Charles W. Dabney, "Woman: Her Education and Service," in folder 325, box 26, ser. 5, subser. 5.2, Charles W. Dabney Papers.

58. J. C. Nagle, "The Influence of Applied Science," *Texas Academy of Science* 4, pt. 2 (Feb. 1902): 10; Francis P. Venable, "Address Before Washington and Lee Univ.," typescript, n.d., in folder 128, box 3, Francis Preston Venable Papers; Francis P. Venable, "Presidential

Address Before the *Southern Educational* Association, Atlanta, Ga., Dec. 30, 1903," typescript, in folder 131, box 3, Francis P. Venable Papers; W. P. Few, "Some Educational Needs of the South," *South Atlantic Quarterly* 3 (July 1904): 201–11; Alderman, *Growing South,* 5; John C. Futrall, "President's Address," *Reprint from the Proceedings of 47th Annual Convention of the Association of Land Grant Colleges and Universities, Chicago, Ill., Nov. 13–15, 1933* (Burlington, Vt.: Free Press, 1934), 28–34; W. P. Trent, *The Study of Southern History* (N.p.: [1896?]), 1–24, reprinted from the Vanderbilt Observer, n.d.; Henneman, "Historical Studies in the South," 320–39; Frederick W. Moore, "The Status of History in Southern Colleges," *South Atlantic Quarterly* 2 (Apr. 1903): 169–71; George T. Winston, *The Influence of Universities and Public Schools on National Life and Character* (N.p.: [1896]), 1–3, located in bound volume entitled "Univ. of Texas Commencement Addresses," Center for American History; Charles W. Dabney, "The State University: The Institution of Democracy," typescript, [1902], in folder 329, box 26, ser. 5, subser. 5.2, Charles W. Dabney Papers.

59. Charles William Dabney, *Universal Education,* 1:154–61; Robert Lewis Dabney, *Life and Campaigns of Lieut. Gen. Thomas J. Jackson* (New York: Blelock and Co., 1866); R. L. Dabney to Dear Charley, 9 Dec. 1881, in folder 67, box 4, ser. 1, subser. 1.4, Charles William Dabney Papers; Charles R. Wilson, *Baptized in Blood*, 11; R. L. Dabney, *New South,* 1–16.

60. Charles W. Dabney, "A Child During the Civil War," typescript, [1939–45?], in folder 280, box 22, ser. 4, Charles W. Dabney Papers; Charles W. Dabney, "Birth and Early Childhood," typescript, [1939–45?], in folder 281, box 22, ser. 4, Charles W. Dabney Papers; Charles W. Dabney, notes for his memoirs, typescript, [1939–45?], in folder 272, box 21, ser. 4, Charles W. Dabney Papers.

61. Draft of Chas. W. Dabney to Board of Trustees of Emory and Henry College, 13 June 1877, in folder 65, box 4, ser. 1, subser. 1.4, Charles W. Dabney Papers; Charles W. Dabney to Jno. A. Campbell, 20 July 1878, in folder 66, box 4, Charles W. Dabney Papers; "In Memory of Professor Mallet," 28.

62. Charles W. Dabney, *Universal Education,* 1:187–88.

63. Draft of Charles W. Dabney to Jas. Comfort, 11 July 1887, in folder 71, box 5, ser. 1, subser. 1.4, Charles W. Dabney Papers; Charles W. Dabney, "State University"; Charles W. Dabney, "Declaration of Educational Principles with Special Reference to the Needs of the South," typescript, [29 Feb. 1904], in folder 321, box 26, ser. 5, subser. 5.2, Charles W. Dabney Papers.

64. Charles W. Dabney, "Progress of Renationalization." See also Charles W. Dabney, "The Task of the Renationalization of the South," typescript of address delivered at the Univ. of South Carolina, 11 Jan. 1917, in folder 319, box 25, ser. 5, subser. 5.2, Charles W. Dabney Papers.

65. Charles Dabney, "Progress of Renationalization"; Charles W. Dabney, *Universal Education.*

66. Hugh C. Bailey, *Liberalism in the New South,* 131; Cobb, "Beyond Planters," 57; Grantham, *Southern Progressivism,* 246; Alderman, *Growing South,* 6; Charles Dabney, "State University"; Charles Dabney, "President Battle and the University," typescript, 1928, in folder 274, box 21, ser. 4, Charles W. Dabney Papers; Edwin A. Alderman, *In Memoriam Charles Duncan McIver* (N.p.: 1907); Charles W. Dabney, *Universal Education;*

Francis P. Venable, "Walter H. Page: Democrat, Statesman, and Man," typescript, n.d., in folder 134, box 3, Francis P. Venable Papers.

67. Charles W. Dabney, "The Consolidation of the Three Colleges of North Carolina," typescript, [1931–32], in folder 283, box 22, ser. 4, Charles W. Dabney Papers; Edwin L. Stephens, "The Story of Acadian Education in Louisiana," *Louisiana Historical Quarterly* 18 (Apr. 1935): 401; Charles W. Dabney, "Bible Instruction in the College," typescript, n.d., in folder 281, box 22, Charles W. Dabney Papers; Chas. Lee Smith, "Mr. Hill's Relation to the Denominational Colleges," *Bulletin of the Univ. of Georgia,* Memorial Number (May 1906): 42–45; James E. Dickey, "Mr. Hill's Relation to the Denominational Colleges," *Bulletin of the Univ. of Georgia,* Memorial Number (May 1906): 46–51; H. C. White, "In What Ways Can the Average American College Best Constitute to the Promotion of the International Peace Movement?" typescript, n.d., in folder 8, box 1, Henry Clay White Collection, Hargrett Rare Books and Manuscript Library, Univ. of Georgia, Athens; Hugh C. Bailey, *Liberalism in the New South,* 118; Grantham, *Southern Progressivism,* 28–32; Foster, *Ghosts,* 180–86.

68. Charles Dabney, "Progress of Renationalization"; "Henry Clay White," typescript, n.d., in folder 1, box 1, Henry Clay White Collection, from a clipping in an unidentified newspaper, folder 2, box 1, Henry Clay White Collection; White, "Peace Movement"; H. C. White to William LeRoy Broun, 23 Sept. 1890, in folder 89, box 6, William LeRoy Broun Collection, Auburn. On the attitudes of late-19th and early-20th-century Southern intellectuals toward race, see Bruce Clayton, *The Savage Ideal: Intolerance and Intellectual Leadership in the South, 1890–1914* (Baltimore, Md.: Johns Hopkins Univ. Press, 1972).

69. Walter B. Hill to Herbert Clay Hill, 13 June 1869, in Walter B. Hill, *Student Correspondence,* 91; Walter B. Hill to Mary Clay Hill, 6 Sept. 1868, in Walter B. Hill, *Student Correspondence,* 65–66; Walter B. Hill to Barnard Hill, 28 June 1868, in Walter B. Hill, *Student Correspondence,* 53–55; Walter B. Hill to Barnard Hill, 20 Sept. 1868, in Walter B. Hill, *Student Correspondence,* 71; Walter B. Hill to Henry Clay Hill, 3 Oct. 1869, in Walter B. Hill, *Student Correspondence,* 124; Walter B. Hill to Mary Clay Hill, 9 Apr. 1871, in Walter B. Hill, *Student Correspondence,* 229; Walter B. Hill to Herbert Clay Hill, 20 June 1868, in Walter B. Hill, *Student Correspondence,* 50–51; "Editor's Preface" to Walter B. Hill, *Student Correspondence,* xi; Thomas Dyer, Univ. of Georgia, 154.

70. Edgar Gardner Murphy, *The Task of the South: An Address Before the Faculty and Students of Washington and Lee Univ., Lexington, Va., Dec. 10th, A.D., 1902* (Montgomery, Ala.: n.p., [1903?]), 1–11; Wilmore, "Phases of Engineering Education," 62; Aldrich, "Engineering Education," 277–78.

71. F. P. V. [Venable] to [Mrs. Venable], 16 Apr. 1886, in folder 31, box 1, Francis P. Venable Papers; F. P. Venable, quoted in Nancy Smith Midgette, *To Foster the Spirit of Professionalism: Southern Scientists and the State Academies of Science* (Tuscaloosa: Univ. of Alabama Press, 1991), 27; Francis P. Venable, "Presidential Address."

72. Frost and Nelson, *LSU College of Engineering,* 124; *Report of the Board of Supervisors of LSU . . .1900–1902,* 13; Alderman, *Growing South,* 7; see also Charles Dabney, "State University." Daniel J. Whitener questions whether an "educational renaissance" actually took place after 1900; see his "Republican Party and Public

Education in North Carolina, 1867–1900," *North Carolina Historical Review* 37 (July 1960): 393.

73. Braden and Mixon, "Epideictic Speaking," 43.

74. Thomas Sheehan, *The First Coming: How the Kingdom of God Became Christianity* (New York: Random House, 1986), 57–69.

75. Stephen D. Lee, quoted in Hattaway, *Stephen D. Lee,* 196.

76. Ayers, *Promise of the New South;* Rabinowitz, *First New South;* Numan V. Bartley, "Another New South?" *Georgia Historical Quarterly* 65 (Summer 1981): 119–37.

Bibliography

I. Primary Sources
A. Manuscript Collections

Auburn University, Special Collections and University Archives, Draghon Library, Auburn, Alabama.

> Boyd, David F. Papers.
> Boyd, Leroy Stafford. Collection.
> Broun, William LeRoy. Collection.
> Lane, James H. Papers.
> Tichenor, Isaac Taylor. Papers.

College of William and Mary, University Archives, Williamsburg, Virginia.

> Ewell, Benjamin Stoddert. Papers.

Duke University, Special Collections Library, Durham, North Carolina.

> Lewis, Burwell Boykin. Papers.

Stephen D. Lee Museum, Columbus, Mississippi.

> Lee, Blewett. Scrapbooks. Volumes 1–3.

Library of Congress, Washington, D.C.

> Maury, Matthew Fontaine. Papers.

Louisiana State University Libraries, Louisiana and Lower Mississippi Valley Collections, Baton Rouge, Louisiana.

Board of Supervisors, Louisiana State University and Agricultural and Mechanical College. Minutes. 1881–86.

> Fleming, Walter L. Collection
> > Bragg, Braxton. Letters.
> > Broun, William LeRoy. Letters.
> > Hebert, P. O. Letters.
> > Lockett, Samuel H. Letters and Related Items.
> > McCullock, [sic] Richard S. Letters and Related Items.
> > Smith, Francis H. Letters.
> > Vallas, Anthony. Letters.
> > Venable, Richard M. Letters and Related Items.

> Nicholson, James W. Papers.
> Pegues, Boykin W. Papers.

Mississippi Department of Archives and History, Jackson, Mississippi.

Hilgard, Eugene W. Papers.
Lee, Robert E. Letters.
Regan, Charles K. Papers.

Mississippi State University, University Archives, Starkville, Mississippi.

Board of Trustees, Mississippi Agricultural and Mechanical College.
   Minutes. 1880–92.
Claiborne, John Francis Hamtramck. Papers. On microfilm. (Originals
   in John Francis Hamtramck Claiborne Papers, Southern Historical
   Collection, University of North Carolina, Chapel Hill, North
   Carolina.)
Commencement Programs.
Lee, Stephen Dill. Papers. On microfilm. (Originals in Stephen Dill Lee
   Papers, Southern Historical Collection, University of North
   Carolina, Chapel Hill, North Carolina.)
President's Letter Books. Volumes 1–4.
Walker, Buz M. President's File.

North Carolina Department of Archives and History, Raleigh, North Carolina.

Hill, Daniel Harvey, Jr. Papers.
Hill, Daniel Harvey [Sr.]. Papers.

Texas Agricultural and Mechanical University, University Archives, College Station, Texas.

Bringhurst W. L. Vertical File.
Dinwiddie, Hardaway Hunt. Vertical File.
McInnis, Louis Lowry. Papers.

Tulane University, Manuscripts and Rare Books, Howard-Tilton Memorial Library, New Orleans, Louisiana.

Johnston, William Preston. Collection.

University of Alabama, Tuscaloosa, Alabama.

Gorgas Library
   Alabama Collection.
   Rare Book Room.
William Stanley Hoole Special Collections Library
   Clayton, Henry DeLamar. Collection.
   Garland, Landon C. Letters.
   Gorgas Family. Papers.
   Lewis, Burwell Boykin. Vertical File.
   Powers, James Knox. Vertical File.
   Smith, Eugene Allen. Collection.

University Archives
   Board of Trustees, University of Alabama. Minutes. 1876–1884.
   Trustee Records.

University of Arkansas, University Archives, Fayetteville, Arkansas.

   Annual Reports.
   Biology and Geology Reports. 1883–97.
   Board of Trustees. Records. 1868–1934.
   Faculty Minutes. 1881–86.
   Letters.

University of Georgia, Athens, Georgia.

   Hargrett Rare Books and Manuscript Library
      Reed, Thomas Walter. "History of the University of Georgia."
         19 volumes. Typescript, n.d.
      White, Henry Clay. Collection.
   University Archives
      Board of Trustees, University of Georgia. Minutes. 1855 77.

University of Mississippi, Archives and Special Collections, Williams Library, Oxford, Mississippi.

   Board of Trustees, University of Mississippi. Minutes. 1860–89.

University of North Carolina, Chapel Hill, North Carolina

   Southern Historical Collection, Wilson Library
      Bailey, John Lancaster. Papers.
      Dabney, Charles W. Papers.
      Edgar, George M. Papers.
      Hardaway, Robert A. "Book." Microfilm #3006.
      Hedrick, Benjamin Sherwood. Papers.
      Hill, Daniel Harvey. Papers.
      Kimberly, John. Papers.
      Lockett, Samuel Henry. Papers.
      McBryde Family. Papers.
      Smith, Edmund Kirby. Papers.
      Stubbs, William C. Papers.
      Venable, Francis Preston. Papers.
   University Archives
      Board of Trustees, University of North Carolina. Minutes. 1859.

University of Texas, Center for American History, Austin, Texas

   Roberts, Oran Milo. Papers.

University of Virginia, Manuscripts Department, Alderman Library, Charlottesville, Virginia.

Board of Visitors, University of Virginia. Minutes. 27 May 1861 to 16
July 1861.
Harrison, Smith, and Kent Family. Papers.

Virginia Military Institute, Archives, Lexington, Virginia.

Smith, Francis Henney. Papers.
Report of the Board of Visitors of the Virginia Military Institute.
1850–1857.

Virginia State Library and Archives, Archives Division, Richmond, Virginia.

Hill, Daniel Harvey. Papers.

Washington and Lee University, University Archives, Lexington, Virginia.

Board of Trustees, Washington College. Minutes. 1865.
Lee, Robert Edward. Papers.
Trustee Papers.

B. Addresses, Books, Papers, and Pamphlets

Adams, Henry. *The Education of Henry Adams: An Autobiography.* 1918. Reprint,
New York: Heritage Press, 1942.
———. *Mont-Saint-Michel and Chartres.* 1905. Reprint, Boston: Houghton
Mifflin Company, 1933.
*An Address on Southern Education Delivered July 18, 1859, Before the Faculty,
Trustees, Students, and Patrons of "Madison College," Sharon, Mississippi.*
Washington, D.C.: n.p., 1859.
Alderman, Edwin A. *The Growing South: An Address Delivered Before the Civic
Forum in Carnegie Hall, New York City, March 22, 1908.* New York: Civic
Forum, 1908.
———. *In Memoriam Charles Duncan McIver.* N.p., 1907.
———. *Sectionalism and Nationality . . . Before the New England Society in the
City of New York, December 22, 1906.* N.p., n.d.
Avery, A. C. *Memorial Address on [the] Life and Character of Lieutenant General D. H.
Hill, May 10th, 1893.* Raleigh, N.C.: Edwards and Broughton, 1893.
Avery, W. W. *Address Delivered Before the Two Literary Societies of the Univ. of
North Carolina, June 4, 1851.* Raleigh, N.C.: William W. Holden, 1851.
Baptist, Edward. *Address Delivered Before the Trustees, Faculty, and Students of
Howard College . . . November 16, 1846.* Tuscaloosa, Ala.: M. D. J. Slade,
1846.
Barksdale, Wm. R. *The True Office of the College: An Address, Delivered Before the
Alumni Association of the University of Mississippi, July 15, 1857.* Mem-
phis, Tenn.: Bulletin Company, 1857.
Barnard, F. A. P. *Improvements Practicable in American Colleges.* Hartford, Conn.:
F. C. Brownell, 1856.
———. *Memoirs of Frederick A. P. Barnard.* Edited by John Fulton. New York:
Macmillan and Company, 1896.

————. *An Oration Delivered Before the Citizens of Tuscaloosa, Ala., July 4th, 1851.* Tuscaloosa, Ala.: J. W. and J. F. Warren, 1851.

Battle, Kemp P. *History of the University of North Carolina.* 2 vols. Raleigh, N.C.: Edwards and Broughton, 1907.

————. *Memories of an Old Time Tar Heel.* Edited by William James Battle. Chapel Hill: Univ. of North Carolina Press, 1945.

————. *Sketches of the History of the University of North Carolina, Together with a Catalogue of Officers and Students, 1789–1889.* N.p.: [Chapel Hill]: Univ. of North Carolina, 1889.

Battle, William H. *Address Delivered Before the Two Literary Societies of the University of North Carolina, June 1st, 1865.* Raleigh, N.C.: Wm. B. Smith and Company, 1866.

Battles and Leaders of the Civil War. 4 vols. New York: Century, 1887.

Bledsoe, Albert T. *Address Delivered at the First Annual Commencement of the University of Mississippi, July 12th, 1849.* Oxford, Miss.: Organizer Office, 1849.

Board of Trustees of the State [Mississippi] University. *Where Shall I Send My Son? An Address to the People of Mississippi.* N.p.: [1876].

Boyd, D. F. *Address of [the] Superintendent, Louisiana State Seminary, to the Graduating Class, Delivered June 30, 1869.* New Orleans: Jas. A. Gresham, 1869.

————. *Address . . . on the Anniversary of the Delta Rifles, 4th Louisiana Regiment, Confederate States Army, at Port Allen, West Baton Rouge, La., May 20th, 1887.* Baton Rouge, La.: Capitolian-Advocate Book and Job Print, 1887.

————. *Address to the Graduating Class, Delivered June 30th, 1869.* New Orleans: Jas. A. Gresham, n.d.

————. *General History of the Seminary Fund and the Agricultural and Mechanical College Fund, and of the Organization and Work of the Institution Founded Thereon by the State of Louisiana.* Baton Rouge, La.: Bauer Printing Company, 1899.

————. *Louisiana State University Scheme to Raise an Endowment Fund.* New Orleans: n.p., 1872.

————. *Reminiscences of the War in Virginia.* Edited by T. Michael Parrish. Baton Rouge, La.: United States Civil War Center, 1994.

Broun, William LeRoy. *Dr. William LeRoy Broun.* Compiled by Thomas L. Broun. New York: Neale Publishing Company, 1912.

————. *Improvements Required in Southern Colleges: Read Before the Teachers' Association of Georgia, in Macon, Decb'r 19th, 1867.* Macon, Ga.: J. W. Burke and Company, 1868.

————. *Science-Education: An Address . . . Delivered at the Annual Commencement of the A. and M. College of Alabama.* Auburn, Ala.: n.p., 1880.

Brown, A. G. *Governor's Message Delivered at the Biennial Session [of the Mississippi State Legislature], January, 1848, and Accompanying Documents.* N.p., [1848?].

Brown, Aaron V. *Address Delivered Before the Literary Societies of the University of North Carolina . . . May 31, 1854.* Nashville: J. F. Morgan, 1854.

Burwell, W. M. *Address Delivered Before the Faculty and Students of the Louisiana*

State University, On Wednesday, 25th June, 1871. N.p.: Price Current, [1871?].

Campbell, John A. *Address Delivered Before the Alumni Society of the University of Georgia.* Athens, Ga.: J. S. Peterson, 1853.

Cappon, Lester J., ed. *The Adams-Jefferson Letters: The Complete Correspondence Between Thomas Jefferson and Abigail and John Adams.* 2 vols. Chapel Hill, N.C.: Institute of Early American History and Culture, 1959.

Clapp, J. W. *Address Delivered at the University of Mississippi on Behalf of the Board of Trustees on Commencement Day, June 29, 1866.* Memphis, Tenn.: Public Ledger Office, n.d.

Clark, Willis G. "The Promise of Education." In *Memorial Record of Alabama.* 2 vols., 154–76. Madison, Wisc.: Brant and Fuller, 1893.

Clayton, Alexander M. *Address Delivered at the First Annual Commencement of the University of Mississippi . . . July 12, 1849.* Oxford, Miss.: Organizer Office, 1849.

———. *Commencement Address . . . Read Before the Law Students of the University of Mississippi on the 26th Day of June, 1860.* Oxford, Miss.: n.p., 1860.

Clemens, Samuel L. [Mark Twain]. *Personal Recollections of Joan of Arc . . .* New York: Harper and Brothers, 1896.

———. "The Private History of a Campaign That Failed." In Samuel L. Clemens [Mark Twain], *The American Claimant and Other Stories and Sketches,* pp. 255–82. New York: P. F. Collier and Son Company, 1899.

Colton, Simeon. *An Address Delivered at His Inauguration to the Presidency of Mississippi College, July 30, A.D. 1846.* Jackson, Miss.: Southron Office, 1846.

Comte, Auguste. *The Essential Comte: Selected from* Cours de Philosophie Positive, *Paris, 1830–42.* Edited by Stanislav Andreski. New York: Barnes and Noble, 1974.

Cooper, Thomas. *Address to the Graduates of the South Carolina College, at the Public Commencement, 1830.* Columbia, S.C.: S. J. M. Morris, 1831.

———. *Address to the Graduates of the South Carolina College, December, 1821.* Columbia, S.C.: D. Faust, 1821.

Croom, Isaac. *Address Delivered Before the Greensboro Agricultural Society on the 2d of May, 1850.* [Greensboro, Ala.]: n.p., [1850?].

Curry, J. L. M. *Address Before the Alabama Polytechnic Institute, Auburn, Alabama, June 14th, 1899.* Montgomery, Ala.: Brown Printing Company, 1899.

———. *Civil History of the Government of the Confederate States, with Some Personal Reminiscences.* Richmond, Va.: B. F. Johnson, 1901.

Dabney, Charles William. *Universal Education in the South.* 2 vols. Chapel Hill: Univ. of North Carolina Press, 1936.

Dabney, Robert Lewis. *Life and Campaigns of Lieut. Gen. Thomas J. Jackson.* New York: Blelock and Company, 1866.

———. *The New South: A Discourse Delivered at the Annual Commencement of Hampden-Sidney College, June 15, 1882, Before the Philanthropic and Union Literary Societies.* Raleigh, N.C.: Edwards, Broughton and Company, 1883.

Davis, Jefferson. *Address Before the Phi Sigma and Hermean Societies, of the University of Mississippi, Oxford, July 15, 1852.* Memphis, Tenn.: Appeal Book and Job Office, 1852.

Dew, Thomas R. *An Essay on Slavery.* Richmond, Va.: J. W. Randolph, 1849.

Dinwiddie, H. H. *Industrial Education in Our Common Schools . . . Paper Read Before the Texas State Teachers Convention . . . at Waco, Texas, July 1, 1885.* Fort Worth, Tex.: Loving Printing Company, 1886.

Egan, Bartholomew. *Address Delivered at the Commencement Exercises of the Louisiana State Seminary and Military Academy.* Alexandria, La.: n.p., 1866.

Elliott, E. N., ed. *Cotton Is King and Pro-Slavery Arguments.* Augusta, Ga.: Pritchard, Abbott, and Loomis, 1860.

Faust, Drew Gilpin, ed. *The Ideology of Slavery: Proslavery Thought in the Antebellum South, 1830–1860.* Baton Rouge: Louisiana State Univ. Press, 1981.

Fleming, Walter L., ed. *General W. T. Sherman as College President.* Cleveland, Oh.: Arthur H. Clark, 1912.

Garland, L. C., and Ormond, J. J. [*Military Department—University of Alabama*]. N.p., [1861].

Goodwin, S. A. *Commencement Sermon Delivered Before the Students of the University of Columbus, Sunday, June 26th, 1876 . . . Subject: Excellency of the Knowledge of Christ.* Columbus, Miss.: Excelsior Book and Job, 1876.

Gorgas, Josiah. *The Journals of Josiah Gorgas, 1857–1878.* Edited by Sarah Woolfolk Wiggins. Tuscaloosa: Univ. of Alabama Press, 1995.

Green, William Mercer. *Address Delivered Before the Board of Trustees of the University of the South, Sewanee, Tenn., Monday of Commencement Week, July 28, 1878.* Sewanee, Tenn.: Mountain News, [1878?].

Grigsby, Hugh Blair. *Oration, Delivered Before the Students of William and Mary College, July 4, 1859.* N.p., n.d.

Hamilton, R. D. *An Address, Delivered Before the Students of Jefferson College, Washington, Mississippi, at the Commencement, July 25, 1855.* Natchez, Miss.: Daily Courier Book and Job Office, 1855.

Hamilton, W[illia]m. T. *Address on the Importance of Knowledge Delivered . . . December 11th, 1841.* Tuscaloosa, Ala.: Office of the Independent Monitor, 1841.

Hammond, James H. *An Oration, Delivered Before the Two Societies of the South Carolina College, on the Fourth of December, 1849.* Charleston, S.C.: Walker and James, 1850.

Harlan, Louis R., ed. *The Booker T. Washington Papers.* 13 vols. Urbana: Univ. of Illinois Press, 1974.

Harris, Nathaniel E. *Autobiography: The Story of an Old Man's Life with Reminiscences of Seventy-Five Years.* Macon, Ga.: J. W. Burke Company, 1925.

Haygood, Atticus G. *The New South: Gratitude, Amendment, Hope: A Thanksgiving Sermon, for November 25, 1880.* Oxford, Ga.: n.p., 1880.

———. *Our Brother in Black: His Freedom and His Future.* New York: Phillips and Hunt, 1881.

Helper, Hinton Rowan. *Compendium of the Impending Crisis of the South.* New York: A. B. Burdick, 1860.

———. *The Impending Crisis of the South: How to Meet It.* New York: Burdick Brothers, 1857.

Herbert, Hilary. *An Address Delivered Before the Society of Alumni of the University of Virginia, on Commencement Day, June 29, 1887.* Lynchburg, Va.: J. P. Bell and Company, 1887.

Hilgard, Eug[ene]. W. *Address on Progressive Agriculture and Industrial Education, Delivered Before the Mississippi Agricultural and Mechanical Fair Association, at Jackson, November 14th, 1872.* Jackson, Miss.: Clarion Book and Job Office, 1873.

Hill, D. H. *The Confederate Soldier in the Ranks: An Address . . . Before the Virginia Division of the Association of the Army of Northern Virginia . . . October 22, 1885.* Richmond, Va.: Wm. Ellis Jones, Book and Job Printer, 1885.

———. *A Consideration of the Sermon on the Mount.* Philadelphia: William S. and Alfred Martien, 1858.

———. *Elements of Algebra.* Philadelphia: J. B. Lippincott and Company, 1857.

———. *The Old South: An Address . . . June 6, 1887, Before the Society of the Army and Navy of the Confederate States in the State of Maryland.* Baltimore, Md.: Andrew J. Conlon, 1887.

———. *University Address by Gen. D. H. Hill of Georgia: Delivered on Commencement Day, June 20, 1888, Before the Regents, Faculty, and Students of the University of Texas.* Austin, Tex.: State Printing Office, 1888.

Hill, Walter B. *College Life in the Reconstruction South: Walter B. Hill's Student Correspondence, University of Georgia, 1869–1871.* Edited by G. Ray Mathis. Miscellanea Publications No. 10. Athens: Univ. of Georgia Libraries, 1974.

Hogg, Alexander. *An Address Prepared for [the] National Educational Association . . . Delivered Also Before the Centennial Bureau of Education, Philadelphia, September 1st, 1876.* Salem, Oh.: W. D. Henkle, 1876.

———. *Industrial Education (Origin and Progress): State Agricultural and Mechanical College of Texas.* Galveston, Tex.: Galveston News, 1879.

Holcombe, J. P. *An Address Delivered Before the 7th Annual Meeting of the Virginia State Agricultural Society, November 4th, 1858.* Richmond, Va.: MacFarlane and Fergusson, 1858.

———. *An Address Delivered Before the Society of Alumni of the University of Virginia, at Its Annual Meeting, Held in the Public Hall, June 29th, 1853.* Richmond, Va.: MacFarlane and Fergusson, 1853.

Holmes, George Fred[eric]k. *Inaugural Address, Delivered on Occasion of the Opening of the University of the State of Mississippi, November 6, 1848.* Memphis, Tenn.: Franklin Book and Job Office, 1849.

Huse, Caleb. *The Supplies for the Confederate Army: How They Were Obtained in Europe and How Paid For.* Boston: T. R. Marvin and Son, 1904.

Jefferson, Thomas. *An Essay Towards Facilitating Instruction in the Anglo-Saxon and Modern Dialects of the English Language for the Use of the University of Virginia.* New York: John F. Trow, 1851.

———. *The Works of Thomas Jefferson.* Edited by Paul Leicester Ford. 12 vols. New York: G. P. Putnam's Sons, 1905.

———. *The Writings of Thomas Jefferson.* Edited by H. A. Washington. 9 vols. Washington, D.C.: Taylor and Maury, 1854.

———. *The Writings of Thomas Jefferson.* Edited by Albert Ellery Bergh. 20 vols. Washington, D.C.: Thomas Jefferson Memorial Association, 1907.

Johnston, W[illia]m. Preston. *An Address Before the Louisiana State Public School Teachers Association . . . December 28th, 1893.* New Orleans: L. Graham and Son, Ltd., 1894.

————. *Decoration Day [Address] at the Graves of Lee and Jackson, June 2nd, 1875.* Lexington, Va.: n.p., 1875.

————. *High Schools in Louisiana and Tulane University.* New Orleans: n.p., 1893.

————. *Problems of Southern Civilization: An Address Delivered Before the Polytechnic Institute of Alabama . . . June 10, 1891.* N.p., [1891].

————. *The University: Its Dangers and the Remedies: An Address . . . at the Commencement of the University of Texas, June 14, 1884.* Austin, Tex.: Warner and Company, 1884.

Joynes, Edward S. *Education After the War: A Letter Addressed to a Member of the Southern Educational Convention, Columbia, S.C., 28th April, 1863.* Richmond, Va.: MacFarlane and Fergusson, 1863.

————. *The Education of Teachers in the South: Embracing a Letter from Prof. Edw'd S. Joynes to Geo. P. Tayloe, Esquire.* Lynchburg: Virginia Power-Press Book and Job Office, 1864.

Junkin, George. *Christianity: The Patron of Literature and Science: An Address Delivered February 22, 1849, on the Occasion of the Author's Inauguration as President of Washington College, Virginia.* Philadelphia: n.p., 1849.

Keyes, F. W. *An Address Delivered Before the Alumni Association of the University of Mississippi on the 5th Day of July, 1859.* Oxford, Miss.: n.p., 1859.

Knight, Edgar W., ed. *A Documentary History of Education in the South Before 1860.* 5 vols. Chapel Hill: Univ. of North Carolina Press, 1953.

LaBorde, M. *History of the South Carolina College.* Charleston, S.C.: Walker, Evans and Cogswell, 1874.

LeConte, Joseph. *The Autobiography of Joseph LeConte.* Edited by William Dallam Armes. New York: D. Appleton and Company, 1903.

Lee, S. D. *The Agricultural and Mechanical College of Mississippi: Its Origin, Object, Management and Results, Discussed in a Series of Papers.* Jackson, Miss.: Clarion-Ledger, 1889.

Lewis, B. B. *Baccalaureate Address: A Plea for Popular Institutions.* N.p., n.d.

————. *Baccalaureate Address Delivered at the 50th Annual Commencement of the University of Alabama, July 7, 1881.* N.p., n.d.

————. *Memorial Address . . . at the Laying of the Memorial Stone of the New University Hall, May 5, 1884; and Baccalaureate Address, Delivered on Commencement Day, June 18, 1884.* N.p., n.d.

Lincoln, Abraham. *The Collected Works of Abraham Lincoln.* Edited by Roy P. Basler. 8 vols. New Brunswick, N.J.: Rutgers Univ. Press, 1953.

Lindsley, Philip. *The Works of Philip Lindsley.* Nashville, Tenn.: W. T. Berry and Company, 1859.

Longstreet, Augustus B. *Address Delivered Before the Faculty and Students of Emory College, Oxford, Georgia.* Augusta, Ga.: W. T. Thompson, 1840.

Lupton, N. T., and Eugene A. Smith. *Addresses Delivered Before the State Agricultural Society in Convention at Selma, Alabama, Feb. 2d, 1888.* Montgomery, Ala.: n.p., 1888.

Mallet, J. W. *Chemistry Applied to the Arts: A Lecture Delivered Before the University of Virginia, May 30, 1868.* Lynchburg, Va.: Schaffter and Bryant, 1868.

Martin, G. H. *Address Delivered Before the Philomathean and Hermenian Societies, at Clinton, Miss., July 25, 1859.* Vicksburg, Miss.: Daily and Weekly Whig Steam Book and Job Office, 1859.

Massie, James W. *An Address Delivered Before the Society of Alumni of the Virginia Military Institute, July 3rd, 1857*. Richmond, Va.: MacFarlane and Fergusson, 1857.

Maury, M[atthew] F[ontaine]. *Address Delivered Before the Literary Societies of the University of Virginia . . . 28th June 1855*. Richmond, Va.: H. K. Ellyson, 1855.

—————. *Physical Survey of Virginia, Her Resources, Climate and Productions: Preliminary Report. No. II . . . July 1, 1877*. Richmond, Va.: N. V. Randolph, 1878.

Maxey, S. B. *University Address . . . Delivered on Commencement Day, June 19, 1889, Before the Regents, Faculty, and Students of the University of Texas*. Austin, Tex.: State Printing Office, 1889.

Mayo, A. D. *Industrial Education in the South*. Washington, D.C.: Government Printing Office, 1888.

—————. *The Third Estate in the South: Address Delivered Before the American Social Science Association, at Saratoga, N.Y., Sept. 2d, 1890*. Boston: George H. Ellis, 1890.

—————. *The Training of Teachers in the South: A Paper Read Before the Normal Department, National Educational Association, Nashville, Tenn., July, 1889*. N.p.: [1889].

McBryde, J. M. *Agricultural Education: An Address Delivered Before the State Legislature, December 12th, 1882*. Columbia, S.C.: Charles A. Calvo, Jr., 1883.

McCleary, J. H. *University [of Texas] Address, June 17, 1890*. N.p., n.d.

McQueen, Hugh. *An Address Delivered Before the Alumni and Graduating Class of the University of North Carolina . . . June 26, 1839*. Raleigh, N.C.: Raleigh Register, 1839.

Monteiro, Walter. *Address Delivered Before the Neotrophian Society of the Hampton Academy, on the 28th of July, 1857*. Richmond, Va.: H. K. Ellyson, 1857.

Morgan, John T. *Address . . . Before the Erosophic and Philomathic Societies of the University of Alabama, July 6th, 1875*. [Tuscaloosa, Ala.?]: n.p., 1875.

Murdoch, John. *Home Education and the Claims of Oakland College: Delivered Before the Belles Lettres Society and Adelphic Institute of Oakland College on Commencement Day, June 29th, 1854*. New Orleans, La.: Office of the Picayune, 1854.

Murfee, James T. *A New Scheme of Organization, Instruction, and Government for the University of Alabama, with Report on Construction of Building*. Tuscaloosa, Ala.: John F. Warren, 1867.

Murphy, Edgar Gardner. *The Task of the South: An Address Before the Faculty and Students of Washington and Lee University, Lexington, Virginia, December 10th A.D., 1902*. Montgomery, Ala.: n.p., [1903?].

Nicholson, J. W. *Higher Education at Public Expense Justified: Address of Col. J. W. Nicholson—President of Louisiana State University and Agricultural and Mechanical College on the Occasion of the 7th Annual Convention of the Louisiana Educational Association, Shreveport, LA., July 25, 1890*. Baton Rouge, La.: Truth, Job, and Book Office, 1890.

—————. *Oration Before the Louisiana State Medical Society*. New Orleans, La.: L. Graham and Son, Ltd., 1895.

Norton, A. B. *Remarks of A. B. Norton in the Texas House of Representatives Upon the University Question.* Austin, Tex.: John Marshall and Company, 1858.

Peeler, A. J. *Address Before the State Agricultural and Mechanical College of Texas, Thursday, June 26, 1877.* Austin, Tex.: Statesman Steam Book and Job Office, 1877.

Polk, Leonidas. *A Letter to the Right Reverend Bishops.* New Orleans, La.: B. M. Norman, 1856.

Polk, Leonidas, and Stephen Elliot. *Address of the Commissioners for Raising the Endowment of the University of the South.* New Orleans, La.: B. M. Norman Publisher, 1859.

Pratt, John Wood. *An Address Delivered Before the Society of the Alumni of the University of Alabama, July 8th, 1850.* Tuscaloosa, Ala.: M. D. J. Slade, 1850.

Rains, Geo[rge] W. *History of the Confederate Powder Works: An Address by Invitation Before the Confederate Survivors Association . . . April 26th, 1882.* Augusta, Ga.: Chronicle and Constitutionalist, 1882.

Record of the Testimony and Proceedings, in the Matter of the Investigation, by the Trustees of the University of Mississippi, on the 1st and 2nd of March, 1860, of the Charges Made by H. R. Branham Against the Chancellor of the University. Jackson, Miss.: Mississippian Office, 1860.

Reed, Thomas Walter. *'Uncle Tom' Reed's Memoir of the University of Georgia.* Edited by Ray Mathis. Miscellanea Publications No. 11. Athens: Univ. of Georgia Libraries, 1974.

Review of the Actions of the Trustees in the Trial of Chancellor F. A. P. Barnard, and Defense of the Prosecutor. N.p.: [1860].

Richardson, Charles. *A New Dictionary of the English Language.* 2 vols. Philadelphia: E. H. Butler and Company, 1847.

Roberts, O. M. *Faculty Address, June 17, 1890: The Relation of Public Education to the Government of Texas.* N.p., n.d.

Scott, W. A. *The Education We Want: A Discourse, Pronounced on the 23rd of November, 1844.* New Orleans, La.: Besancon, Ferguson and Company, 1845.

Sherman, William T. *Memoirs of General William T. Sherman.* 2 vols. New York: D. Appleton and Company, 1875.

Smith, Ashbel. *Address Delivered in the Chapel at West Point Before the Officers and Cadets of the United States Military Academy . . . June 16, 1848.* New York: W. L. Burroughs, 1848.

———. *Letter from Doctor Ashbel Smith to the Trustees of the Memphis University.* [Memphis, Tenn.]: Enquirer, n.d.

Smith, Francis H[enney]. *Discourse on the Life and Character of Lt. Gen. Thos. J. Jackson (C.S.A.), Late Professor of Natural and Experimental Philosophy in the VMI.* Richmond, Va.: Ritchie and Dunnavant, 1863.

———. *Gymnastic and Technical Education in the Virginia Military Institute . . . Introductory Lecture on the Resumption of Academic Exercises in the Institution, September 5th, 1871.* New York: D. Van Nostrand, 1871.

———. *Introductory Address to the Corps of Cadets of the Virginia Military Institute, on the Resumption of Academic Duties, September 2nd, 1856.* Richmond, Va.: MacFarlane and Fergusson, 1856.

———. *Introductory Address to the Corps of Cadets of the Virginia Military*

Institute, on the Resumption of the Academic Exercises, September 10, 1866. N.p.: Published by Order of the Board, [1866].

————. *Introductory Lecture Read Before the Corps of Cadets, on the Resumption of the Academic Duties of the Virginia Military Institute, at the Alms House, Richmond, Va., December 28, 1864.* Richmond, Va.: MacFarlane and Fergusson, 1865.

Smith, Francis H[enry]. *Thoughts on the Discord and Harmony Between Science and the Bible: Delivered Before the American Institute of Christian Philosophy, 27th July 1888.* New York: Wilbur B. Ketchum, [1888].

Soule, George. *Address by Col. Geo. Soule, President of Soule Commercial College and Literary Institute, New Orleans, La., at the 32nd Anniversary and Commencement, June 30th, 1888.* N.p., [1888].

State [Mississippi] Grange and A. and M. College: Compiled from the Official Proceedings by Secretary of State Grange. N.p.: [1886].

Stiles, William H. *Southern Education for Southern Youth: An Address Before the Alpha Pi Delta Society of the Cherokee Baptist College, Delivered at the Commencement on the 14th July, 1858.* Savannah, Ga.: Power Press of George N. Nichols, 1858.

Strong, George Templeton. *The Diary of George Templeton Strong.* Edited by Allan Nevins and Milton Halsey Thomas. 4 vols. New York: Macmillan, 1952.

Sutherlin, William T. *Address Delivered Before the Mechanics' Association of Danville, Va., March 11, 1867.* Richmond, Va.: Enquirer Steam Presses, 1867.

Tappan, Henry P. *University Education.* New York: George P. Putnam, 1851.

Taylor, Joseph W. *Address Before the Literary Societies of Washington and Lee University, on Commencement Day, June 22, 1871.* Baltimore, Md.: J. Murphy, 1871.

————. *The Young Men of the New South: Their Education, Duties and Rewards: An Address Delivered Before the Phi Sigma and Hermean Societies, at Commencement of the University of Mississippi, on June 23, 1869.* Memphis, Tenn.: Hite and Corwine, 1869.

Terrell, A. W. *Address of Judge A. W. Terrell.* N.p.: [1884].

Thompson, Jacob. *Address Delivered on Occasion of the Opening of the University of the State of Mississippi . . . November 6, 1848.* Memphis, Tenn.: Franklin Book and Job Office, 1849.

Thornwell, J. H. *Letter to His Excellency Governor Manning on Public Instruction in South Carolina.* Columbia, S.C.: R. W. Gibbes and Company, 1853.

Tucker, J. Randolph. *Life and Character of Col. William Allan, Late Principal of McDonogh School. An Address Delivered November 21, 1889.* McDonogh, Md.: Published by Boys of the School, 1889.

University of Alabama Prize Exhibition Orations by Members of the Senior Class, Tuesday, July 3, 1877. N.p.: J. F. Warren, [1877].

University of the South Papers. Sewanee, Tenn.: Univ. of the South Press, 1888.

Vallas, Anthony. *History of the Louisiana State Seminary, 1864.* Baton Rouge, La.: n.p., 1935.

Venable, C. S. *An Address Delivered Before the Society of Alumni of the University of Virginia.* Richmond, Va.: MacFarlane and Fergusson, 1859.

Waddel, John N. *Historical Discourse Delivered on the Quarter-Centennial Anniver-*

sary of the University of Mississippi on Wednesday, June 25th, 1873. Oxford, Miss.: Board of Trustees, 1873.

Wailes, B. L. C. *Address Delivered in the College Chapel Before the Agricultural, Horticultural, and Botanical Society, of Jefferson College.* Natchez, Miss.: Daily Courier Office, 1841.

Walthall, W. T. *First Annual Address: Delivered Before the Mobile Teachers' Institute, December 15th, 1856.* Mobile, Ala.: Daily Register, 1857.

Washington, Booker T. *Up from Slavery: An Autobiography.* 1900; reprint, Williamstown, Mass.: Corner House Publishers, 1978.

Wayland, Francis. *The Educational Demand of the People of the United States.* Boston: Phillips, Sampson and Company, 1855.

————. *Elements of Moral Science.* New York: Cooke and Company, 1835.

————. *Report to the Corporation of Brown University and Changes in the System of Collegiate Education.* Providence, R.I.: George H. Whitney, 1850.

————. *Thoughts on the Present Collegiate System in the United States.* Boston: Gould, Kendall and Lincoln, 1842.

Webster, Noah. *An American Dictionary of the English Language.* 2 vols. New York: S. Converse, 1828.

Wightman, W. M. *Inaugural Address Delivered at the Opening of the Southern University, Greensboro, Alabama.* Marion, Ala.: George C. Rogers, 1859.

Wiley, C. H.; F. M. Hubbard; W. M. Wingate; B. Craven; V. C. Barringer; D. H. Bittle; R. DeSchweintz; L. F. Siler; T. M. Jones; A. McDowell; A. Wilson; and Daniel Johnson. *Address to the People of North Carolina.* N.p.: [ca. 1861–65].

Winston, George T. *The Influence of Universities and Public Schools on National Life and Character.* N.p.: [1896].

Wood, Thomas Newton. *An Address Delivered Before the Two Literary Societies of the University of Alabama, in the Rotunda, July 4th, 1840.* Tuscaloosa, Ala.: M. D. J. Slade, 1840.

Woods, Alva. *Valedictory Address, Delivered December 6, 1837, at the Close of the 7th Collegiate Year of the University of the State of Alabama.* Tuscaloosa, Ala.: Marmaduke J. Slade, 1837.

Worcester, J. E. *Comprehensive Pronouncing and Explanatory Dictionary of the English Language.* Burlington, Vt.: Chauncey Goodrich, 1831.

C. Addresses and Articles in Books and Periodicals

"Agricultural Requirements of the South." *De Bow's Review* 7 (Jan.-Feb. 1862): 87–103.

"Agricultural Schools." *Farmer's Register* 1 (Jan. 1843): 16–17.

Bishop, A. W. "Farewell Address." In *Third Report of the Arkansas Industrial University.* Fayetteville, Ark.: Democrat Book and Job, 1875.

Bittle, T. C. "Address." *Battalion* [Texas A&M] Memorial volume (Jan. 1898): 13.

Bledsoe, Albert T. "Liberty and Slavery; or, Slavery in the Light of Moral Political Philosophy." In *Cotton Is King and Pro-Slavery Arguments . . . ,* edited by E. N. Elliott, 268–458. Augusta, Ga.: Pritchard, Abbott, and Loomis, 1860.

Boyd, David F. "Appeal to the People of Louisiana." In *Official Register of the*

Louisiana State University . . . 1871–1872, pp. 74–75. New Orleans: A. W. Hyatt, 1872.

———. "William Tecumseh Sherman: First Superintendent of the Louisiana State Seminary, Now the Louisiana State University." *Alumnus* [Louisiana State Univ.] 5 (Oct. 1909): 3–11.

Brewer, Fisk Parsons. "South Carolina University—1876." Edited by William P. Vaughn. *South Carolina Historical Magazine* 76 (Oct. 1975): 225–31.

Bringhurst, W. L. "Recollections of the Old Seminary." *Alumnus* [Louisiana State Univ.] 5 (Oct. 1909): 15–18.

Broun, William LeRoy. "Address Delivered on Memorial Day Before the Students of the Alabama Polytechnic Institute in May, 1891." In William LeRoy Broun, *Dr. William LeRoy Broun,* compiled by Thomas L. Broun. New York: Neale Publishing Company, 1912.

———. "Confederate Ordnance During the War." *Journal of the United States Artillery* 9 (Jan.–Feb. 1898): 1–13.

———. "The Red Artillery: Confederate Ordnance During the War." *Southern Historical Society Papers* 26 (1898): 365–76.

Burwell, William M. "General Lee as Teacher." *De Bow's Review* 6 (July 1869): 540–47.

Cartwright, Samuel A. "The Education, Labor, and Wealth of the South." In *Cotton Is King and Pro-Slavery Arguments . . .,* edited by E. N. Elliott, 879–96. Augusta, Ga.: Pritchard, Abbott, and Loomis, 1860.

Clarkson, A. "The Basis of Northern Hostility to the South." *De Bow's Review* 3 (Jan. 1860): 7–13.

Clopton, A. G. "From the Eulogy on the Life and Character of Ashbel Smith." In *Catalogue of the University of Texas for 1886–87.* Austin, Tex.: State Printing Office, 1887.

Curry, J. L. M. "Annual Report of the Hon. J. L. M. Curry, General Agent of the Peabody Fund." *Texas Journal of Education* 1 (Oct. 1881): 240–42.

———. "Education at the South." *Texas Journal of Education* 2 (Mar. 1882): 80–83.

"The Dead Languages." *De Bow's Review* 5 (Mar. 1861): 316–20.

De Bow, J. D. B. "Commerce and Agriculture Subjects of University Instruction." *De Bow's Review* 3 (June 1847): 502–16.

[Dew, Thomas Roderick]. "Abolition of Negro Slavery." *American Quarterly Review* 12 (Sept. 1832): 189–265.

Dickey, James E. "Mr. Hill's Relation to the Denominational Colleges." *Bulletin of the University of Georgia,* Memorial Number (May 1906), pp. 46–51.

"Education of Southern Women." *De Bow's Review* 6 (Oct.–Nov. 1861): 381–90.

"Faculty Notes." *Longhorn* [Texas A&M], Memorial volume (1903): 20.

Few, W. P. "Some Educational Needs of the South." *South Atlantic Quarterly* 3 (July 1904): 201–11.

Fitzhugh, George. "Southern Thought." *De Bow's Review* 23 (Oct. 1857): 338–50.

Ford, Spencer. "Address." *Battalion* [Texas A&M], Memorial volume (Jan. 1898): 19–22.

"Future Revolution in Southern School Books." *De Bow's Review* 5 (May–June 1861): 606–14.

Gorgas, Josiah. "Notes on the Ordnance Department of the Confederate Government." *Southern Historical Society Papers* 12 (Jan.–Feb. 1884): 67–94.

Graham, George Mason. "The Autobiography of George Mason Graham: Contributed by His Grandson, Dr. G. M. Stafford." *Louisiana Historical Quarterly* 20 (Jan. 1937): 43–57.

Graham, Richard N. "The Economic Man." *Ozark* [Arkansas Industrial University] 4 (May 1897): 346–51.

"Great Southern Convention in Charleston." *De Bow's Review* 16 (June 1854): 632–41.

Harper, William. "Memoir on Slavery." In *The Pro-Slavery Argument as Maintained by the Most Distinguished Writers of the Southern States,* 1–98. Philadelphia: Lippincott, Gramb and Company, 1853.

Henneman, J. B. "Historical Studies in the South Since the War." *Sewanee Review* 1 (May 1893): 320–39.

Hilgard, Eugene. "A Confederate Scientist at War." Edited by Walter E. Pittman. *Civil War Times Illustrated* 25 (Mar. 1986): 20–37.

Hill, Benjamin H. "Address Delivered Before the Southern Historical Society, at Atlanta, Ga., February 18, 1874." In Benjamin H. Hill, *Senator Benjamin H. Hill of Georgia: His, Life, Speeches and Writings,* compiled by Benjamin H. Hill, Jr., 399–414. Atlanta: T. H. P. Bloodworth, 1893.

———. "Speech Delivered Before the Alumni Society of the University of Georgia . . . July 31, 1871." In Benjamin H. Hill, *Senator Benjamin H. Hill of Georgia: His, Life, Speeches and Writings,* compiled by Benjamin H. Hill, Jr., 334–49. Atlanta: T. H. P. Bloodworth, 1893.

Hill, D. H. "Address before the Mecklenburg (N.C.) Historical Society," *Southern Historical Society Papers* 1 (1876): 389–98.

———. "Education." Pt. 1. *Land We Love* 1 (May 1866): 1–11.

———. "Education." Pt. 2. *Land We Love* 1 (June 1866): 83–91.

———. "Education." Pt. 3. *Land We Love* 1 (Aug. 1866): 235–39.

H[olmes], G[eorge] F. "Sir William Hamilton's Discussions." *Southern Quarterly Review* 8 (Oct. 1853): 299–336.

Johnston, William Preston. "Higher Education in the South." *Regents' Bulletin* 9 (Aug. 1892): 12–25.

———. "History: Its Place in a Liberal Education. Address of Wm. Preston Johnston, of Washington and Lee University, Before the Educational Association of Virginia, at Staunton, Va., July 10, 1872." In William Preston Johnston, *Addresses and Essays, First President of Tulane.* N.p., n.d.

———. "Zagony's Charge with Fremont's Body-Guard—A Picturesque Fol-de-rol," *Southern Historical Society Papers* 3 (1877): 195–96.

Joynes, Edward S. "Lee, the College President." In *Robert E. Lee: Centennial Celebration of His Birth, Held Under the Auspices of the University of South Carolina on the 19th Day of January, 1907.* Columbia, S.C.: State Company, 1907.

Lee, S. D. "The Second Battle of Manassas—A Reply to General Longstreet." *Southern Historical Society Papers* 6 (1878): 59–70.

———. "The South Since the War." In *Confederate Military History,* vol. 12, edited by Clement Anselm Evans, 267–368. Atlanta: Confederate Publishing Company, 1899.

Lipscomb, Dabney. "General Stephen D. Lee: His Life, Character, and Services." *Publications of the Mississippi Historical Society* 10 (1909): 13–33.

Mallet, J. W. "Work of the Ordnance Bureau." *Southern Historical Society Papers* 37 (Jan.–Dec. 1909): 1–20.

Mell, P. H. "Dr. William LeRoy Broun." *Confederate Veteran* 10 (May 1902): 225.

"In Memory of Professor Mallet." *Alumni Bulletin* [Univ. of Virginia] 6 (Jan. 1913): 5–47.

Moore, Frederick W. "The Status of History in Southern Colleges." *South Atlantic Quarterly* 2 (Apr. 1903): 169–71.

Nagle, J. C. "The Influence of Applied Science." *Texas Academy of Science* 4, pt. 2 (Feb. 1902): 3–16.

Nott, Josiah C. "Two Lectures on the Natural History of the Caucasian and Negro Races." In *The Ideology of Slavery: Proslavery Thought in the Antebellum South, 1830–1860,* edited by Drew Gilpin Faust, 206–38. Baton Rouge: Louisiana State Univ. Press, 1981.

"On Public Education in Virginia." *Southern Literary Messenger* 13 (Nov. 1847): 685–87.

"Original Papers in Relation to a Course of Liberal Education [Yale Report]." *American Journal of Science and Arts* 15 (1829): 297–351.

"Our School Books." *De Bow's Review* 3 (Apr. 1860): 434–40.

"Polytechnic Education." *De Bow's Review* 2 (Oct. 1859): 486.

"Richard Morton Venable." *Louisiana State University Quarterly* 6 (Apr. 1911): 86–88.

Shepard, Henry E. "Gen. D. H. Hill—A Character Sketch." *Confederate Veteran* 25 (Sept. 1917): 411–13.

Smith, Ashbel. "Address on the Laying of the Corner Stone of the University of Texas." In *Catalogue of the University of Texas for 1883–84,* 53–65. Austin: E. W. Swindells, State Printer, 1984.

Smith, Charles Forster. "Southern Colleges and Schools." *Atlantic Monthly* 54 (Oct. 1884): 542–57.

Smith, Cha[rle]s Lee. "Mr. Hill's Relation to the Denominational Colleges." *Bulletin of the University of Georgia,* Memorial Number (May 1906): 42–45.

Smith, Mrs. Francis W. "Lieut.-Colonel Francis W. Smith, C.S.A.: Professor of Chemistry and Geology and Commandant of Cadets at the Louisiana State Seminary." *Alumnus* [Louisiana State Univ.] 5 (Oct. 1909): 12–14.

"Southern School-Books." *De Bow's Review* 1 (Sept. 1852): 258–66.

"The Times and the War." *De Bow's Review* 6 (July 1861): 1–13.

Trent, W. P. *The Study of Southern History.* N.p., [1896?].

"University Lectures." *De Bow's Review* 2 (Mar. 1852): 336.

"University of Louisiana." *De Bow's Review* 1 (May 1846): 430–33.

Williams, Ch[arles] H. "Agricultural Education." *Southern Planter* 13 (July 1853): 217–19.

D. Catalogues, Programs, Registers, Regulations, and Reports

Annual Announcement of the University of Georgia. Athens, Ga.: Banner Job Print., 1891.

Annual Catalogue of the Officers and Students of the Agricultural and Mechanical College of Mississippi, 1880–81. Jackson, Miss.: Clarion Steam Publishing House, 1881. Various publishers and years.

Babbitt, B. B. *Report of the Chairman of the Faculty of the University of South*

Carolina in Response to a Resolution of the House of Representatives and of the Senate, Passed February 18, 1875. Columbia, S.C: Republican Printing Company, 1875.

Barnard, F. A. P. Report on the Organization of Military Schools, and to the Trustees of the University of Mississippi, November, 1861. Jackson, Miss.: Cooper and Kimball, 1861.

Biennial Report of the Superintendent of Public Instruction to the Governor of the State of Arkansas for the Two Years Ending September 30, 1872. Little Rock, Ark.: Price and McClure, 1872.

Biennial Report of the Trustees, President, and Other Officers of the Agricultural College of Mississippi for the Years 1890 and 1891. Jackson, Miss.: R. H. Henry, 1891.

Board of Trustees for the Univ. of Georgia. Present Organization and Proposed Plan of Expansion of the University of Georgia. Athens, Ga.: Southern Banner, 1872.

"Branch Normal College of the Arkansas Industrial University, Pine Bluff, Arkansas." In Eighth Catalogue of the Arkansas Industrial University . . . for the Year Ending June 10th, 1880. Little Rock, Ark.: Democrat, 1880.

Broun, William LeRoy. "Industrial Education." In Report of the Board of Supervisors of the Louisiana State University . . . 1878. New Orleans, La.: Office of the Democrat, 1878.

By-Laws of the University of South Carolina, as Revised and Adopted by the Board of Trustees at the Annual Meeting in 1866. Columbia, S.C.: W. W. Deane, 1867.

Catalogue of the Arkansas Industrial University. Little Rock, Ark.: A. H. Sevier, 1878. Various publishers, titles, and years.

Catalogue of the Officers and Students of Furman University for 1860–61. Charleston, S.C.: Evans and Cosswell, 1861.

Catalogue of the Officers and Students of Mercer University, 1860–61. Penfield, Ga.: n.p., 1861.

Catalogue of the Officers and Students of the University of Alabama for 1860–1861. Nashville, Tenn.: Southern Methodist Publishing House, 1861. Various publishers, titles, and years.

Catalogue of the Officers and Students of the University of Georgia, Athens, Georgia, Seventy-Third Year, 1874. Macon, Ga.: J. W. Burke and Company, 1874. Various publishers, titles, and years.

Catalogue of the Officers and Trustees of the University of Mississippi at Oxford, Mississippi, Twenty-second Session. Oxford, Miss.: n.p., 1874.

Catalogue of the Officers of North Carolina College at Mount Pleasant . . . Second Collegiate Year Ending July, 1861 . . . Chartered January 1859. Salisbury, N.C.: North Carolina Watchman Office, 1861.

Catalogue of the State Agricultural and Mechanical College of Alabama, 1883–1884. N.p., n.d.

Catalogue of the State Agricultural and Mechanical College of Texas, Session of 1876–1877. Bryan, Tex.: Pilot Book and Job Office, 1877.

Catalogue of the Trustees, Faculty and Students of the University of North Carolina, 1860–61. Chapel Hill, N.C.: John B. Neathery Book, Job and Card, 1861. Various publishers, titles, and years.

Catalogue of the Trustees, Faculty and Students, Wofford College, Spartanburg, S.C., 1861. Spartanburg, S.C.: Express Office, 1861.

Catalogue of the Trustees, Officers, and Alumni of the University of Georgia, from 1785 to 1894. Atlanta, Ga.: Foote and Davies Company, 1894.

Catalogue of the University of South Carolina, 1872–73. N.p., n.d. Various publishers, titles, and years.

Catalogue of the University of Virginia, Session of 1860–61. Richmond, Va.: Chas. H. Wynne, 1861. Various publishers and years.

Catalogue of the University of Texas for 1883–84. Austin, Tex.: E. W. Swindells, 1884. Various publishers and years.

Catalogue of Washington College, Lexington, Virginia . . . 1866. Richmond, Va.: MacFarlane and Fergusson, 1866. Various publishers and years.

Cohn, M. A. "Report of the Secretary of the Board of Trustees, Arkansas Industrial University, December 31, 1872." In *Biennial Report of the Superintendent of Public Instruction to the Governor of the State of Arkansas . . . 1872.* Little Rock, Ark.: Price and McClure, Public Printers, 1872.

Constitution and Statutes of the University of the South. Nashville, Tenn.: Bang, Walker and Company, 1860.

Copes, J. S. *Report of a Committee of the Board of Administrators of the University of Louisiana, Upon the Organization of the Collegiate Department, Read December 23d, 1856.* New Orleans, La.: E. C. Wharton, 1857.

Draft of the Constitution and Statutes of the University of the South. New Orleans, La.: Bulletin Book and Job Office, 1860.

Edgar, George M. *Biennial Report of the Board of Trustees of Arkansas Industrial University to His Excellency, Simon P. Hughes, Governor of Arkansas.* Little Rock, Ark.: A. M. Woodruff, 1886.

"Georgia State Industrial College for Colored Youths." In *University of Georgia, General Catalogue, 1900–1901.* Atlanta, Ga.: Foote and Davies Company, 1901.

Hilgard, Eug[ene]. *Report on Organization of the Department of Agriculture and the Mechanic Arts, August 29, 1871.* N.p., n.d.

Historical Catalogue of the Officers and Alumni of the University of Alabama, 1821 to 1870. Selma, Ala.: Armstrong and Martin, 1870.

Historical Catalogue of the University of Mississippi, 1849–1909. Nashville, Tenn.: Marshall and Bruce Company, 1910.

James, J. G. "President's Report." In *Fourth Annual Report of the President of the Agricultural and Mechanical College of Texas, with Accompanying Documents,* [Nov. 22, 1879–July 1, 1880]. College Station, Tex.: n.p., 1880.

Johnston, William Preston. "The Definition of History." In *Annual Report of the American Historical Association for the Year 1893.* Washington, D.C.: Government Printing Office, 1894.

———. *Report . . . to the Board of Administrators on the Plan of Organization of Tulane University, June 4th, 1883.* New Orleans, La.: A. W. Hyatt, 1883.

Lee, Stephen D. "President's Report to the Honorable Trustees." In *Biennial Report of the Trustees, President and Other Officers of the Agricultural and Mechanical College of Mississippi for the Years 1884–85.* Jackson, Miss.: Clarion Steam Publishing Establishment, 1885.

———. "Report of the President." In *Report of the Trustees, President and Other Officers of the Agricultural and Mechanical College of Mississippi, from the*

Organization of College to Dec. 1st, 1883. Jackson, Miss.: Clarion Steam Printing Establishment, 1883.

Lockett, Samuel H. "Report of Visit to Various Schools, Colleges, Universities and Public Works in the Northern States and Canada." In *Annual Report to the Board of Supervisors [of Louisiana State University] for 1871–1872.* New Orleans, La.: n.p., 1872.

Manly, Basil. *Report on Collegiate Education, Made to the Trustees of the University of Alabama, July 1852.* Tuscaloosa, Ala.: M. D. J. Slade, 1852.

Murfee, E. H. "Biennial Report of the President." In *Biennial Report of the Board of Trustees of the Arkansas Industrial University to His Excellency, Simon P. Hughes, Governor of Arkansas.* Little Rock, Ark.: Press Printing Company, 1889.

Official Register of the Faculty, or Academic Staff, and Military Staff, with the Rules and Regulations of the Alabama Military and Scientific Institute, Near Tuskegee, Alabama. Tuskegee, Ala.: Macon Republican, 1845.

Official Register of the Louisiana State University and Agricultural and Mechanical College, 1877–1878. New Orleans, La.: A. W. Hyatt, 1878. Various publishers, titles, and years.

Official Register of the Officers and Cadets of the State Seminary of Learning and Military Academy of Louisiana, Near Alexandria, Parish of Rapides, for 1860–61 and [186]2. Alexandria, La.: Louisiana Democrat Office, 1862. Various publishers and titles.

Program, Commencement Exercises, A. and M. College of Mississippi, 1891. Starkville, Miss.: O'Brien's Book and Job Office, [1891].

Prospectus of the University of South Carolina, 1866. Columbia, S.C.: Southern Presbyterian Review, 1866.

Regulations for the University of Alabama at Tuscaloosa. Nashville, Tenn.: Southern Methodist Publishing House, 1861.

Reorganization of the University of South Carolina in 1873, and Catalogue for 1872–73. N.p., n.d.

Report of the Agricultural and Mechanical College of Texas, Session 1880–1881. Brenham, Tex.: Sentinel Print, 1881. Various publishers and years.

Report of the Alabama History Commission to the Governor of Alabama, December 1, 1900. Montgomery, Ala.: Brown Printing Company, 1901.

Report of the Arkansas Industrial University. Fayetteville, Ark.: Democrat Book and Job, 1875. Various publishers and years.

Report of the Board of Supervisors for the Louisiana State Seminary . . . 1870. New Orleans, La.: n.p., 1870.

Report of the Board of Supervisors of the Louisiana State University and Agricultural and Mechanical College . . . 1878. New Orleans, La.: Office of the Democrat, 1878. Various publishers and years.

"Report of the Board of Visitors to the Secretary of War, United States Military Academy, 20 June 1839." *Army and Navy Chronicle* 9 (4 July 1839): 1–5.

Report of the Board of Visitors of the Virginia Military Institute. 1850–57. VMI Archives, Lexington, Va.

Report of the Joint Committee on Charitable and Public Institutions to the General Assembly of Louisiana, January 1869. New Orleans: n.p., 1869.

Report of the Louisiana State University for the Year 1874, to the Governor of Louisiana. New Orleans, La.: Republican Office, 1875.

Report of the Prairie View Normal School Located in Waller County [Texas]. Austin, Tex.: Smith, Hicks and Jones, 1889.

Report of the Sub-Committee on Public and Charitable Institutions, Appointed January 20, 1876. New Orleans, La.: n.p., [1876?].

Report of the Trustees of the University of Mississippi [1861]. N.p., n.d. [1861?].

Reports, Southern University, 1899–1900. New Orleans, La.: n.p., n.d. [1900?]. Various publishers and years.

Second Decennial Catalogue of the Mississippi Agricultural and Mechanical College, 1890–1900. Meridian, Miss.: Meridian News, n.d.

Smith, Francis H[enney]. *Special Report of the Superintendent of the Virginia Military Institute, on Scientific Education in Europe.* Richmond, Va.: Ritchie, Dunnavant and Company, 1859.

E. Proceedings, Published Minutes, and Transactions

Aldrich, William S. "Engineering Education and the State University." *Proceedings of the Society for the Promotion of Engineering Education* 2 (1894): 268–92.

"Constitution of the Texas Agricultural Society." *Transactions of the Texas State Agricultural Society* 1 (1853): 6.

Futrall, John C. "President's Address." In *Reprint from the Proceedings of 47th Annual Convention of the Association of Land Grant Colleges and Universities, Chicago, Ill., November 13–15, 1933.* Burlington, Vt.: Free Press, 1934.

Garrett, W[illia]m R. "The Work of the South in the Building of the United States." *Transactions of the Alabama Historical Society* 3 (1898–99): 27–45.

Hogg, Alexander. "Lacks and Needs of the South Educationally: The Development of Her Natural Resources, the Remedy." In *Addresses and Journal of Proceedings of the National Educational Association . . . 1876.* Salem, Oh.: Office of the National Teacher, 1876.

Minutes of the Convention, Which Formed the Alabama Educational Association . . . July 24–25, 1856. Selma, Ala.: Selma Reporter and Job Printing Office, 1857.

Proceedings of the Agricultural Convention and of the State Agricultural Society of South Carolina from 1839 to 1845. Columbia, S.C.: Summer and Carroll, 1846.

Proceedings of the Alabama Industrial and Scientific Society 1 (1891).

Proceedings of the Annual Convention of the Association of American Agricultural Colleges and Experiment Stations . . . 1889. Washington, D.C.: Government Printing Office, 1890.

Proceedings of the Convention of Teachers of the Confederate States, Assembled at Columbia, South Carolina, April 28th, 1863. Marion, Ga.: Burke, Boykin and Company, 1863.

Proceedings of the Farmers' State Alliance of Texas, Ninth Regular Session, Held in Dallas, Texas . . . 1888. Dallas, Tex.: Circular Letter Office, 1888.

Proceedings of the Sixth Annual Convention of the Association of American Agricultural Colleges and Experiment Stations, Held at New Orleans, Louisiana, November 15–19, 1892. Washington, D.C.: Government Printing Office, 1893.

Proceedings of the Texas State Grange . . . 1888. Dallas, Tex.: Texas Farmer, 1888. Various publishers and years.

Proceedings of the Third Session of the State Grange of the Patrons of Husbandry of South Carolina. Columbia, S.C.: Wm. Sloane, 1875.

Transactions of the Alabama Historical Society 2 (1897–98).

University of Alabama, 53rd Annual Commencement, June 18, 1884. N.p.: M. I. Burton, [1884].

Wilmore, John J. "Some Phases of Engineering Education in the South." *Proceedings of the Society for the Promotion of Engineering Education* 6 (1898): 56–68.

F. Newspapers

Louisiana Democrat (Alexandria, La.)
Baton Rouge (La.) Daily Reveille
Louisiana Capitolian (Baton Rouge, La.)
Baton Rouge (La.) Tri-Weekly Advocate
Charleston (S.C.) News and Courier
Charleston (S.C.) Weekly News and Courier
Columbus (Miss.) Patron of Husbandry
Jackson (Miss.) Clarion
Jackson (Miss.) Clarion-Ledger
Knoxville (Tenn.) Daily Tribune
Lexington (Va.) Southern Collegian
Montgomery (Ala.) Advertiser
Montgomery (Ala.) Daily Advertiser
New Orleans (La.) Picayune
New Orleans (La.) Republican
New Orleans (La.) Times-Democrat
Raleigh Register and North Carolina Gazette
Starkville (Miss.) College Reflector
Starkville (Miss.) Dialectic Reflector
Tallahassee Floridian
Tallahassee Floridian and Journal
Tuscaloosa (Ala.) Independent Monitor

G. Government Documents

Acts Passed at the Twelfth Session of the General Assembly of the State of Arkansas, [1858–1859], Little Rock: Johnson & Yerkes, 1859.

Journal of the House of Representatives . . . of the State of Arkansas. Little Rock: State Printer, 1842.

Roberts, Oran M. *General Message on the Judiciary, Education, the Department of Insurance, Statistics and History, Railroads, Etc., to the Seventeenth Legislature of the State of Texas . . . January 11, 1881.* Galveston, Tex.: News Book and Job, 1881.

II. Secondary Sources

A. Books

Abernethy, T. P. *Historical Sketch of the University of Virginia.* Richmond, Va.: Dietz Press, 1948.

Auburn's First 100 Years, 1856–1956. N.p.: Auburn Univ., 1956.

Ayers, Edward L. *The Promise of the New South: Life After Reconstruction.* New York: Oxford Univ. Press, 1992.

Bailey, Hugh C. *Liberalism in the New South: Southern Social Reformers and the Progressive Movement.* Coral Gables, Fla.: Univ. of Miami Press, 1969.

Banning, Lance. *The Jeffersonian Persuasion: Evolution of a Party Ideology.* Ithaca, N.Y.: Cornell Univ. Press, 1978.

Barringer, Paul Brandon; James Mercer Garnett; and Rosewell Page, eds. *University of Virginia: Its History, Influence, Equipment and Characteristics.* 2 vols. New York: Lewis Publishing Company, 1904.

Bennett, Charles Alpheus. *History of Manual and Industrial Education, 1870–1917.* Peoria, Ill.: Manual Arts Press, 1937.

Berkeley, Edmund, and Dorothy Smith Berkeley. *A Yankee Botanist in the Carolinas: The Reverend Moses Ashley Curtis, D.D. (1808–1872).* Berlin: J. Cramer, 1986.

Bernstein, John Andrew. *Progress and the Quest for Meaning: A Philosophical and Historical Inquiry.* Rutherford, N.J.: Farleigh Dickinson Univ. Press, 1993.

Bettersworth, John K. *People's College: A History of Mississippi State University.* University, Ala.: Univ. of Alabama Press, 1953.

Bledstein, Burton J. *The Culture of Professionalism: The Middle Class and the Development of Higher Education in America.* New York: W. W. Norton, 1976.

Boatner, Mark Mayo, III. *The Civil War Dictionary.* New York: David McKay Company, 1959.

Boller, Paul F., Jr. *American Thought in Transition: The Impact of Evolutionary Naturalism, 1865–1900.* Lanham, N.Y.: University Press of America, 1981.

Bond, Horace Mann. *Negro Education in Alabama: A Study in Cotton and Steel.* Washington, D.C.: Associated Publishers, 1939.

Boorstin, Daniel J. *The Lost World of Thomas Jefferson.* 1948. Reprint, Chicago: Univ. of Chicago Press, 1981.

Booth, Andrew B., ed. *Records of Louisiana Confederate Soldiers and Louisiana Commands.* 3 vols. Spartanburg, S.C.: Reprint Company, 1984.

Bridges, Hal. *Lee's Maverick General: Daniel Harvey Hill.* New York: McGraw-Hill Company, 1961.

Brooks, Robert Preston. *The University of Georgia Under Sixteen Administrations, 1785–1955.* Athens: Univ. of Georgia Press, 1956.

Brubacher, John S., and Willis Rudy. *Higher Education in Transition: A History of American Colleges and Universities, 1636–1968.* New York: Harper and Row, 1968.

Bruce, Philip Alexander. *History of the University of Virginia, 1819–1919.* 5 vols. New York: Macmillan Company, 1920.

Buck, Paul H. *The Road to Reunion, 1865–1900.* Boston: Little, Brown and Company, 1947.

Bury, J. B. *The Idea of Progress.* London: Macmillan, 1928.

Cabaniss, James Allen. *A History of the University of Mississippi.* University, Miss.: Univ. of Mississippi, 1949.

————. *The University of Mississippi: Its First Hundred Years.* Hattiesburg: University and College Press of Mississippi, 1971.

Calhoun, Daniel Hovey. *The American Civil Engineer: Origins and Conflict.* Cambridge, Mass.: Technology Press, Massachusetts Institute of Technology, 1960.

Calvert, Monte A. *The Mechanical Engineer in America, 1830–1910.* Baltimore, Md.: Johns Hopkins Univ. Press, 1967.

Carter, Dan T. *When the War Was Over: The Failure of Self-Reconstruction in the South, 1865–1867.* Baton Rouge: Louisiana State Univ. Press, 1985.

Cash, W. J. *The Mind of the South.* New York: Vintage Books, 1941.

Chitty, Arthur Benjamin, Jr. *Reconstruction at Sewanee: The Founding of the University of the South and Its First Administration, 1857–1872.* Sewanee: University Press, 1954.

Chute, William J. *Damn Yankee! The First Career of Frederick A. P. Barnard, Educator, Scientist, Idealist.* Port Washington, N.Y.: National University Publications, Kennikat Press, 1978.

Clark, James C. *The Murder of James A. Garfield: The President's Last Days and the Trial and Execution of His Assassin.* Jefferson, N.C.: McFarland, 1993.

Clayton Bruce. *The Savage Ideal: Intolerance and Intellectual Leadership in the South, 1890–1914.* Baltimore, Md.: Johns Hopkins Univ. Press, 1972.

Cofer, David Brooks. *First Five Administrators of Texas A&M College, 1876–1890.* College Station, Tex.: Association of Former Students of Texas A&M College, 1952.

Connelly, Thomas L. *The Marble Man: Robert E. Lee and His Image in American Society.* Baton Rouge: Louisiana State Univ. Press, 1977.

Conrad, Glenn R., ed. *A Dictionary of Louisiana Biography.* 2 vols. New Orleans: Louisiana Historical Association, 1988.

Coulter, E. Merton. *College Life in the Old South.* Athens: Univ. of Georgia Press, 1951.

Cremin, Lawrence A. *American Education: The Metropolitan Experience, 1876–1980.* New York: Harper and Row, 1988.

————. *American Education: The National Experience, 1783–1876.* New York: Harper and Row, 1980.

Cubberly, Ellwood P. *The History of Education.* Boston: Houghton Mifflin, 1920.

Curti, Merle. *The Social Ideas of American Educators.* New York: Charles Scribner's Sons, 1935.

Dabney, Virginius. *Liberalism in the New South.* Chapel Hill: Univ. of North Carolina Press, 1932.

————. *Mr. Jefferson's University: A History.* Charlottesville: Univ. Press of Virginia, 1981.

Delvaille, Jules. *Essai sur l'Histoire de l'Idée de Progrès jusqu'à la Fin du XVIIIe Siècle.* 1910. Reprint, Geneva, Switzerland: Slatkine Reprints, 1969.

Dethloff, Henry C. *A Centennial History of Texas A&M University, 1876–1976.* 2 vols. College Station: Texas A&M Univ. Press, 1975.

Dodd, William G. *History of West Florida Seminary.* Tallahassee, Fla.: n.p., 1952.

Dyer, John P. *Tulane: The Biography of a University, 1834–1965.* New York: Harper and Row Publishers, 1966.

Dyer, Thomas G. *The University of Georgia: A Bicentennial History, 1785–1985.* Athens: Univ. of Georgia Press, 1985.

Ekirch, Arthur Alphonse, Jr. *The Idea of Progress in America, 1815–1860.* New York: Columbia Univ. Press, 1944.

Fairbanks, George R. *History of the University of the South at Sewanee, Tennessee, from Its Founding by the Southern Bishops, Clergy, and Laity of the Episcopal Church in 1857 to the Year 1905.* Jacksonville, Fla.: H. and W. B. Drew Company.

Farnham, Christie Anne. *The Education of the Southern Belle: Higher Education and Student Socialization in the Antebellum South.* New York: New York Univ. Press, 1994.

Faulkner, William. *Absalom, Absalom!* New York: Random House, 1936. Reprint, New York: Vintage Books, 1987.

Faust, Drew Gilpin. *The Creation of Confederate Nationalism: Ideology and Identity in the Civil War South.* Baton Rouge: Louisiana State Univ. Press, 1988.

———. *A Sacred Circle: The Dilemma of the Intellectual in the Old South, 1840–1860.* Baltimore: Johns Hopkins Univ. Press, 1977.

Finch, James Kip. *A History of the School of Engineering, Columbia University.* New York: Columbia Univ. Press, 1954.

Fleming, Walter L. *Louisiana State University, 1860–1896.* Baton Rouge: Louisiana State Univ. Press, 1936.

Foner, Eric. *Free Soil, Free Labor, Free Men: The Ideology of the Republican Party Before the War.* London: Oxford Univ. Press, 1970.

Forman, Sidney. *West Point: A History of the United States Military Academy.* New York: Columbia Univ. Press, 1950.

Foster, Gaines M. *Ghosts of the Confederacy: Defeat, the Lost Cause, and the Emergence of the New South.* New York: Oxford Univ. Press, 1987.

Franklin, John Hope. *The Militant South, 1800–1861.* Cambridge, Mass.: Belknap Press of Harvard Univ. Press, 1956.

Frost, Dan R., and Kou K. Nelson. *The LSU College of Engineering: Origins and Establishment, 1860–1908.* Baton Rouge: College of Engineering, Louisiana State Univ., 1995. Distributed by Louisiana State Univ. Press.

Gaston, Paul M. *The New South Creed: A Study in Southern Mythmaking.* New York: Alfred A. Knopf, 1970.

Genovese, Eugene D. *The Political Economy of Slavery: Studies in the Economy and Society of the Slave South.* New York: Pantheon Books, 1965.

———. *Roll, Jordan, Roll: The World the Slaves Made.* New York: Vintage Books, 1974.

———. *The Slaveholders' Dilemma: Freedom and Progress in Southern Conservative Thought, 1820–1860.* Columbia: Univ. of South Carolina Press, 1992.

Gillespie, Neal C. *The Collapse of Orthodoxy: The Intellectual Ordeal of George Frederick Holmes.* Charlottesville: Univ. of Virginia Press, 1972.

Godbold, Albea. *The Church College of the Old South.* Durham, N.C.: Duke Univ. Press, 1944.

Goodenow, Ronald K., and Arthur O. White, eds. *Education and the Rise of the New South.* Boston: G. K. Hall and Company, 1981.

Goodwyn, Lawrence. *The Populist Moment: A Short History of the Agrarian Revolt in America.* Oxford, England: Oxford Univ. Press, 1978.

Grantham, Dewey. *Southern Progressivism: The Reconciliation of Progress and Tradition.* Knoxville: Univ. of Tennessee Press, 1983.

Hale, Harrison. *University of Arkansas, 1871–1948.* Fayetteville: Univ. of Arkansas Alumni Association, 1948.

Hattaway, Herman. *General Stephen D. Lee.* Jackson: Univ. Press of Mississippi, 1976.

Heatwole, Cornelius J. *A History of Education in Virginia.* New York: Macmillan Company, 1916.

Heitmann, John Alfred. *The Modernization of the Louisiana Sugar Industry, 1830–1910.* Baton Rouge: Louisiana State Univ. Press, 1987.

Hellenbrand, Harold. *The Unfinished Revolution: Education and Politics in the Thought of Thomas Jefferson.* Newark, DE.: Univ. of Delaware Press, 1990.

Henderson, Archibald. *The Campus of the First State University.* Chapel Hill: Univ. of North Carolina Press, 1949.

Hesseltine, William B. *Confederate Leaders in the New South.* Baton Rouge: Louisiana State Univ. Press, 1950.

Hill, Joseph M. *Biography of Daniel Harvey Hill: Lieutenant General, Confederate States of America; Educator; Author; Editor.* [Little Rock, Ark.?]: Official Publications of the Arkansas History Commission, n.d.

Hofstadter, Richard. *Social Darwinism in American Thought, 1860–1915.* Philadelphia: Univ. of Pennsylvania Press, 1945.

Hofstadter, Richard, and C. DeWitt Hardy. *The Development and Scope of Higher Education in the United States.* New York: Columbia Univ. Press, 1952.

Hofstadter, Richard, and Walter P. Metzger. *The Development of Academic Freedom in the United States.* New York: Columbia Univ. Press, 1955.

Hollis, Daniel Walker. *University of South Carolina.* 2 vols. Columbia: Univ. of South Carolina Press, 1951.

Honeywell, Roy J. *The Educational Work of Thomas Jefferson.* New York: Russell and Russell, 1964.

Johnson, Allen, ed. *Dictionary of American Biography.* 10 vols. New York: Charles Scribner's Sons, 1935.

Johnson, Charles D. *Higher Education of Southern Baptists.* Waco, Tex.: Baylor Univ. Press, 1955.

Johnson, Michael P. *Toward a Patriarchal Republic: The Secession of Georgia.* Baton Rouge: Louisiana State Univ. Press, 1977.

Johnson, Sid S. *Texans Who Wore the Gray.* [Tyler, Tex.: n.p., 1907].

Kasson, John F. *Civilizing the Machine: Technology and Republican Values in America, 1776–1900.* New York: Grossman Publishers, 1976.

Kinnear, Duncan Lyle. *The First Hundred Years: A History of Virginia Polytechnic Institute and State University.* Blacksburg, Va.: VPI Educational Foundation, 1972.

Knight, Oliver. *Fort Worth: Outpost on the Trinity.* Norman: Univ. of Oklahoma Press, 1953.

Kolchin, Peter. *American Slavery, 1619–1877.* New York: Hill and Wang, 1993.

———. *Unfree Labor: American Slavery and Russian Serfdom.* Cambridge, Mass.: Belknap Press of Harvard Univ. Press, 1987.

Lasch, Christopher. *The True and Only Heaven: Progress and Its Critics.* New York: W. W. Norton and Company, 1991.

Leach, Josiah Granville. *History of the Bringhurst Family, with Notes on the Clarkson, De Peyster and Boude Families.* Bossier City, La.: Everett Companies, 1989.

Lee, Robert E., Jr. *Recollections and Letters of General Robert E. Lee, by His Son Captain Robert E. Lee.* New York: Doubleday, Page and Company, 1909.

Leflar, Robert A. *The First 100 Years: Centennial History of the University of Arkansas.* Fayetteville: Univ. of Arkansas Foundation, 1972.

Leloudis, James L. *Schooling the New South: Pedagogy, Self, and Society in North Carolina, 1880–1920.* Chapel Hill: Univ. of North Carolina Press, 1996.

Linderman, Gerald. *Embattled Courage: The Experience of Combat in the American Civil War.* New York: Free Press, 1987.

Link, William A. *The Paradox of Southern Progressivism, 1880–1930.* Chapel Hill: Univ. of North Carolina Press, 1992.

Lloyd, Allen Alexander, and Pauline O. Lloyd. *History of the Town of Hillsborough, 1754–1982.* N.p., n.d.

Loveland, Anne C. *Southern Evangelicals and the Social Order, 1800–1860.* Baton Rouge: Louisiana State Univ. Press, 1980.

Maddex, Jack P., Jr. *The Virginia Conservatives, 1867–1879: A Study in Reconstruction Politics.* Chapel Hill: Univ. of North Carolina, 1970.

Malone, Dumas. *The Public Life of Thomas Cooper, 1783–1839.* Columbia: Univ. of South Carolina Press, 1961.

Marcus, Alan I. *Agricultural Science and the Quest for Legitimacy: Farmers, Agricultural Colleges, and Experiment Stations, 1870–1890.* Ames: Iowa State Univ. Press, 1985.

McCoy, Drew. *The Elusive Republic: Political Economy in Jeffersonian America.* New York: W. W. Norton and Company, 1980.

McGivern, James Gregory. *First Hundred Years of Engineering Education in the United States (1807–1907).* Spokane, Wash.: Gonzaga Univ. Press, 1960.

McKale, Donald M., ed. *Tradition: A History of the Presidency of Clemson University.* Macon, Ga.: Mercer Univ. Press, 1988.

McMath, Robert C., Jr.; Ronald H. Bayor; James E. Brittain; Lawrence Foster; Augustus W. Giebelhaus; and Germaine M. Reed. *Engineering the New South: Georgia Tech, 1885–1985.* Athens: Univ. of Georgia Press, 1985.

Meigs, W[illia]m M. *Life of Josiah Meigs.* Philadelphia: n.p., 1887.

Midgette, Nancy Smith. *To Foster the Spirit of Professionalism: Southern Scientists and the State Academies of Science.* Tuscaloosa: Univ. of Alabama Press, 1991.

Montgomery, James Riley; Stanley J. Folmsbee; and Lee Seifert Green. *To Foster Knowledge: A History of the University of Tennessee, 1794–1970.* Knoxville: Univ. of Tennessee Press, 1984.

Moore, James R. *The Post-Darwinian Controversies: A Study of the Protestant Struggle to Come to Terms with Darwin in Great Britain and America, 1870–1900.* London: Cambridge Univ. Press, 1979.

Morrison, James L., Jr. *"The Best School in the World": West Point, the Pre–Civil War Years, 1833–1866.* Kent, Oh.: Kent State Univ., 1986.

Nisbet, Roger. *History of the Idea of Progress.* New York: Basic Books, 1980.

Noble, David F. *America by Design: Science, Technology, and the Rise of Corporate Capitalism.* New York: Alfred A. Knopf, 1977.

Norrell, Robert J. *A Promising Field: Engineering at Alabama, 1837–1987.* Tuscaloosa: Univ. of Alabama Press, 1990.

Novick, Peter. *That Noble Dream: The "Objectivity Question" and the American Historical Profession.* New York: Cambridge Univ. Press, 1988.

Paludan, Phillip S. *"A People's Contest": The Union and the Civil War, 1861–1865.* New York: Harper and Row, 1988.

Parks, Joseph Howard. *General Edmund Kirby Smith, C.S.A.* Baton Rouge: Louisiana State Univ. Press, 1954.

Parrish, T. Michael. *Richard Taylor: Soldier Prince of Dixie.* Chapel Hill: Univ. of North Carolina Press, 1992.

Pirie, Madsen. *Trial and Error and the Idea of Progress.* London: Open Court, 1978.

Pocock, J. G. A. *The Machiavellian Moment: Florentine Political Thought and the Atlantic Republican Tradition.* Princeton, N.J.: Princeton Univ. Press, 1975.

Posey, Josephine M. *Against Great Odds: The History of Alcorn State University.* Jackson: Univ. Press of Mississippi, 1994.

Rabinowitz, Howard N. *The First New South, 1865–1920.* Arlington Heights, Ill.: Harlan Davidson, 1992.

Reagan, Alice Elizabeth. *North Carolina State University: A Narrative History.* Ann Arbor, Mich.: Edwards Brothers, 1987.

Reed, Germaine M. *David French Boyd: Founder of Louisiana State University.* Baton Rouge: Louisiana State Univ. Press, 1977.

Reynolds, John Hugh, and David Yancey Thomas. *History of the University of Arkansas.* Fayetteville: Univ. of Arkansas, 1910.

Rosenberg, Charles E. *No Other Gods: On Science and American Social Thought.* 1961. Reprint, Baltimore, Md.: Johns Hopkins Univ. Press, 1976.

Ross, Earle D. *Democracy's College: The Land-Grant Movement in the Formative State.* Ames: Iowa State College Press, 1942.

Royster, Charles. *The Destructive War: William Tecumseh Sherman, Stonewall Jackson, and the Americans.* New York: Alfred A. Knopf, 1991.

Rudolph, Frederick. *The American College and University: A History.* New York: Alfred A. Knopf, 1962.

Sampson, Ronald Victor. *Progress in the Age of Reason: The Seventeenth Century to the Present Day.* Cambridge, Mass.: Harvard Univ. Press, 1956.

Sellers, James B. *History of the University of Alabama.* 2 vols. University, Ala.: Univ. of Alabama Press, 1953.

Sheehan, Thomas. *The First Coming: How the Kingdom of God Became Christianity.* New York: Random House, 1986.

Shugg, Roger W. *Origins of Class Struggle in Slavery and After, 1840–1875.* 1936. Reprint, Baton Rouge: Louisiana State Univ. Press, 1968.

Silber, Nina. *The Romance of Reunion: Northerners and the South, 1865–1900.* Chapel Hill: Univ. of North Carolina Press, 1993.

Silverthorne, Elizabeth. *Ashbel Smith of Texas: Pioneer, Patriot, Statesman, 1805–1886.* College Station: Texas A&M Univ. Press, 1982.

Snay, Mitchell. *Gospel of Disunion: Religion and Separatism in the Antebellum South.* New York: Cambridge Univ. Press, 1993.

Spadafora, David. *The Idea of Progress in Eighteenth-Century Britain.* New Haven, Conn.: Yale Univ. Press, 1990.

Staples, Thomas S. *Reconstruction in Arkansas, 1862–1874.* New York: Longmans, Green and Company, 1923.

Stevens, Hazard. *The Life of Isaac Ingalls Stevens.* 2 vols. Boston: Houghton Mifflin and Company, 1900.

Tewksbury, Donald G. *The Founding of American Colleges and Universities Before* the Civil War: With Particular Reference to the Religious Influences Bearing Upon the College Movement. New York: Columbia Univ. Press, 1932.

Thomas, Emory M. The Confederacy as a Revolutionary Experience. Englewood Cliffs, N.J.: Prentice-Hall, 1971.

―――. The Confederate Nation, 1861–1865. New York: Harper and Row, 1978.

Tuveson, Ernest Lee. Redeemer Nation: The Idea of America's Millennial Role. Chicago: Univ. of Chicago Press, 1968.

Tyler, Lyon Gardiner, ed. Encyclopedia of Virginia Biography. 5 vols. New York: Lewis Historical Publishing Company, 1915.

Vandiver, Frank E. Ploughshares into Swords: Josiah Gorgas and Confederate Ordnance. Austin: Univ. of Texas Press, 1952.

Veysey, Laurence R. The Emergence of the American University. Chicago: Univ. of Chicago Press, 1965.

Virginia Agricultural and Mechanical College: Its History and Organization. N.p., n.d.

Wade, John Donald. Augustus Baldwin Longstreet: A Study of the Development of Culture in the South. Athens: Univ. of Georgia Press, 1969.

Wagar, W. Warren. Good Tidings: The Belief in Progress from Darwin to Marcuse. Bloomington: Indiana Univ. Press, 1972.

Wagstaff, Henry McGilbert. Impressions of Men and Movements at the University of North Carolina. Chapel Hill: Univ. of North Carolina Press, 1950.

Wiebe, Robert H. The Opening of American Society: From the Adoption of the Constitution to the Eve of Disunion. New York: Alfred A. Knopf, 1984.

Wiener, Jonathan M. Social Origins of the New South: Alabama, 1860–1885. Baton Rouge: Louisiana State Univ. Press, 1978.

Wilson, Charles Reagan. Baptized in Blood: The Religion of the Lost Cause, 1865–1920. Athens: Univ. of Georgia Press, 1980.

Woodward, C. Vann. Origins of the New South, 1877–1913. 1951. Reprint, Baton Rouge: Louisiana State Univ. Press, with the Littlefield Fund for Southern History, Univ. of Texas, 1971.

Wright, Gavin. The Political Economy of the Cotton South: Households, Markets, and Wealth in the Nineteenth Century. New York: W. W. Norton and Company, 1978.

Wyatt-Brown, Bertram. Honor and Violence in the Old South. New York: Oxford Univ. Press, 1986.

B. Articles in Books and Periodicals

Altsetter, Mabel, and Gladys Watson. "Western Military Institute, 1847–1861." Filson Club History Quarterly 10 (Apr. 1936): 100–115.

Anderson, L. F. "The Manual Labor School Movement." Educational Review 46 (June–Dec.): 369–86.

Andrew, Rod, Jr. "Soldiers, Christians, and Patriots: The Lost Cause and Southern Military Schools, 1865–1915." Journal of Southern History 64 (Nov. 1998): 677–710.

Axtell, James. "The Death of the Liberal Arts College." History of Education Quarterly 11 (Winter 1971): 339–52.

Bailey, Fred A. "Oliver Perry Temple and the Struggle for Tennessee's Agricultural College." Tennessee Historical Quarterly 36 (Spring 1977): 44–61.

————. "The Textbooks of the 'Lost Cause': Censorship and the Creation of Southern State Histories." *Georgia Historical Quarterly* 75 (Fall 1991): 507–8.

Bartley, Numan V. "Another New South?" *Georgia Historical Quarterly* 65 (Summer 1981): 119–37.

Bauman, Mark K. "Confronting the New South Creed: The Genteel Conservative as Higher Educator." In *Education and the Rise of the New South,* edited by Ronald K. Goodenow and Arthur O. White, 92–113. Boston: G. K. Hall and Company, 1981.

Bettersworth, John K. "'The Cow in the Front Yard': How a Land-Grant College Grew in Mississippi." *Agricultural History* 53 (Jan. 1979): 62–70.

Blackburn, Robert T., and Clifton F. Conrad. "The New Revisionists and the History of Higher Education." *Higher Education* 15 (1986): 211–30.

Brabham, Robin. "Defining the American University: The University of North Carolina, 1865–1875." *North Carolina Historical Review* 57 (Oct. 1980): 427–55.

Braden, Waldo W. "'Repining Over an Irrevocable Past': The Ceremonial Orator in a Defeated Society, 1865–1900." In *Rhetoric of the People: "Is There Any Better or Equal Hope in the World?,"* edited by Harold Barrett, 273–301. Amsterdam, Netherlands: Rodopi NV, 1974.

Braden, Waldo W., and Harold Mixon. "Epideictic Speaking in the Post–Civil War South and the Southern Experience." *Southern Communication Journal* 54 (Fall 1988): 40–57.

Bridges, Hal. "D. H. Hill's Anti-Yankee Algebra." *Journal of Southern History* 22 (May 1956): 220–22.

Brittain, James E., and Robert C. McMath, Jr. "Engineers and the New South Creed: The Formation and Early Development of Georgia Tech." *Technology and Culture* 18 (Apr. 1977): 175–201.

Calhoun, Robert M. "James Woodrow." In *American National Biography.* New York: Oxford Univ. Press, 1999.

Carter, Allan M. "The Role of Higher Education in the Changing South." In *The South in Continuity and Change,* edited by John C. McKinney and Edgar T. Thompson, 277–97. Durham, N.C.: Duke Univ. Press, 1965.

Chambers, Clarke A. "The Belief in Progress in Twentieth-Century America." *Journal of the History of Ideas* 19 (Apr. 1958): 197–224.

Cobb, James C. "Beyond Planters and Industrialists: A New Perspective on the New South." *Journal of Southern History* 54 (Feb. 1988): 45–68.

————. "Does *Mind* No Longer Matter? The South, the Nation, and *The Mind of the South,* 1941–1991." *Journal of Southern History* 57 (Nov. 1991): 681–718.

Coulter, E. Merton. "A Famous University of Georgia Commencement, 1871." *Georgia Historical Quarterly* 57 (Fall 1973): 347–61.

————. "The New South: Benjamin H. Hill's Speech Before the Alumni Society of the University of Georgia, 1871." *Georgia Historical Quarterly* 57 (Summer 1973): 179–99.

Cunningham, Horace H. "The Southern Mind Since the Civil War." In *Writing Southern History: Essays in Historiography in Honor of Fletcher M. Green,* edited by Arthur S. Link and Rembert W. Patrick. Baton Rouge: Louisiana State Univ. Press, 1965.

Donald, David. "The Proslavery Argument Reconsidered." *Journal of Southern History* 37 (Feb. 1971): 3–18.

Donnelly, Ralph W. "Scientists of the Confederate Nitre and Mining Bureau." *Civil War History* 2 (Dec. 1956): 88–89.

Dyer, Thomas G. "Higher Education in the South Since the Civil War: Historiographical Issues and Trends." In *The Web of Southern Social Relations: Women, Family, and Education,* edited by Walter J. Fraser, Jr., and Jon L. Wakelyn, 127–45. Athens: Univ. of Georgia Press, 1985.

Ezell, John S. "A Southern Education for Southrons." *Journal of Southern History* 17 (Aug. 1951): 303–25.

Fleming, Walter L. "Industrial Development in Alabama During the Civil War." *South Atlantic Quarterly* 3 (July 1904): 260–72.

Flynt, Wayne. "Southern Higher Education and the Civil War." *Civil War History* 14 (Sept. 1968): 211–25.

"Forty Years Ago." *Alumni Bulletin of the University of Virginia* 4 (Oct. 1904): 286–92.

Frazier, Donald S. "Losses and Numbers." In *Encyclopedia of the Confederacy,* edited by Richard N. Current, vol. 1, 337–40. New York: Simon and Schuster, 1993.

Gass, W. Conard. "Kemp Plummer Battle and the Development of Historical Instruction at the University of North Carolina." *North Carolina Historical Review* 45 (Jan. 1968): 1–22.

Geiser, S. W. "George Washington Curtis and Frank Arthur Gulley: Two Early Agricultural Teachers in Texas." *Field and Laboratory* 14 (Jan. 1946): 1–13.

Gianniny, O. Allan, Jr. "The Overlooked Approach to Engineering Education: One and a Half Centuries at the University of Virginia, 1836–1986." In *Proceedings of the 150th Anniversary Symposium on Technology and Society,* edited by Howard L. Hartman, 144–76. Tuscaloosa, Alabama: Univ. of Alabama College of Engineering, 1988.

Gilstrap, Marguerite. "Daniel Harvey Hill, Southern Propagandist." *Arkansas Historical Quarterly* 2 (Mar.–Dec. 1943): 43–50.

Good, H. G. "New Data on Early Engineering Education." *Journal of Educational Research* 29 (Sept. 1935–May 1936): 37–46.

Graves, C. A. "General Lee at Lexington." In *General Robert E. Lee After Appomattox,* edited by Frank L. Riley, 22–31. New York: Macmillan Company, 1922.

Hale, Harrison. "Glimpses of University of Arkansas History." *Arkansas Historical Quarterly* 6 (Winter 1947): 430–39.

Herbst, Jurgen. "The Eighteenth-Century Origins of the Split Between Private and Public Education in the United States." *History of Education Quarterly* 15 (Fall 1975): 273–82.

Idol, John L., Jr. "The Controversial Humanities Professor, Edwin Booth Craighead, 1893–1897." In *Tradition: A History of the Presidency of Clemson College,* edited by Donald M. McKale, 35–52. Macon, Ga.: Mercer Univ. Press, 1988.

Kabat, Ric A. "Before the Seminoles: Football at Florida State College, 1902–1904." *Florida Historical Quarterly* 70 (July 1991): 20–37.

Kelley, Maurice. "Additional Chapters on Thomas Cooper." *University of Maine Studies* 33 (Aug. 1930): 5–100.

Kincheloe, Joe L. "Building God's Kingdom: The Holy Mission of Antebellum Evangelical Colleges." *Southern Studies* 2 (Summer 1991): 103–12.

Lambert, Robert S. "The Builder of a College, Henry Aubrey Strode." In *Tradition: A History of the Presidency of Clemson University,* edited by Donald M. McKale, 21–34. Macon, Ga.: Mercer Univ. Press, 1988.

Lane, Jack C. "The Yale Report of 1828 and Liberal Education: A Neorepublican Manifesto." *History of Education Quarterly* 27 (Fall 1987): 325–38.

London, H. A. "The University During the War." *University of North Carolina Record* (June 1911): 75–89.

Luraghi, Raimondo. "The Civil War and the Modernization of American Society: Social Structure and Industrial Revolution in the Old South Before and During the War." *Civil War History* 18 (Sept. 1972): 230–50.

Maddex, Jack P., Jr. "Proslavery Millennialism: Social Eschatology in Antebellum Southern Calvinism." *American Quarterly* 31 (Spring 1979): 46–62.

Mahan, Harold Eugene. "The Final Battle: The Southern Historical Society and Confederate Hopes for History." *Southern Historian* 5 (Spring 1984): 27–37.

Mathews, Joseph J. "The Study of History in the South." *Journal of Southern History* 31 (Feb. 1965): 3–20.

Maxcy, Spencer J. "Progressivism and Rural Education in the Deep South, 1900–1950." In *Education and the Rise of the New South,* edited by Ronald K. Goodenow and Arthur O. White, 47–71. Boston: G. K. Hall and Company, 1981.

Moger, Allen W. "General Lee's Unwritten 'History of the Army of Northern Virginia.'" *Virginia Magazine of History and Biography* 71 (1963): 341–63.

Neufeldt, Harvey, and Clinton Allison. "Education and the Rise of the New South: An Historiographical Essay." In *Education and the Rise of the New South,* edited by Ronald K. Goodenow and Arthur O. White, 250–94. Boston: G. K. Hall and Company, 1981.

Nichols, Guerdon D. "Breaking the Color Barrier at the University of Arkansas." *Arkansas Historical Quarterly* 27 (Spring 1968): 3–21.

Numbers, Ronald L., and Janet S. Numbers. "Science in the Old South: A Reappraisal." *Journal of Southern History* 48 (May 1982): 163–84.

Pannabecker, John R. "Industrial Education and the Russian System: A Study in Economic, Social, and Technical Change." *Journal of Industrial Teacher Education* 24 (Fall 1986): 19–31.

Persons, Stow. "The Cyclical Theory of History in Eighteenth-Century America." *American Quarterly* 6 (Summer 1954): 147–63.

Potts, David B. "American Colleges in the Nineteenth Century: From Localism to Denominationalism." *History of Education Quarterly* 11 (Winter 1971): 363–80.

Reed, Germaine M. "David Boyd, LSU, and Louisiana Reconstruction." *Louisiana Studies* 14 (Fall 1975): 259–76.

Reesman, John A. "A School for Honor: South Carolina College and the Guard House Riot of 1856." *South Carolina Historical Magazine* 84 (Oct. 1983): 195–213.

Riley, Frank L. "What General Lee Read After the War." In *General Robert E. Lee*

After Appomattox, edited by Frank L. Riley, 157–81. New York: Macmillan Company, 1922.

Roberts, Derrell. "The University of Georgia and Georgia's G.I. Bill." *Georgia Historical Quarterly* 49 (Dec. 1965): 418–23.

Rogers, William Warren. "The Founding of Alabama's Land Grant College at Auburn." *Alabama Review* 40 (Jan. 1987): 14–37.

Sloan, Douglas. "Harmony, Chaos, and Consensus: The American College Curriculum." *Teachers College Record* 73 (Dec. 1971): 221–51.

Starnes, Richard D. "Forever Faithful: The Southern Historical Society and Confederate Historical Memory." *Southern Cultures* 2 (Winter 1996): 177–94.

Stephens, Edwin L. "The Story of Acadian Education in Louisiana." *Louisiana Historical Quarterly* 18 (Apr. 1935): 397–406.

Stephenson, Wendell H. "Herbert B. Adams and Southern Historical Scholarship at the Johns Hopkins University." *Maryland Historical Magazine* 42 (Mar. 1947): 2–19.

Stetar, Joseph M. "In Search of a Direction: Southern Higher Education after the Civil War." *History of Education Quarterly* 25 (Fall 1985): 341–67.

Thomas, Milton Halsey. "Professor McCulloh of Princeton, Columbia, and Points South." *Princeton Library Chronicle* 9 (Nov. 1947): 17–29.

Thomas, Peter C. "Matthew Fontaine Maury and the Problem of Virginia's Identity." *Virginia Magazine of History and Biography* 90 (Apr. 1982): 213–37.

Thomson, Robert Polk. "Colleges in the Revolutionary South: The Shaping of a Tradition." *History of Education Quarterly* 10 (Winter 1970): 399–412.

Towns, W. Stuart. "Atticus G. Haygood: Neglected Advocate of Reconciliation and a New South." *Southern Studies* 26 (Spring 1987): 30–40.

Urofsky, Melvin I. "Reforms and Response: The Yale Report of 1828." *History of Education Quarterly* 5 (Mar. 1965): 53–67.

Wagoner, Jennings L. "Higher Education and Transitions in Southern Culture: An Exploratory Apologia." *Journal of Thought* 18 (Fall 1983): 104–18.

Whitener, Daniel J. "Republican Party and Public Education in North Carolina, 1867–1900." *North Carolina Historical Review* 37 (July 1960): 382–96.

Wilson, Carl B. "The Baptist Manual Labor School Movement in the United States: Its Origin, Development ,and Significance." *Baylor Bulletin* 40 (Dec. 1937): 9–159.

Wilson, Charles Reagan. "The Religion of the Lost Cause: Ritual and Organization of the Southern Civil Religion." *Journal of Southern History* 46 (May 1980): 219–38.

C. Unpublished Works

Foerster, Alma Pauline. "The State University in the Old South: A Study of Social and Intellectual Influences in State University Education." Ph.D. dissertation, Duke Univ., 1939.

Goode, James Moore. "The Confederate University: The Forgotten Institution of the American Civil War." Master's thesis, Univ. of Virginia, 1966.

May, John B. "The Life of John Lee Buchanan." Ph.D. dissertation, University of Virginia, 1937.

Paskoff, Paul F. "Invention and Culture in the Old South, 1790–1860." Unpublished paper delivered at Works-in-Progress Seminar, Louisiana State Univ., 1993.

Richard, Dinah Daniel. "The Southern Oratory of William Preston Johnston." Ph.D. dissertation, Louisiana State Univ., 1982.

Scafidel, J. R., ed. "The Letters of Augustus Baldwin Longstreet." Ph.D. dissertation, Univ. of South Carolina, 1976.

Stetar, Joseph M. "Development of Southern Higher Education, 1865–1910: Selected Case Studies of Six Colleges." Ph.D. dissertation, State Univ. of New York at Buffalo, 1975.

Stillman, Rachel Bryan. "Education in the Confederate States of America, 1861–1865." Ph.D. dissertation, Univ. of Illinois, 1972.

Toles, Caesar F. "Regionalism in Southern Higher Education." Ph.D. dissertation, Univ. of Michigan, 1953.

Watson, Joel Colley. "Isaac Taylor Tichenor and the Administration of the Alabama Agricultural College, 1872–1882." Master's thesis, Auburn Univ., 1968.

Webb, Lester Austin. "The Origin of Military Schools in the United States Founded in the Nineteenth Century." Ph.D. dissertation, Univ. of North Carolina, 1958.

Wiley, Wayne Hamilton. "Academic Freedom at the University of Virginia: The First Hundred Years—From Jefferson Through Alderman." Ph.D. dissertation, Univ. of Virginia, 1973.

Index

Thinking Confederates was designed and typeset on a Macintosh computer system using PageMaker software. The text and chapter openings are set in Amerigo. This book was designed by David Alcorn, typeset by Kimberly Scarbrough, and manufactured by Thomson-Shore, Inc. The paper used in this book is designed for an effective life of at least three hundred years.